Bleeding Manipur

By the same author

Insurgency Movement in North Eastern India

Drug Abuse and Illicit Trafficking in North Eastern India

Bleeding Manipur

Phanjoubam Tarapot

HAR-ANAND PUBLICATIONS PVT LTD
E-49/3, Okhla Industrial Area, Phase-II, New Delhi-110020
Tel.: 41603491
E-mail: info@haranandbooks.com/haranand@rediffmail.com
Shop online at: www.haranandbooks.com

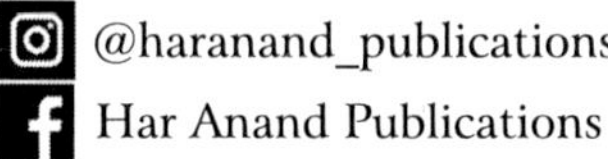

Published by Ashok Gosain and Ashish Gosain for
Har-Anand Publications Pvt Ltd

Printed in India Megha Enterprises

In the loving memories of
my mother, Phanjoubam Ibetombi
&
my niece, Phanjoubam Maipaksana Chanu
whom we affectionately called Pakpi.

Preface

Unceasing insurgency-related violence, years-long ethnic feuds among major tribes, underground factional fights and ceaseless attempts to tear apart Manipur by some sections of the militant-backed tribes have put the 'sensitive' north eastern state on the limelight for several years. There is, at present, no sign of ending the violence. Common people are sandwiched in the armed conflicts and, in a predicament. Thousands of civilians have lost their lives in these clashes in the past one or two decades.

The book traces the root cause of the ethnic clashes, its historical background, and reveals the deep-hatredness among some tribes. It also mentions about the plight of the affected peoples. The book also depicts how civilians are used sometimes as human shields in the ongoing fights among armed groups or between the security forces and underground cadres; and it points out the unhealthy relations among some communities over the attempts to divide Manipur by some tribes in the hills.

As a senior representative of the nation's premier newsagency, the *Press Trust of India,* I have been able to talk to various kinds of people. In the course of doing my work, I have interviewed several persons from different communities, visited various interior places, reported the clashes among major tribes and within the underground factions, observed the growing tension among some communities, mingled with people from different walks of life, done stories on insurgent activities, seen how the issues were tackled in a lackadaisical manner, and witnessed the deteriorating situation over the years. The book is an outcome of these activities. It intends to tell the readers concisely of what is happening in the tiny state.

I thank those who helped me during my research for the book. Especially, I would like to thank Laishram Binodkumari Devi, librarian of the Tribal Research Centre, and Abul Kalam, a staff member of the Manipur State Archives for their wholehearted support and for making some background materials available to me for an unspecified period. I am also thankful to Minister of Industries, Manipur, Thoudam Debendra Singh, who is a senior political leader of the state, for encouraging me all the time to write the book.

I also thank the editor-in-chief and general manager of *PTI*, M.K. Razdan for encouraging me in the work of *PTI* which has greatly contributed in writing this book.

I would also like to thank human rights activist Babloo Loitongbam, associate professor Konsam Ibo Singh, journalist Sobhapati Samom and politician Loitongbam Iboyaima Singh for hunting out some materials on my behalf. I also thank my wife Phanjoubam Ongbi Jamini without whose persevering support the book would not have been possible. Lastly, I would very much welcome any suggestion for improvement of the book which, I feel, is not exhaustive on the subject.

PHANJOUBAM TARAPOT

Contents

Introduction

Nowhere in the world various tribes or sub-tribes are fighting for formation of smaller states along the ethnic lines as in Manipur, where as many as nine underground outfits are separately trying to carve up this small state which has a total area of 22,327 sq km and a 2000-year old written history in India's north eastern region. While some want a portion of it to integrate with a neighbouring state which was born only in 1963, others demand creation of different what they called 'homelands' by reorganising its territories. Interestingly, some of the groups are only in name, and believed to have been formed to serve the interests of a few persons. On the other hand, there are also at least four known insurgent organisations which have been separately waging armed struggles for an 'independent Manipur' for the past three decades or so. They say Manipur is 'forcibly merged' with the Indian union in October 1949.

In its millennia-old history, there had not been such tribe as 'Naga' or 'Kuki' in Manipur. In the state, the tribes were (or are) known as Kabui, Maring, Tangkhul, Mao, Maram, Chiru, Khongjai, Thadou, Paite, Hmar, Monsang, Moyon, etc,. Some scholars have pointed out that the 'generic terms' such as 'Naga' or 'Kuki' were introduced only after the advent of the British in the state less than two centuries ago to identify different tribes in the hills for their own 'convenience.' In fact, the name Manipur itself is also of recent origin. The state was named 'Manipur' some three centuries ago during the reign of King Pamheiba. Are not the terms 'Naga' or 'Kuki' misnomer for the purpose of identification of different tribes in the state? Were the terms, 'Naga' or 'Kuki,' used in the state to 'incorporate more tribal areas' and sow the seeds of division between the people in the hills and valley? These questions which will remain unanswered have come up following the demand by some tribal organisations including underground outfits for formation of small states by dividing Manipur.

Unlike in neighbouring Assam where the plain people, according to T.C. Hodson's *The Naga Tribes of Manipur,* used to call some hill-tribes in hinterland in interior areas of the state as 'Noga' (the term Naga is said to be derived from Noga), the people in Manipur valley used to call the tribes in the state by their tribal names. At present, the state government has recognised twenty nine tribes which are: Aimol, Anal, Angami, Mizo, Chiru, Chothe, Gangte, Hmar, Kabui (Puimei and Rongmei), Kacha Naga (Zemei and Liangmei), Koirao, Koireng, Kom, Lamkang, Maram, Maring, Mao, Monsang, Moyon, Paite, Purum, Ralte, Sema, Simte, Salhte, Tanghkul, Thadou, Vaiphei and Zou. Both Kabui and Kacha Naga come under Zeliangrong. According to a state government publication, some major Naga tribes are Zeliangrong, Mao, Maram, Tangkhul, Maring, etc. While major Chin-Kuki-Mizo tribes are Thadou (Kuki), Gangte, Hmar, Mizo, Paite, Simte, Vaiphei, Zou, etc. The numerically smaller tribes which are linguistically nearer to the Chin-Kuki-Mizo group are Aimol, Chiru, Koireng, Kom, Anal, Chothe, Lamkhang, Koirao, Purum, Monsang, Moyon, etc,. Sometimes, they are also known as old Kukis. Some of the small tribes who wanted to maintain their own separate identity have also been forced by some big tribes either to denote themselves as 'Naga' or 'Kuki.'

While it is for the wiser minds to comment on the armed struggle of some underground organisations for an 'independent Manipur,' or, as some termed it, 'Indo-Burma region' (some major underground groups have formed Indo-Burma Revolutionary Front to what they termed liberate Indo-Burma region comprising north eastern region of India and north western part of upper Myanmar); a question which has come up now is why some tribal underground and over ground outfits want to break up Manipur, which lost its independence after British conquest in 1891 and later merged with the Indian union in October 1949. It appears that some of the major tribes or communities are still sharply divided along the ethnic lines in spite of living in propinquity for centuries together. Unless the mindsets of different sections of the people are changed and adjusted themselves to living in communities and in harmony in this violence-marred state, action by any group against another's interests would be detrimental and mutually destructive to one another. Moreover, many observers feel that it is only a few sections of the people with vested interests that are trying to divide this historic state. They expressed the view that the protection of territorial integrity would be the interests of all sections of the people and a prerequisite for bringing peace and communal harmony in the insurgency ravaged state. For some decades, underground National Socialist Council of Nagaland (NSCN) has been fighting for 'an independent Nagaland' which, according to them, should include apart from Nagaland four hill districts of Manipur—Ukhrul, Chandel, Senapati and Tamenglong, where Nagas of different tribes formed parts of the population in these districts. Kukis, some other communities and tribes have also settled in these districts. The demand for a 'greater Nagaland' also included Naga-settled areas of Assam and Arunachal Pradesh apart from the four hill districts of Manipur. What is to be understood is that the history of Manipur is totally different from that of Assam, present Nagaland state and Arunachal Pradesh. It may be stated that some Nagas of Manipur, allegedly supported by some Naga underground group, expressed their wish either to merge the four hill districts with Nagaland which was carved out of Assam and became a state in 1963, or form a 'separate state' within Manipur.

It is not only the NSCN which broke into two in 1988 — NSCN Isac and Muivah (NSCN-IM) and NSCN Khaplang (NSCN-K) who is demanding disintegration of this former kingdom. The Myanmar-based underground Kuki National Army (KNA) also wants to form what it called 'an independent sovereign Kuki state' by carving out Kuki-populated areas of Myanmar and, sardonically, some portions of Thoubal, Ukhrul and Chandel districts of Manipur. Two other Kuki underground groups—Kuki National Front Presidium. KNF-P, and Kuki National Front Military Council, KNF-MC, are separately demanding formation of what they called 'Kukiland' or 'Kuki homeland' by incorporating all the Kuki-settled areas of Manipur and want to have separate administration, court, economic rights, etc, according to the customary laws of the Kukis. Obviously, the KNA militants, who are active in parts of Chandel district, can not operate in Manipur without the support of some Kukis in the state. Less-known Zomi Revolutionary Army (ZRA) wants to unite all Zomis 'scattered in different parts of India (mostly in Churachandpur district of Manipur), Bangladesh and Myanmar' while little-known Kuki Liberation Army (KLA) and United Kuki Liberation Front (UKLF) are fighting for 'liberation of Kuki areas of north eastern region including Manipur, Assam, Tripura, Bangladesh and Myanmar' and for a separate Kuki homeland comprising Kuki areas of India (mostly Manipur) and Myanmar respectively. The UKLF, according to intelligence sources, has also developed links with NSCN-IM and is locked in an internecine clashes with KNA, which also acts as the armed wing of the Kuki National Organisation (KNO). Underground Hmar People's convention Democrats, HPC-D, is fighting for a Hmar autonomous district council to be formed by carving out Hmar-settled portions of Churachandpur district of Manipur, Mizoram and Assam. It means these underground groups, although fighting separately for separate states, want to tear apart all the five hill districts—Ukhrul, Senapati, Chandel, Tamenglong and Churachandpur, which together have a total area of 20,089 sq km, from Manipur. The remaining four valley districts—Imphal East, Imphal West, Bishenpur and Thoubal—have a total area of 2,238 sq km but what is to be pointed out here is that KNA's demand for an 'independent sovereign state' included some portions of Thoubal district. If these 'demands' were fulfilled, the total area of Manipur which had once extended its boundaries upto Chindwin river in Myanmar, present Cachar in Assam and Doyena/Dhunsiri (see A. Mackenzie's 'The North-East Frontier of Bengal') in the then Naga hills (now Nagaland) would be reduced to less than 2,238 sq: km. While these demands would remain far-fetched dreams (or will the central government divide Manipur?), many wondered why some tribes wanted to disintegrate the historic state which had been built by the forefathers over the centuries by sacrificing their lives, bloods etc.

According to 2001 census report, four valley districts, which together accounts for an area of 2,238 sq km representing merely 10.02 per cent of the total area of the state viz., 22,327 sq km have a population representing 58.85 per cent of the total population in Manipur. The total population of the state, the report points out, is 23,88,634 including 11,81,296 females. In the hills, Senapati has the highest figure with 3,79,214 followed by Churachandpur 2,28,707, Ukhrul 1,40,946, Chandel 1,22,714 and Tamenglong 1,11,493. It is the socio-cultural and economic ties that have bound the hill and valley people together since time immemorial, and both the people know that they are interdependent. Why the social relationship is lacking among ethnic groups and others communities now needs to be studied, as elsewhere in the world ethnic groups or people of different religious faiths, cultural identities or customs are living in pluralistic societies. In the hill districts, Nagas and Kukis live side by side along with other communities or tribes. Attempt to divide Manipur along the ethnic lines was considered the main reason of the decade-old Kuki-Naga clashes which broke out in early 1990s and involved large scale violence of mass killings, executions, forced expulsions, etc in major hill districts of the state. It was considered the worst feud between the two groups who follow the faith of Christianity but differ in terms of culture, physical features and language. The conflict left thousands of persons homeless, produced hundreds of orphans and widows, turned several women as sex workers to earn livelihood, changed the demography in hills, increased crimes at many places, etc. One can imagine the plight of the victims of the ethnic clashes because thousands of villagers could not harvest the crops during the feud. And some tribal organisations appear to be transgressing the history to whip up their campaign for division of Manipur. They are trying to break up Manipur by twisting and distorting historical facts to suit their demands.

When the government of India and NSCN-IM entered into a 'cease-fire agreement' in August 1997 to begin 'peace talks,' it was believed that the Naga underground group which has been fighting for an 'independent Nagaland' was prepared to settle the issues within the framework of the constitution of India because the central government was not likely to secede the Nagaland state from the union. How can the settlement be brought between the two? Many observers viewed that the centre was likely to concede to the demand of the underground outfit for a 'greater Nagaland' comprising adjoining areas of Manipur, Assam and Arunachal Pradesh. Besides, the centre, like it did in Mizoram, seemed to be prepared for spending huge amount of money on Nagaland to wean away the Naga underground members. This appeared to be a way for settlement between the centre and NSCN-IM though the 'peace process' did not involve other Naga underground factions. Even if a settlement was reached, the observers felt, the problems would continue to dog the north eastern region including Nagaland since some of the other major underground outfits were not involved in the peace process.

While people in Manipur supported the peace initiatives in Nagaland, they had apprehensions in their mind that there was what some social organisations termed as 'a clandestine design' to divide Manipur. And on 4 August 1997, more than five lakh people organised a rally throughout the state capital to show solidarity and fight to finish against any attempt to divide Manipur's territorial integrity. The rally was organised by the All Manipur United Clubs Organisation (AMUCO), a body of several local clubs. The

AMUCO-sponsored rally sent a clear message that the people of Manipur will not allow disintegration of the state 'at all costs.'

At first the Centre—NSCN-IM 'cease-fire' for a period of one year from 1 August 1997 was limited to only in the state of Nagaland. But, the Naga underground group persisted for extension of the truce to other adjoining areas including four hill districts of Manipur. This caused serious apprehension in the minds of the people that efforts were being continuously made to divide the state. Their apprehension and anxieties were compounded with fear when reports attributing to NSCN-IM Chairman Isak Chishi Swu appeared in a section of the national press on 13 August and 15 August, 1997 that the government of India had agreed to the demand of a 'bigger Naga state' comprising the adjoining areas of Assam, Arunachal Pradesh and Manipur. The report, though denied by the central government sources at that time, added fuel to the fire. Did it reveal, as later events proved, that the centre had been prepared to accept the terms dictated by some underground organisation(s), asked many observers. Some of the mandarins in New Delhi involved in the north eastern affairs, they felt, seemed to have lacked utter knowledge and historical background of the region they were dealing with. How far their concepts were clear on issues they were tackling or how honestly attempts were being made to bring peace in the region came up following large scale discontentment among wide sections of the people over extension of cease-fire beyond Nagaland to other parts of the north eastern states.

Towards the end of 1997, the Nagaland Chief Minister S.C. Jamir on two or three occasions stated that the 'talk with NSCN-IM' was confined in Nagaland state only. However, the government of Manipur, it seemed, was kept in the dark as far as the talk between the centre and NSCN-IM was concerned. Since there was, however, no clear-cut clarification from the centre on the above-stated news report that the government of India had agreed the demand of greater Nagaland, people in Manipur became restless.

Various social organisations, clubs or associations started despatching memoranda to the central leaders seeking assurances from them that the territorial integrity of Manipur would not be disturbed while settling issues with any underground outfit or outfits in the north eastern region. As there were wide protests from the various organisations and groups, and growing tension among some communities; Chief Minister Rishang Keishing wrote a letter to the Prime Minister on 13 August 1997 conveying that the state cabinet had taken a serious view of the 'provocative statement' published in some sections of the press that the centre had accepted 'in principle the need to unify Naga areas of Nagaland's neighbouring states under a single administrative unit.' The state government sought clarification from the Prime Minister.

Sensing the mood of the entire population, an all political party delegation led by Chief Minister Rishang Keishing called on the Prime Minister, I.K. Gujral on 21 August 1997 in New Delhi. The delegation conveyed to the Prime Minister that 'any political settlement arrived at between the government of India and insurgent outfits should not affect the territorial integrity of the state of Manipur.' 'It is a historical fact that Manipur with her long history of independent existence for nearly two thousand years has always maintained her territorial entity,' the delegation informed the Prime Minister pointing out that sovereignty of Manipur was recognised by the 'Treaty of Yandaboo in 1826' executed between the British and the Burmese empire. Her political boundary remains intact since 1834 when Kabaw valley was transferred to Burma,' the delegation told the centre seeking a written assurance from the government of India.

As the movement against the demand of greater Nagaland was gaining momentum, the NSCN-IM in a not-so-detailed statement on 29 August 1997 said, reports under the caption 'Government has accepted Naga demand' claims Isak Swu had 'appeared' in a section of the press. The reports said, 'the centre has accepted in principle the need to unify Naga inhabited areas of Nagaland's neighbouring states under single administrative unit claims the NSCN Chairman. This is entirely baseless; it is a total invention,' said the NSCN-IM statement signed by Swu and General Secretary Thuingaleng Muivah (a Tangkhul from Manipur's Ukhrul district). "The truth is that Mr. Isak, Chairman NSCN has not met in Geneva any press people belonging to the particular paper' in which the reports had appeared, nor has he ever made such a statement anywhere," the statement said. It continued that the press reports were intended to 'disturb the peace process' by creating pretext for the government of India and added that one should never forget the fact that hatred does not hold things together.'

'Meiteis (of the valley) and Nagas must know that the India government is not the final authority,' the statement said. 'The ultimate authority is the Meiteis and the Nagas themselves. For us, Meiteis and Nagas are brothers and sisters of the same parents beyond dispute. They are inseparable under any circumstances... Therefore anyone who attempts to break this oneness is a reactionary... This is our unquestionable principle and aim,' said the NSCN-IM statement.

Notwithstanding the large scale protests by various organisations, political parties, the state government; there was no firm or convincing written assurance from the centre except Manipur delegation being told by national leaders on different occasions that cease-fire with NSCN-IM would not be extended to Manipur, and its territorial integrity not disturbed while settling issues with any underground group. Did the verbal assurances pacify the people? As the cease-fire went on extending year after year, and demand for increasing area coverage intensified, different sections of the people wanted a firm commitment from the central government about the protection of territorial integrity of Manipur. Various organisations also demanded declaration of policy of the government of India in dealing with the underground organisations operating in the north eastern region. To show to the world that the people of Manipur would never allow the division of their state, the biggest ever rally and public meeting in the recent years was jointly organised by All Manipur Kanba Ima Lup (AMKIL) (roughly in English mothers association to protect Manipur) and National Identity Protection Committee (NIPCO) on 28 September 2000 in Imphal. More than eight lakh people participated in the rally and attended the historic public meeting at the Imphal pologround where the first ever polo match in the world had been played two millennia ago. The rallyists who carried placards 'save Manipur,' 'do not break Manipur boundary,' 'hill and plain people are one,' marched across Imphal and shouted slogans 'do not extend centre-NSCN-IM cease-fire to Manipur.' A resolution adopted in the 28 September public meeting said 'the people strongly opposed any move to disintegrate Manipur which has a 2000-year old history by some national leaders and NSCN-IM and declared that every available means will be utilised to prevent the disintegration.

On four occasions, the Manipur legislative assembly had passed resolutions to protect the territorial integrity of the state, and to oppose any move to extend the centre-NSCN-1M cease-fire to the territories of Manipur. People's concern was evident following the passing of a private member's motion in the Nagaland state legislative assembly in September 1994 to form a 'greater Nagaland' with areas including that of Manipur. The four resolutions passed unanimously on different occasions by the Manipur legislative assembly were:

- 24 March 1995: The House is also aware of the demands of various groups, both in the hills and the plain, for homelands. This sitting of the sixth Manipur legislative assembly strongly condemns the said resolution of the Nagaland legislative assembly (September 1994 resolution). This sitting expresses its opposition to the demands of homelands by various groups and strongly warns against continuance of movements for the same. It is resolved that the territorial boundary of Manipur, which has been in existence long before India got independence, cannot be under any circumstance compromised and any effort from any quarter to threaten this territorial integrity shall be faced collectively and unitedly.

- 14 March 1997: Welcoming the decision of the Prime Minister to have talks with the insurgents of the north east without any condition, the Manipur legislative assembly reiterates its resolution number two adopted on 24 March 1995 that the territorial integrity of Manipur shall be inviolate. The government of India as well as the leaders of all national parties be apprised of this resolution within this month of March by the hon'ble speaker and all members informed about the action taken in this regard.
- 17 December 1998: It is resolved that the cease-fire to facilitate Naga peace talks should not be extended into the territory of Manipur and that while implementing the outcome of the peace talk the boundary of Manipur can not be compromised under any circumstances. The house resolved to inform the government of India accordingly.
- 22 March 2001: The people of Manipur are opposed to the extension of the cease-fire between the Naga insurgents and the government of India. Therefore, it is resolved unanimously to appeal to the government of India to start negotiation with all insurgent outfits after declaring cease-fire with all of them.

Not only these resolutions had been conveyed (or was it really conveyed?) to the centre but also the demonstrations and rallies of the public organised against any move to extend the cease-fire between the government of India and NSCN-IM to territories of Manipur. (Controversial statements came up during the hearing of an inquiry commission probing into the 18 June 2001 incident in which 14 persons, opposing the extension of cease-fire between Government of India and underground National Socialist Council of Nagaland Isac and Muivah faction to the territories of. Manipur, were killed when Central Reserve Police Force personnel opened fire at the protesters in Imphal. Altogether 18 persons were killed during the month long anti-cease-fire agitation. It was said before the commission that the assembly resolution had been forwarded to the centre, but it was soon discovered that there was no official record to prove it. The state government has been urged by different organisations including the All Manipur Students Union (AMSU) to order an inquiry into the matter. The real picture will be known only after proper investigation.) What has been pointed out before the centre was that Manipur which had its own written constitution and well-defined internationally recognised boundary had entered into agreements, treaties, etc with foreign powers in the past. The 1470 agreement between king Kiyamba of Manipur and Khekhomba of Pong in upper Myanmar under which the boundaries of the state had once extended upto the present Kabaw valley in upper part of the neighbouring country was considered the first of its kind in the annals of the state. Under the Anglo-Manipuri treaty of 14 September 1762, the first such treaty with the British empire, the latter agreed to help Manipur recover its lands or drive away the Burmese from the state. It was followed by another Anglo-Manipuri defence protocol of 1763. Manipur had also entered into an agreement with Ahoms of Assam under which the state once extended its help to a former Ahom ruler. Under the Treaty of Yandaboo in February 1826, both the British and Burma (now Myanmar) recognised the independence of Manipur while the 1833 agreement with the British set the western boundary of the state. Under the 1834 agreement, the Kabaw valley was transferred to Burma from Manipur. After signing the stand still agreement and instrument of accession in August 1947, the Manipur merger agreement was signed on 21 September 1949. Prior to this, elections based on universal adult franchise had been held under the Manipur State Constitution Act 1947. This was followed by the formation of a popular government. All these years after the 1834 agreement, the boundaries of the state remained unchanged when Manipur merged with the union in October 1949 after the merger agreement. It still remains intact.

It may be emphasised that manipur must not be linked with any other state or states while settling Issues with any underground organisation or group. Unfortunately, the education which spread far and wide over the years has not helped much in bringing the people together and some tribes in the hills want to separate themselves from the state. It is not common people or the villagers who wanted to tear apart the state but some 'leaders' who misled the former. There are excellent relations/rapport between the common people both in hills and valley. Being the majority community. Meiteis must realise why 'some people' want to divide Manipur and ponder on how to bring everlasting harmonious relations among various sections of the people. On the other hand, it must also be realised by those who want to break up the state that it is not only majority Meiteis but various tribes also who are prepared to protect the territorial integrity of this tiny and historic state for all time to come. It is unfortunate to mention that thousands of Nagas and Kukis who joined the anti-cease-fire agitation in June/July 2001 in Manipur were termed by some Naga organisations that they had been 'forced to join the stir.' Time has come for all to rethink about the past mistakes and work for a common cause to hold the state from drifting towards an uncertain future. What is required is to look at issues not from one track of mind but from various angles as many complex problems are confronting the state.

When some Naga villages in then Naga hills of Assam sought British protection from the plain people in early 20th century, they began expansion of their villages. In, a memorandum submitted to the 'Simon Commission' in 1929, the 'Nagas Club' said their country within the administered area (of the British) consisted of more than eight tribes 'quite different from one another with quite different languages which can not be understood by each other, and there are more tribes outside the administered area which are not known at present.' It said Nagas were locked in intermittent warfare with the Assamese of Assam valley to the north and west, and Manipuris to the south. The memorandum said there was 'no unity among the Nagas and it is only the British Government that is holding us together now' and urged the latter to 'safeguard' them against all encroachment from other people. The then Naga hills district of Assam comprised of only two subdivisions—Kohima and Mokokchung. The district was later placed under the sixth schedule of the constitution as an autonomous district within the state of Assam in 1950, and the territory of the district expanded under the 'Naga Hills Tuensang Areas Act 1957' with the addition of Tuensang frontier division of the North East Frontier Agency. And the district became a state of Indian union called 'Nagaland' in 1963. From tribal villages to a district and then to a statehood. However, some Naga organisation still maintain that they had distinct identity, history and areas in the part. When Nagaland became a state, Manipur still remained a union territory. A partial policy the centre had adopted in dealing with people in the north east. History recalls how people in Manipur had to fight for several years to press their rightful demand for granting statehood to Manipur and for constitutional recognition of Manipuri language.

As the period of extended cease-fire between the centre—NSCN-IM was to expire on 31 August 2001, the government of India's emissary K. Padmanabhaih from May first week began shuttling between New Delhi and Bangkok where NSCN-IM General Secretary Thuingaleng Muivah was lodged in a jail for entering Thailand by using a forged passport. The two discussed many times about the extension of the cease-fire which was, as stated before, confined in the state of Nagaland. This time, the Naga underground organisation insisted that the area of coverage should include Nagaland's adjoining areas in other states where Nagas have settled. The government of India at first did not accept the condition put forward by the NSCN-IM. The underground Naga group said if the cease-fire was to be extended, the area coverage should include the adjoining areas of Nagaland.

When the former interlocutor of the central government Swaraj Kaushal had reportedly stated in 1998 that the centre was prepared to extend the area coverage of the cease-fire with NSCN-IM, the government contradicted his statement stating that the cease-fire was limited to the boundaries of Nagaland. Efforts to persuade the NSCN-IM continued since the government viewed the outfit as the main insurgency group operating in the north eastern region. Right from the beginning, attempts were made by some Naga underground groups to include Manipur's territories under the cease-fire between the centre and Naga underground outfit. When parts of Manipur such as Ukhrul, Mao-Maram and Tamenglong were included in the cease-fire agreement with underground Naga government 'Federal Government of Nagaland' (forerunner of the NSCN-IM's present government of people's republic of Nagaland) in 1964, the All Manipur People's Convention (AMPC) strongly objected to it. In a memorandum to the Prime Minister in September 1965, the AMPC President. Laishram Manaobi said the 'hostiles (Naga) in the cease-fire areas of Ukhrul, Mao-Maram and Tamenglong sub-divisions of Manipur have taken the law into their own hands and set up a parallel government while civil administration in these areas is heading for collapse.' Manaobi (who is no more) had said the law and order situation had 'extremely deteriorated' in the hills after inclusion of certain areas of Manipur in the cease-fire agreement. He had also stated that it had also become 'increasingly difficult for other tribes such as Kukis and loyal tribals to live in disturbed areas.' The AMPC pointed out before the centre that people in the hills were 'at the mercy of the hostiles who move freely with arms in the cease-fire areas and announce from the house tops that Ukhrul, Mao-Maram and Tamenglong have been merged with Nagaland and are no longer under the government of Manipur.

They (the Naga underground members) proclaim that Nagaland including Ukhrul, Mao-Maram and Tamenglong will soon be made an independent country... the AMPC memorandum said pointing out that 'this highly provocative misguided and harmful propaganda has produced a deterrent effect on the masses in the hill areas.' The memorandum strongly demanded among others: (1) The cease-fire agreement should cease to operate in Ukhrul, Mao-Maram and Tamenglong sub-divisions of Manipur as these areas do not form a part of Nagaland. (2) The entire population of Manipur would rule out even the remotest possibility of giving the smallest patch of land to Nagaland, let alone big areas like Ukhrul, Mao-maram and Tamenglong. The ceding of these three hill sub-divisions will be tantamount to dismemberment of Manipur. Any such arrangement will be fraught with grave consequences. None would brook the territorial disintegration of this ancient state of Manipur ... The government of India should also in their own interest rule out completely such an unrealistic suggestion.'

Padmanabhaih held talks with Muivah but the latter insisted the expansion of area coverage of cease-fire. Since the people of Manipur had on various occasions demonstrated against any move to extend the centre-NSCN-IM cease-fire to the state, the centre's emissary wanted a condition from NSCN-IM's leadership that there must not be demand for greater Nagaland. The Naga underground group refused to accept the condition and threatened to review the cease-fire with the government of India. Ultimately, the centre in spite of strong protests and objection from the people of Manipur conceded to the NSCN-IM pressure and extended the cease-fire by including the words 'without territorial limits' in the agreement. The 14 June 2001 joint statement read as: "In continuation of the ongoing peace process, a meeting was held on 13 and 14 June, 2001 in Bangkok between the representatives of the government of India and the NSCN and the following points are mutually agreed upon: (1) The cease-fire agreement is between the government of India and the NSCN as two entities without territorial limits. (2) Both the parties would abide by the ground rules as revised on 13 January 2001, both in letter and in spirit. (3) It is agreed to further extend the cease-fire for a period of one year with effect from 1 August 2001. (4) The government of India and the NSCN agree to proceed with the peace process on substantive issues to bring about a lasting political solution to the issue. It is recognised that there is a need for mutual trust and respect. (5) The next round of talks would be held in the last week of July/first week of August 2001." It was jointly signed by K. Padmanabhaih, representative of the government of India and Th. Muivah, General Secretary of the NSCN.

Soon after the agreement, Padmanabhaih and Union Home Minister L.K. Advani stated that 'without territorial limits' did not have any reference to the reorganisation of the territories of the north eastern states. How would the people of Manipur believe this because on several occasions earlier Prime Minister A.B. Vajpayee and Advani had said cease-fire would not be extended to Manipur. What was the motive or 'hidden agenda' behind extension of cease-fire to territories of Manipur, Assam or Arunachal Pradesh? Why did the centre ignore 'democratic' voice of the entire people of Manipur against move to extend cease-fire to appease a banned underground outfit? The centre's decision drove a wedge between the people in hill and valley. The extension of the cease-fire against the wishes of people raised serious doubts in their minds that it was a first step to divide their state. Moreover, the state governments concerned in the region did not have as per the agreement any role in deciding the modalities of implementation of the ground rules.

The total area of Nagaland state is 16,579 sq km while NSCN-IM has claimed a large area of 1,20,000 sq km as their territory. Political observers asked where are the remaining areas. The claimed area, it may be pointed out, transcends the boundaries of Assam, Manipur, Arunachal Pradesh and Nagaland and includes upper part of neighbouring Myanmar. Since the agreement for cease-fire extension was 'without territorial limits' together with agreed ground rules, the NSCN-IM cadres can set up their designated camps anywhere in the area, and move freely between the such designated camps. This will legitimise the NSCN-IM's claim for territorial expansion at the cost of Manipur and other neighbouring states. It will also give the NSCN-IM cadres license to freely move with arms in Manipur and other states while the state government concerned will remain as mere spectators.

While Rome was burning, was Nero fidling? Are some of the politicians in Manipur utterly selfish, opportunist, self-centered? Are some of them hopelessly corrupt, parochial, short-sighted or are only a few good? Most of these so-called public leaders in Manipur have 'no principle or ideology' and will do 'whatever is possible to come to power after elections. 'But, interestingly, whenever they change sides to grasp power, they say they are doing it in the interests and for the welfare of the common people in the state.' Unfortunately and very sadly, the state has not been able to produce a leader worth-mentioning his name—a man who can forsee the future, shape the things to come, brave all kinds of difficulties to keep Manipur solidly united, mobilise the people and resources effectively for bringing about an all round developments despite obstacles, bring emotional and physical integration among various sections of the people. It is time for those in the powers to realise the present condition and situation, and put the state on the right track. If the present situation is not tackled properly, the future of Manipur appears to be doomed.

Many people in the country have seen how unstable was the government formed in Manipur in the past some years because of frequent changing of sides by the legislators. No government formed after any fresh elections has completed its tenure of five years so far in Manipur. In the past, when there was no threat to the territorial integrity of Manipur, people tolerated all kinds of 'political activities' of the legislators even if these had not been in the interests of the common people.

So far Manipur has had eighteen ministries since it became a state of the Indian Union in 1972. After the February 2000 assembly elections, a 34-member United

Front Manipur (UFM) ministry headed by Manipur State Congress Party (MSCP) leader and Chief Minister Wahengbam Nipamacha Singh was sworn in on 2 March 2000. The strength of the UFM of the then seventh legislative assembly was MSCP 23, Federal Party of Manipur (FPM) 6, Independent 1 and 9 others. Of the 9, four had been elected under Nationalist Congress Party (NCP), 3 under Manipur People's Party (MPP), 1 under Rashtraiya Janata Dal (RJD) and 1 under Janata Dal United (JDU). The 9 legislators soon merged with the MSCP. On the opposition front, the congress had 11 members. Bharatiya Janata Party (BJP) 6, MPP 1, NCP 1, Samata Party (SP) 1 and Janata Dal Secular (JDS) 1. Like in the past, political bickering began some months after the formation of the ministry following 'differences' among some senior leaders of the ruling front particularly between Chief Minister and Speaker of the legislative assembly, Sapam Dhananjoy. Attempts were made to dethrone each other by their supporters. Two motions had been moved in the house—opposition-sponsored no-confidence motion against the UFM ministry led by Nipamacha Singh and UFM-sponsored no confidence motion against the Speaker. Leaders of ruling front and Speaker-backed opposition hurled charges and counter charges. As Governor Ved Marwah for the third time asked the Speaker and Chief Minister in separate letters on 7 February 2001 to 'immediately reconvene' the house to discuss the 'pending' no confidence motion against the ruling front, the Speaker said he could not do so because of what he termed as 'heightened tension' between the ruling front and opposition. Speaker on 1 December 2000 had admitted the no confidence motion against the UFM ministry but the house was adjourned sine die after admitting the motion, and without fixing the date for discussion on the motion. He later said the date was to be fixed by the business advisory committee of the house. However, the provisions of the rules of business warrants the assembly to discuss the motion within ten days of admission of the motion.

Since Speaker adjourned the house sine die without fixing date for discussion of the motion, there was a clash between the ruling front and opposition members on 1 December 2000 resulting in the damage of microphones, chairs, etc, of the assembly. Dhananjoy had earlier said without repairing the damaged microphones, chairs, he could not fix date for discussion of the no confidence motion against Nipamacha Singh ministry which, many political observers felt, had commanded a solid strength and majority in the house. Tussles for capturing ... powerwent on.

On 10 February 2001, eight MSCP MLAs (Members of the Legislative Assembly) switched over side and announced their support to the six-party 'disjointed' opposition whose declared aim and object was nothing but to pull down the UFM ministry led by Nipamacha Singh for what it termed 'failure' on all fronts—an oft-used word by any opponent group while attempting to topple a ministry in the recent political history of Manipur. The eight MLAs except one were ministers or holding equivalently ministerial posts in the UFM ministry. This, many observers felt, indicated that they had 'revolted' against the ministry since they were not given portfolios of their choice. The eight were sports Minister Moirangthem Hemanta Singh, Revenue Minister Thounaojam Bira Singh. Sericulture Minister Hangkhangpao, Minister of State for Works Z. Mangaibou, Minister of State for Public Health Engineering On Jamang Haokip, Minister of State for Backward Classes Allaudin, Deputy Chairman of the State Planning Board (a cabinet ranking post) Laisram Jatra Singh and MLA M. Chungkhosei. Some of them were senior cabinet ministers who, along with known MSCP functionaries, had built up the regional party recently as an alternative to the national parties.

People in Manipur, it was viewed, felt that national parties had dominated the state politics for several years. Some local politicians believed these parties had overlooked the regional interests and 'realised' the necessity of having a united regional party which, some thought, would cater to the needs of local people. But the oft—quoted phrase 'the same old wine in a new bottle' applied in the case of Manipur also as most of the senior members of he MSCP were from different national parties, The organisational level members were also sharply divided with a section of the MSCP supporting the Chief Minister, Nipamacha Singh and the other group siding with the Working President of the party, Th. Chaoba Singh who was once a former Union Minister of State for Sports and Food processing,

Next day, on 11 February 2001, while 'welcoming the desertion of the eight MLAs from MSCP (Nipamacha Camp) and their supporting the opposition camp'. Chaoba Sigh told media persons at the official residence of the Speaker that eight other MSCP MLAs—Chief Minister Nipamacha Singh, Deputy Chief Minister Leisangthem Chandramani Singh, Urban Development Minister Paonam Achou Singh, Agriculture Minister S. Rajen Singh, Tribal Development Minister Samuel Jendai, Irrigation and Flood Control Minister Kshetrimayum Biren Singh, Information Minister M. Kunjo Singh and Former Finance Minister H. Lokhon Singh were expelled for six years from the party. A question came up whether the Working President who was appointed by the MSCP President Nipamacha Singh could expel the party president (an elected post) and other members of the party or not. But, as many have said, in politics the numbers matter.

In between horse-trading among the MLAs was encouraged and many switched over side from ruling front to the opposition camp. Lokhon Singh also switched over to opposition camp. It may be pointed out that the SP (Samata Party) which had a lone member increased its strength to eleven as ten MLAs from the Congress left the party and joined SP under the leadership of Radhabinod Koijam. Things went very fast. On 13 February 2001, UFM ministry headed by Nipamacha Singh resigned, and some hours later united democratic alliance (UDA) was formed by MSCP, FPM and SP. There must not be any confusion about the strength of different parties as MLAs often changed sides.

On 14 February 2001, the UDA split as SP withdrew from it and formed People's Front (PF). The strength of the PF was SP 12, MSCP 23, BJP 6, NCP 2, JDS 1, MPP 1, FPM 4 and an independent member. Koijam was elected leader of the PF, Meanwhile, MSCP President Nipamacha Singh after an Executive meeting of the party expelled Working President Chaoba Singh. Vice President Loitongbam Amuiao Singh, General Secretary Y. Mangi Singh for six years from the party. The fight for supremacy within the MSCP ultimately led both the warring groups to the court.

It appeared that some of the senior—level leaders who were not in favour of the regional party becoming powerful hastened the political process in Manipur. On 15 February 2001, Radhabinod Koijam was sworn in as the 24th Chief Minister of Manipur heading the PF ministry. It temporarily ended the months long political crisis following frequent changing of sides by the legislators. One finds it very difficult to study the political scenario in Manipur as it may change any moment. Hours after the portfolios were allotted to the new ministers, Medical Minister Nimaichad Luwang, Veterinary Minister M. Manihar Singh and Cooperation Minister Kh. Amutombi Singh resigned citing 'reasons' that senior NCP leader Chungkhokai Doungel and some break away MSCP legislators who had toppled the Nipamacha Singh ministry had not been given ministerial berths.

However, it may be noted that they resigned only after the allocation of portfolios to the ministers. Their resignations were not accepted by the Chief Minister. Meanwhile, K. Raina who resigned from the post of Deputy Speaker of the state assembly on 24 February 2001 announced the formation of 'Democratic Federal Party of Manipur' (DFPM). Both were elected under the FPM tickets and for the first time. Manipur cabinet under the leadership of Chief Minister Koijam took a decision to declare unilateral cease-fire to all insurgent organisations operating in the state for one month from 1 March 2001 though some observers were sceptical about this. Some viewed it as a prelude to extend the centre-NSCN-IM cease-fire to Nagaland's adjoining areas in other states.

On 27 March 2001, all major political parties in the state during a meeting convened by Chief Minister agreed to extend the unilateral cease-fire to all insurgent groups for one more month from 1 April 2001. The meeting had been convened to seek opinion of the political parties on the proposal to extend the period of cease-fire. However, the state government's decision on the issue was not accepted by the Government of India as it was evident from Koijam's announcement on 30 March 2001 in New Delhi after meeting with Union Home Minister Advani that 'one-month-long unilateral cease-fire may not be extended further.'

Hardly three months have passed, the PF ministry faced a serious political crisis as its main constituent, 31-member MSCP, was split with 18 of them forming 'progressive MSCP' (PMSCP). MSCP's original strength was 23, it rose to 32 and again came down to 31. It further needs no elaboration. On 13 May 2001, the 18-member PMSCP merged with the BJP increasing latter's strength in the 60-member Manipur legislative assembly to 26. Since it increased its strength, the BJP under the leadership of former Chief Minister R.K. Dorendra Singh began its 'toppling game' to capture power from the PF. Both BJP and SP were partners of the ruling National Democratic Alliance (NDA) in New Delhi but the two were sharply divided in Manipur. BJP was able to garner support from small parties in its attempt to topple the ministry.

As the political crisis was deepening, crippling the normal administrative work, and to assert his position, Chief Minister Radhabinod Koijam who had soon lost popularity moved a motion of confidence. BJP central leadership instructed state unit and legislators to support the Samata Party-led PF ministry. However, the 3-month old PF ministry was voted out on 21 May 2001 on the floor of the assembly. At the time of voting, 17 members favoured the vote of confidence and they were SP 13, MPP 1, MSCP (Nipamacha faction) 1, BJP 1 and an independent. Those who opposed the motion were BJP 24, MSCP (Chaoba faction) 10, NCP 2, FPM 2 and Janata Dal (Loken group) 1. BJP legislature wing leader Dorendra Singh abstained from voting. Hours later, progressive democratic alliance (PDA) was formed by BJP 25 (including Dorendra Singh), MSCP (Chaoba faction) 10, NCP 2, FPM 2 and Janata Dal (Loken group) 1. Of 26 BJP legislators, only former Higher Education Minister Haobam Bhuban Singh followed the central leadership's directive and voted in favour of the PF. The PDA demanded installation of a BJP-led ministry but SP angered over ally's stabbing in the back lambasted its NDA partner whose central leadership announced that BJP would not take part in the ministry formation in Manipur. All the legislators belonging to the PDA went to Delhi on 23 May 2001 but BJP President Jana Krishnamurthi refused to see the Manipur MLAs on 25 May 2001. BJP central leadership reiterated its stand that the party would not take part in ministry formation.

As BJP's decision became clear, Speaker Dhananjoy submitted a list of 41 supporters to the Governor on 28 May 2001 and staked his claim to form the ministry. Speaker claimed that he had been elected new PDA leader. At the same time, MSCP (Chaoba faction) leader M. Hemanta Singh also in a letter to the Governor staked his claim to form a ministry. In the meantime, Dhananjoy withdrew his claim to form the ministry because of internal squabble within the PDA. And, ultimately Manipur was placed under president's rule on 2 June 2001, and its assembly later dissolved. While all these political crises, defections by legislators, horse-trading of MLAs, etc, were taking place, the centre and NSCN-IM were discussing about the extension of cease-fire between the two to other parts of north eastern states including Manipur.

When a news agency report from Bangkok about the signing of the centre NSCN-IM cease-fire agreement on 14 June 2001, and extending it to parts of Manipur and other north eastern states, flashed across the country, people in the state were not only confounded and dumbfounded but utterly shocked. The ignorance of the central government about the wishes of the people, and not taking them into account, deeply hurt the sentiments of the Manipuris both in the hills and valley. They felt more alienated when the government of India, apprehending troubles after the cease-fire extension, rushed more central troops in addition to the already-stationed more-than-required forces and deployed them particularly in the valley and interior parts of the state.

How much people were shocked and concerned were reflected in a 'declaration' on 26 June 2001 made by major organisations which spearheaded the anti-cease-fire agitation in the state—AMSU (All Manipur Students Union), AMUCO, AMKIL, NIPCO, United People's Front (UPF) and International Peace and Social Advancement (IPSA). They said the people of Manipur supported 'peace process in Nagaland' but considered the extension of the centre-NSCN-IM cease-fire to Manipur and allowing the opening of designated camps and free movement of armed cadres (under the agreement) of the NSCN-IM was a 'step towards the disintegration of the territorial integrity of Manipur.' The organisations said extension of cease-fire to Manipur was an 'act to escalate the colonial divide and rule policy aiming to infuse hitherto non-existent communal division to the symbiotic society of Manipur' and declared that any attempt and subsequent alteration to the existing boundary by the government of India would 'necessarily initiate the process of the disintegration of the republic of India duly constituted in 1950.'

Enraged people viewed that their 'unworthy' representatives who had always indulged in trying to grasp power from one another were responsible for the extension of area coverage of the truce from Nagaland to parts of Manipur, Assam and Arunachal Pradesh. However, it was the same people who had elected whom they now called 'unworthy' representatives. Had a 'united' state government firmly opposed any such move to extend the area coverage of the truce, it was thought, the centre would not have 'conceded' to the pressure of the Naga underground outfit. Veracity of the newspaper reports attributing to Union Home Minister Advani that the response from Assam and

Manipur Chief Ministers P.K. Mahanta and Radhabinod Koijam (to the centre's proposal to extend cease-fire to parts of other north eastern states) were positive could not be confirmed because Koijam strongly denied having agreed to the proposal.

As the 14 June report spread like a wild fire among the population within a few hours, Manipur government as a 'precautionary measure' imposed prohibitory orders under criminal procedure code preventing gathering of four or more persons in Imphal and greater Imphal areas. Under the orders, the people were also not allowed to carry any arm or lethal weapon. On the same day, the AMUCO expressed strong opposition to the cease-fire extension to Manipur. The Assam government also strongly opposed the cease-fire extension without territorial limits.

Soon things started hotting up. AMUCO called for a 66-hour 'general strike' from 15 June midnight while Manipur Students Federation (MSF) locked offices of different political parties. Legislators of all parties condemned the cease-fire extension to Manipur. Effigies of Prime Minister Vajpayee, Home Minister Advani, government's emissary Padmanabhaih, Home Secretary Kamal Pande, NSCN-IM leaders Swu and Muivah, were set on fire at various places in Manipur as all members of Manipur assembly took out a short rally on 16 June and Submitted a memorendum to the Governor demanding immediate withdrawal of cease-fire from Manipur. More and more people and social organisations came out in open in protest against the cease-fire extension which was to be effective from 1 August 2001. The wrath of the people quickly directed on their 'representatives.'

On 17 June, the AMSU, the biggest body of the students, demanded members of Parliament from Manipur and members of the state assembly to resign immediately to lodge strong protest with the central government against the truce extension while Arunachal Pradesh Chief Minister Mukut Mithi said the centre-NSCN-IM cease-fires extension 'will not be honoured' in his state. Apart from entire Manipuri Muslim community, various Naga and Kuki tribes and their organisations who strongly opposed the area coverage of the cease-fires joined in the anti-cease-fire's agitations launched by people in the state.

After an emergency joint meeting, five social organisations—AMSU, AMKIL, NIPCO, UPF and IPSA—called a 24-hour 'Manipur bandh' from 17 June midnight as wide-ranging protests against the cease-fires extension were reported from across the state. In the past, hardly any one dared to come out either during the 'Manipur bandh' or 'general strike' called by any social organisation. Tension was running high in the valley as wide protests were continuing day and night amid heavy deployment of security and police forces. Everyone whether young or old was concerned and restless since the extension of the cease-fire to Manipur, and the state government under the leadership of Governor Ved Marwah (Manipur was under central rule), notwithstanding the growing widespread protests, only conveyed the 'assurance' from Union Home Minister Advani that boundary of Manipur would be protected. An assurance which the people of Manipur will never believe because of past experiences.

In the beginning, soon after signing the Bangkok agreement, some of the statements made by some central leaders were 'harsh and provocative.' 'Some threats,' they remarked, 'will not move the government.' 'The protests will subside after the deployment of the forces.' It didn't. The statement of Union Minister of State for Home Affairs I.D. Swamy that a resolution may be adopted in Parliament to protect the boundaries of Manipur failed to pacify the Manipuries. Will any patriotic person remain silent when their motherland which has a 2000-year-old written history was, they thought, being torn apart either to integrate the divided portion with a state which was born only in 1963 or form a separate state' asked some political observers. When a mass uprising broke out to prevent such move, would the people's action be termed 'politically motivated' or 'engineered by insurgents,' they said.

The atmosphere was thick and heavy in Imphal on 18

June 2001. People wore gloomy face as Manipur faced an uncertain future. Unlike in the past, persons stopped their routine work and swore to fight together against the extension of the centre-NSCN-IM cease-fires to Manipur as they viewed this as a first step to break up their state. Even people who lived on daily wages did not bother about their work and were prepared to join the stir against the extension of area coverage of the truce.

The weather was dull that day and sky over Imphal as overcast with heavy clouds being rainy season. There was heavy deployment of forces at all vulnerable points in Imphal and greater Imphal areas, and people could not communicate to each other because of 'Manipur bandh' and prohibitory orders which were in force. The state government authorities, following a chain of protests after the announcement of the cease-fire extension, put up police and security barricades at all important roads and points in Imphal, Both the central forces and police were instructed to effectively deal with any 'unwanted situation.' Some senior-ranking police officials in private conversation wondered why the centre had taken such a 'sentimentally—hurt step' against the wishes of the general people. Despite heavy security measures that day, irate people in droves came out spontaneously at different localities defying prohibitory orders, burnt effigies of central and NSCN-IM leaders and shouted slogans 'don't break Manipur,' 'we will shed blood for Manipur,' 'we will shed blood for Manipur,' 'don't divide hill and valley people.' 'Kill as many as you want but we will not allow disintegration of our motherland,' etc, at all important roads in the state capital,

First it was a few hundreds, but within hours the number swelled into thousands at various localities and soon, without anybody telling them, thousands and thousands of people trooped towards Raj Bhavan from different directions with effigies of Prime Minister Vajpayee, Home Minister Advani, NSCN-IM leaders Swu and Muivah. As thousands of people broke through major barricades at Palace Gate, Keisampat Bridge, Moirangkhom, Khuyathong, Uripok, etc, police and Central Reserve Police Forces (CRPF) burst a number of tear gas shells to quell the crowds but the determined protestors in spite of hundreds of them being injured in security action proceeded towards the Raj Bhavan in the heart of Imphal town. The scenes were pathetic and touching at all points with young protestors removing their shirts and asking the security men to shoot them first before dividing Manipur. Their anger, helplessness, frustration, thirst for protection of Manipur, were reflected in their faces.

What is the use if we can't protect our motherland, shouted the protestors. Will our forefathers forgive us if we can't protect our territorial boundaries formed by shedding their blood? The slogans 'we will protect our own motherland,' 'we say no to the centre-NSCN-IM cease-fire extension to Manipur,' filled the air. The government statements why people have been provoked so much because there was no question of disturbing the boundary of Manipur could not pacify the people.

At Sanjenthong bridge on Imphal river in the heart of the town, where people from the Palace Gate on way to Raj Bhavan were first blocked, the angry protestors did not retreat even an inch when the police used forces to stop them. At one point of time, the scene became somewhat emotional when both male and female protestors shouted slogans and asked the police whether they will continue to beat the people while the state was being torn apart or not. Some of the police personnel posted there were even 'moved,' The police could no longer control the crowds as similar instances were reported simultaneously from other entry points at Keisampat, Moirangkhom, Uripok and Khuyathong despite bursting tear gas shells, opening fire in the air. And within minutes, lakhs of people who overcame the security barricades at different points converged in front of the eastern gate of Raj Bhavan and burnt the effigies they had carried. And that 18 June 2001 protest turned out to be the biggest ever 'mass uprising' against the government in the past some decades. This day will stand out glaringly in the annals of modern Manipur.

First they wanted the Governor to address them and tell them about how the state government was going to react on cease-fire extension to Manipur. When the Governor wanted a team of representatives to meet him, the protestors turned down the suggestion, and the rest was the history. Angry protestors went towards Manipur assembly complex, set afire the assembly hall and secretariat, pulled out the Speaker, Dhananjoy from his office chamber, roughed him up, forcibly brought him to the gate of Raj Bhavan, sent him to meet Governor Marwah to convey the feelings of the people. The Speaker had played an important role in dethroning the Nipamacha Singh ministry and in the installation of the Koijam ministry. Then, thousands of irate people moved out in different directions and burnt down Chief Minister's secretariat building, party offices of Congress, MSCP, MPP, SP, destroyed the BJP office (not burnt down since it was located next to a petrol pump), official residences of several political leaders including Speaker Dhananjoy, former Union Minister of State for Sports Th. Chaoba Singh (he was the lone representative from Manipur in the NDA ministry), former Deputy Chief Minister L. Chandramani Singh, Adviser to Manipur Governor, K. Kipgen, number of government vehicles, etc,.

The setting ablaze of the state assembly building, according to some analysts, indicated the anger of the people about the ignorance of state assembly resolutions against move to extend the cease-fire to Manipur by the centre and possible threat to territorial integrity of the state while burning of residential quarters of the elected persons showed that the common people were fed up with the activities of these 'leaders' who were always concerned about capturing power. A defiant protestor also hoisted a pre-merger seven-colour' Manipur flag atop the traffic post near the main gate of Raj Bhavan while angry crowds were awaiting a word from the Governor on people's demand for an audience with him. Two MLAs—K. Tomba Singh of Khundrakpam and N. Bihari Singh of Khurai-sustained burn injuries at the assembly complex. Soon there was a heavy downpour but it did not dampen the spirits of the protestors who sneaked into the heavily-guarded VIP complex at Babupara and started setting on fire the residential quarters of the elected members. In such circumstances, some of the security guards naturally remained mere spectators. They had not only been far out numbered but the 'cause' for which the people were fighting 'moved' them, some analysts pointed out.

The target of the angry protestors directed soon on the elected persons. As hundreds of angry youths attempted to set afire the author's office inside the VIP complex, it was, of course, a difficult task to convince the importance of a news agency and that it was the only office located inside the complex.' 'If you are telling lie, Tamo (big brother), we will come and finish your house in the night.' This was the mood of the young protestors. They were again told that it was an office and not the house of an elected person. Around this time, the CRPF posted at Chief Minister's office complex and at Raj Bhavan opened fire killing thirteen persons that day and injuring several others.

While a critically wounded youth died on 22 June, four other persons were also killed in the month-long anti-ceasefire agitation during which widespread sit-in protests, demonstrations, rallies, public meetings, and other democratic forms of stir were organised across the state. While all the eighteen victims—Laishram Ongbi Tamphasana, Khoisnam Singhajit, Nishikanta Yumnam (Nganthoi), Thokchom Wilson (Pappu), Gurumayum Dutta (Richie), Kshetrimayum Jiban (Gocha), Sagolshem Surchandra (Boicha), Thokchom Lalit (Thethe), Bachaspatimayum Naocha (Atang), Konsam Kameshwor, Kshetrimayum Romio (Romi), Mayanglambam Manikanta. Thoudam Guneshwor, Amom Rajendra (Rajen), Thingom Birendra, Laitonjam Rajkumar, Chabungbam Bhagat (Bharat) and Okram Ramananda (Nanao)—who sacrificed their lives for protection of territorial integrity, have become martyrs in the eyes of Manipuris, more than 562 injured persons will also never be forgotten. Two protestors—Sorokhaibam Ongbi Sobita whose right leg was amputated following a bullet injury and Brahmacharimayum Biju (Taiton) who sustained serious bullet wound at the left leg-remain handicapped persons for the rest of their lives. It may be pointed out that bodies of all the eighteen victims were cremated at the historic Kekrupat on the banks of Imphal river.

With more and more local clubs, social groups, different tribal 'organisations joining the anti-cease-fire movement, people intensified the anti-truce stir. An apex social body, United Committee Manipur (UCM) was formed by AMSU, AMKIL, NIPCO, IPSA, UPF and AMUCO on 14 July 2001 while United Naga Council (UNC), also a body of some Naga organisations, organised rallies and public meetings at some parts of the hill areas in support of the cease-fires extension. On 21 June 2001, before forming the UCM, the AMSU, AMKIL, NIPCO, IPSA, UPF and AMUCO had called social boycott of all 60 MLAs and members of Parliament from Manipur. Following pressure from the people, the legislators had also decided to resign en masse if the cease-fires was not withdrawn from the state by 31 July 2001. Legislators from the state camping at New Delhi called on several national leaders of different political parties and urged them to exert pressure on the NDA government to withdraw the cease-fires from Manipur, Assam and Arunachal Pradesh.

For the first time, concerns of the central government were noticed when Union Minister of State for Home Affairs, I.D. Swamy and Additional Home Secretary P.D. Shenoy were sent to study the Manipur situation on 5 July 2001. In the meantime, the UCM had also submitted a memorendum to the centre giving historical backgrounds of the state, and it was followed by discussions between Manipur leaders on one side and Prime Minister Vajpayee, Home Minister Advani and central officials on the other. After receiving the report on the state situation from Swamy, Prime Minister Vajpayee during a meeting with elected representatives from Manipur on 8 July 2001 in New Delhi said, the government of India would review the cease-fires agreement including the words 'without territorial limits.' Advani and other officials also attended the meeting.

On the other hand UNC intensified pressure on the central government not to withdraw the ceasefire extension from Manipur. A UNC-sponsored 'Naga People's Convention' (NPC) on 28 June 2001 'welcomed, appreciated and supported the extension of the ceasefire without territorial limits.' Resolutions adopted in the convention blamed Meitei community for what it termed 'belligerent and confrontationist approach' by launching anti-ceasefire agitation and claimed that 'the traditional homeland of the Nagas was arbitrarily divided by the former colonial rulers (the British).' As stated earlier, the British came to Manipur less than 200 years ago, and before their advent the state had remained as an independent kingdom for centuries. History reveals that people both in hills and valley had jointly fought together against any foreign invasion. They also made joint military expeditions to other countries on many occasions. Some analysts feel that it would be highly improper to exaggerate the things, concoct stories and distort facts while attempting to tear apart a historic state like Manipur as these would lead to nothing but deep misunderstanding among different communities and create unfavourable situation for all.

A resolution adopted in the convention said, the state government would be urged to 'look into the reported coercive steps taken, by the Meitei organisations in the valley to force the Nagas and other non-Meitei communities to toe their line.' The UCM later circulated a printed form seeking information from village chiefs and individuals to inform any instance of 'coercive steps' by Meitei organisations or of Nagas fleeing the valley during the anti-ceasefire agitation but the response was, UCM sources said, 'almost nil.' Various social organisations appealed to all sections of the people to protect the territorial integrity and tirelessly worked for communal harmony. On several occasions, Governor Ved Marwah praised the non-communal attitude and nature displayed by majority community during the 'tense situation' following intensification of anti-truce stir in June and July 2001. True, some Nagas fled the valley out of fear. The UCM and many local organisations made repeated appeals to those Nagas who fled the valley to return to their homes as the agitation was not directed on them. Many heeded to the appeal.

There are at least 24 tribes in Nagaland known as 'Naga tribe' but they have sharply different dialects and communicate each other in 'Nagamese,' a pidgin Assamese. In case of Manipur, there are many similarities between Manipuri language and dialects of the 29 recognised tribes in the state since inhabitants in the state originated from the same stock of people. It might be expected that the present language of the people, united under the name of Meithei, would have a very apparent likeness to these languages (of some major tribes), and such is the case, wrote Maj. W. McCulloch, the then Political Agent in Manipur, in his book 'Account of the Valley of Munnipore and of the Hill Tribes.' All these tribes also have traditions amongst themselves, that the Munniporees are off-shoots from them.

Meanwhile, the announcement that the cease-fires agreement would be reviewed did not pacify the people who continued month-long wide spread sit-in protests, rallies, public meetings, processions, burning of effigies of the leaders, social boycott of elected members, civil disobedient movement, etc... And finally the government of India announced on 27 July 2001 that the three words 'without territorial limits' in the agreement between the centre and NSCN-IM would be deleted and status quo ante of 14 June restored. Soon the ceasefire from Manipur and other parts of Assam and Arunachal Pradesh was withdrawn limiting it, ultimately, to the state of Nagaland. Going by the indications revealed during the anti-ceasefire agitation, one can imagine what will be situation in the state if Manipur is 'forcibly' divided against the wishes of the people. Manipur had witnessed bloody ethnic clashes, and one of the main reasons was because of attempts by some section of the tribes to divide the state along the ethnic lines. Can one imagine what will be situation if Manipur is 'forcibly' divided along the ethnic lines?

Why do some sections of the tribes want to disintegrate Manipur? Or why some sections of the tribes demand extension of the provisions of the sixth schedule of the constitution of India to tribal areas (for separate administration of tribal areas) in the state? In a proposed administrative structure to be formed under the sixth schedule of the constitution in tribal areas of Manipur (if the schedule is extended to the state) submitted to the National Commission for Schedule Castes and Schedule Tribes, the Sixth Schedule Demand Committee Manipur (SSDCM) in October 2000 said tribals in Manipur were suffering from what it termed 'untold miseries and relegated to the background in every socio-economic development because of the biased policy adopted towards the tribals.' The SSDCM said the grievances of the tribes under the government of Manipur were: forcible extension of Manipur Land Revenue and Land Reforms (MLR and LR) Act 1960 to tribal areas, imposition of Manipuri language upon tribals, violation of service quotas and promotion rules, gross misuse and diversion of funds of tribals, monopoly of All India Radio (AIR) and Doordarshan, non initiation for extension of the sixth schedule to hills, constant transfer of tribal government servants, etc..' Some of the points the SSDCM had raised are not correct.

While people are demanding a uniform land laws both in the hills and valley so that every tribal individual can also own land in his or her name in the hills, a close look at the problems faced by the 'common hill villagers' is necessary. The MLR and LR Act 1960 is not extended to the hills except some areas of border town of Moreh, Churachandpur, etc, while Manipuri, according to Manipur government sources, is the official language of the state. The tribal students can opt for alternative English from class nine and it must also be mentioned that different tribal dialects are also taught in the schools. The AIR and Doordarshan are not under the control of the state government. Under the existing land laws, tribals from the hills can purchase lands and settle in any part of the valley while no inhabitant from the valley is allowed to purchase lands in the hills and settle there. Under existing rules, lands in the hills are either owned by community or by chief of the village. The Manipur (Village Authorities in Hill Areas) Act, 1956 and the Manipur (Hill Areas) District Councils Act, 1971 provide ample powers to the village authorities and district councils at tribal area in the hills for proper development of the region and for maintaining customs, traditions, etc. The powers and functions under the Manipur (Hill Areas) District Councils Act, 1971 are more or less the same as provided under the sixth schedule of the constitution. What may be pointed out, however, is that under the provisions of the sixth schedule the constitution, the state government is not likely to have much role in the administration of the scheduled areas. What is required is to make honest effort to work for development of both the tribal and non-tribal areas equally under the system without keeping different sections of the people apart.

Some senior tribal leaders had also been working for extension of the sixth schedule to hill districts for many years. Accordingly, the central government authorities also began studying the proposals before taking any step in this regard.

Provisions under the sixth schedule relate to administration of some tribal areas, after the amendments of the constitution, in the states of Assam, Meghalaya, Tripura and Mizoram. Autonomous districts are to be formed in the areas. The areas included in the autonomous districts are not outside the executive authority of the state government concerned but provision is made for the creation of district councils and regional councils. Barring such functions as law-making in certain specified fields, such as managements of any forest other than a reserved forest, inheritance of property, marriage and social customs and certain judicial functions which are to be exercised by the district or regional councils, the authority of Parliament as well as that of the concerned state legislature extends over these areas, under the general provisions of Article 245 (1) of the constitution of India, unless the governor, by notification; directs to the contrary. Article 245 (1) says: ... subject to the provisions of this constitution, Parliament may make laws for the whole or any part of the territory of India, and the Legislature of a state may make laws for the whole or any part of the state. And all such laws made by these district or regional councils, are to have no effect, unless assented to by the Governor. What is the historical background of the sixth schedule?

It may be stated that before 1947, there were 25 chiefs in the former Khasi areas (in Assam) but they had very limited powers. It has also been pointed out that recognition of the chief whether the succession was hereditary or was elected by the people was necessary by the British government before the chief could exercise any powers. The recognition was conveyed by an edict of the British government. As the paramount power, the British government reserved the right to remove them, and they were also under the control of the deputy commissioner of the district. These chiefs, after the lapse of paramountcy on the passing of the Indian Independence Act 1947, acceded to the dominion of India by executing Instruments of Accession. However, the administrative arrangements were continued under these instruments though these were subject to certain exceptions. The legislative powers of the central and state legislatures were extended to them (the Khasi areas etc). As the Khasi areas were later merged in the state of Assam after the constitution came into being, the administrative powers of the chiefs came to an end. But under Article 244(2), read with the sixth schedule, special provisions were made as regards the governance of these territories though forming a part of the state of Assam. The Article 244 (2) says: the provisions of the sixth schedule shall apply to the administration of the tribals areas, after amendments of the constitution, in the states of Assam, Meghalaya, Tripura and Mizoram. So far it is meant only for these states. Except the state of Tripura, the two others—Meghalaya and Mizoram—were carved out of Assam. Obviously, Manipur had a different historical background.

In a letter to the former Union Home Minister S.B. Chavan on 23 May 1995, former Manipur Chief Minister Rishang Keishing wrote in details about how the district councils should be formed when the sixth schedule is introduced in the state.

In his letter, Keishing wanted the formation of 'four autonomous district councils and two autonomous regions'. They were: autonomous district councils of Churachandpur, Tamenglong, Ukhrul and Senapati and two autonomous regional councils—Chandel autonomous regional council within Ukhrul autonomous district council and Sadar Hills autonomous regional council within Senapati autonomous district council. Former Chief Minister also suggested the amendment of the schedule as follows: (i) keeping in view the principle of the equity, democratic ethos, social harmony, ecological concerns and sustainable development should be inserted under para 3 after the words 'law making power.' (ii) under para 3 (1) (a), the word 'transfer' may be included in between words 'allotment' and 'occupation,' (iii) all the subjects mentioned in the 11th schedule (of the constitution) should come under the purview of the district council. It may here be pointed out that the All Tribal Students' Union (ATSUM) in a memorendum to the President of India demanded creation of a union territory for the tribal people by carving out hill portion of Manipur and the state cabinet on 20 October 1999 made it clear that territorial integrity of Manipur would be safeguarded' at all costs.' In a memorendum to the late Prime Minister Indira Gandhi on 26 July 1968, the then Naga Integration Committee (NIC) demanded integration of Manipur Naga areas with the state of Nagaland. 'It may not be out of place to mention here, in brief the mal-administration and exploitation carried on by the Manipur government in regard to hill people,' said the memorendum signed by NIC Vice-President Mono, General Secretary Rishang Keishing (later Chief Minister), Joint

Secretary S. Larho, Joint Secretary of Tangkhul Naga long (a Tangkhul organisation) R.S. Changson and General Secretary of Zeliangrong Naga Union N.K. Sim. And the United Naga Integration Council (UNIC) of which Rishang Kiehsing was an important member at the time of its merging with the Congress signed an agreement on 4 August 1972 saying: 'It is agreed upon that the Congress party does not oppose Naga integration movement and does not consider Naga integration movement as anti party, anti-national, anti-state and unconstitutional activity.' Of course, there are now no NIC or UNIC but efforts of some section of hill people are still on to break up the state because the seeds for division of the people had been sown years ago.

The subjects included under the 11th schedule of the constitution are agriculture, land improvement, implementation of land reforms, land consolidation, soil conservation, minor irrigation, water management, animal husbandry, fisheries, social forestry, small scale industries including food processing, rural housing, rural electrification, roads, culverts, bridges, waterways, fuel and fodder, etc, etc. If accepted, will it mean two separate administrations in the state which had produced Keishing as the longest-serving Chief Minister (about ten years). While he was the chief Minister, Keishing, who was the former NIC general secretary, wrote to Chavan: 'my colleague, Prof. Gangmumei Kamei, Minister of Higher Education and Prof. M. Horam. Chairman of the Hill Areas Committee along with Prof. B.K. Roy Burman, who is Chairman of the Madhya Pradesh Government Committee on problems of introduction of 6th Schedule in the State and who has agreed to be the Chairman of Manipur government committee on social policy would meet you according to your convenience during 29th May and 1st June, 1995 to provide any clarification that you may require.' However, this time, he did not mention about the 'maladministration' or 'exploitation carried on by the government in regard to the hill people.' Keishing who hails from Ukhrul hill district is a senior and respected political leader in the state.

As mentioned earlier, autonomous district will be formed in the tribal area as per provisions of the sixth schedule and if there are different Scheduled Tribes in an autonomous district, the Governor, by public notification, will divide the area or areas inhabited by them into autonomous regions. Also, the Governor may, by public notification, include or exclude any area, create a new autonomous district, increase or diminish the area of an autonomous district, or unite two or more autonomous districts or parts thereof so as to form one autonomous district.

Action was initiated towards extension of the sixth schedule to tribal areas in Manipur. Joint Secretary to union home ministry B.N. Jha as a sequel to Keishing's letter to Chavan wrote a letter to state Chief Secretary K.K. Sethi on 29 August 1995 asking for a 'detailed note for examining the proposal.' The letter continued: 'further, while indicating that the annual expenditure on the ADCs (autonomous district councils) will go up from Rs 1744.73 lakhs to Rs 5705.58 lakhs after their inclusion under the sixth schedule, a large number of subjects have been mentioned which are perhaps proposed to be delegated to the ADCs. This. may be confirmed and the list of subjects proposed to be delegated maybe examined with respect to the seventh schedule of the constitution. It may be noted that subjects under list one (Union list) cannot be delegated to the ADCs. Similarly, the items under list three (Concurrent list),' it said adding that a careful consideration should be given as consultations with the central ministers would be required to be undertaken for any such delegation to the ADCs. The letter suggested to consider delegating only subjects under list two (State list). If any legislative powers were proposed, the approval of the state legislative assembly would be necessary, the letter pointed out. On the proposal for certain judicial powers for the ADCs, the letter said 'this proposal needs to be elaborated upon in view of the fact that matters pertaining to the inheritance of property, marriage and divorce and social customs are already included under para 3 (1) of the sixth schedule. The letter emphasised the need for no additional financial liability for the central government after inclusion of the ADCs under the sixth schedule and wanted the list of the subjects proposed to be delegated to the ADCs under the sixth schedule was furnished at an early date. It may be pointed out that district councils formed under the Manipur (Hill Areas) District Councils Act, 1971 are fragile and now not functioning properly for various reasons including objection of holding of elections by sections of the people who preferred to have district councils under the sixth schedule. What seems to be important is a thorough discussion about subjects, powers, etc. to be delegated to the ADCs as similar Subjects Powers, Areas, etc. are also dealt under the Manipur (Hill Areas) District Councils Act, 1971. If the demand for extension of sixth Schedule was meant for more central funds, the state government should propose various schemes to be implemented in the hill districts and secure funds for these developmental works. For instance, the central government organised a 'special seminar on problems of development in Tamenglong district' of Manipur on 10 and 11 November 2000 at the district headquarters to study the problems faced by the district, and thereafter several schemes were implemented for the backward districts. Why can't such similar actions be taken up in other districts?

According to a note prepared by the state planning department, about 40 per cent of the total outlay was spent on the development of hill region where a little less than 40 per cent of the total population reside. The level of development between different districts in the hill areas does also vary. So also the level of development between different communities, tribes and problems associated with them. The state government, the note says, has been making consistent effort for development of all regions and 'balanced development' has been one of the important objectives of the five year plans. Steps had been taken for flow of fund to tribal sub plan area more than the population percentage (see appendix). The flow of the state plan fund to the tribal sub plan area has been around 40 per cent. This estimate was arrived from the investment! allocation made for divisible schemes/projects. There are many common facilities, which are located at Imphal (being the capital city), the benefit of which is also shared by schedule tribe population and others. The expenditure/ investment on Manipur university, engineering college, establishment charges in the directorate/head quarter offices are for common benefit. However, while calculating the flow of fund to tribal sub-plan area (considering that benefits are shared) then percentage share of fund flow to tribal sub-plan area in all the years/annual plans would be much higher than 40 percent. Officials pointed out that the funds from north eastern council (NEC) for the state during 1997-99, 1999-2000 and 2000-2001 were Rs 247 lakhs, Rs 466 lakhs, Rs 153 lakhs and Rs 490 lakhs respectively. As major works were taken up in the hill areas the percentage of fund flows to the tribal sub-plan under NEC plan may be treated as 90 per cent. They also said apart from normal flow of funds, huge amount of money is spent on hill districts by the ministries of Home and Defence in connection with infrastructure development for deployment of forces, construction of roads, etc, in interior hill areas.

The underdevelopment is not only in the hills but also in the valley. Major chunk of the inadequate funds from the centre has either gone down the drain or into the pockets of many unwanted elements. It is also a wrong perception by some hill people that the state government has paid attention to the development of valley area only. What is to be remembered also is that it was hill and minority leaders who have occupied the post of Chief Minister over nine times spanning about 16 years since Manipur became a state in 1972. The hill district of Ukhrul bordering with Nagaland and Myanmar has produced two Chief Ministers—Rishang Keishing and Yangmasho Shaiza while the first Chief Minister after Manipur became a state was Alimudin who was from Muslim community having about five per cent of the total population. There are reservation of jobs in government departments for tribal candidates, seats in higher educational institutions for the tribal students and special scholarships for hill students. An important point which can be mentioned is that it is the officers mostly from hill districts and from outside the state who are holding key positions in Manipur secretariat—the backbone of the state administration. It may again be pointed out that there are many officers from hill districts who are holding senior-ranking positions in the state government after getting through all India competitive examinations like Indian Administrative Service and India Police Service directly. In fact, the number of officers from majority Meitei community holding key positions in the state secretariat or in the police department is 'far below the expectation.'

Who are to blame for overall underdevelopment both in the hills and the valley? The answer appears to be obvious. While it is all the more important to develop the hill region as it still remains backward, it must be ensured that the money meant for the development reach its targets. It is not to say that the situation in the valley is better. The funds meant for the development hardly reach the targets in the valley also. However, any 'misunderstanding' between the people in the hill and valley must be removed through constant and frequent interactions at all levels.

It may be pointed out the central government has been meeting about 90 per cent of the state budget but there has hardly been any economic or industrial development. It is sad to mention that apart from those self-centered, corrupt politicians who colluded with those officials who can see nothing beyond the four walls of their offices in 'pocketing' the public money, various insurgent groups and businessmen have also swindled out of these funds meant for development of the state. No effective measures have been initiated so far to effectively monitor the utilisation of funds by the state government. Cases of misappropriation of funds, excess and irregular expenditure, unauthorised withdrawal of funds, excess payment, improper planning, diversion of funds, unauthorised expenditure, irregular payments of grants, poor utilisation of funds, loss of revenue, irregular financial assistances, etc are detected every year in the report of the Comptroller and Auditor General of India. Huge extortion from the public as well as from the government departments by various underground organisations also caused serious concern and impediment to the development works in the state. Various underground organisations including United National Liberation Front (UNLF), Revolutionary People's Front (RPF), People's Revolutionary Party of Kangleipak (PREPAK), Kangleipak Communist Party (KCP), NSCN-IM, both factions of the KNF, etc. used to collect 'monthly donations' from thousands of government employees. According to intelligence reports, the underground members in the guise of government contractors or suppliers also used to get work orders for various government projects involving lakhs of rupees. Both NSCN-IM and Kuki militants collected 'taxes' from vehicles passing through the national highways. Although the NSCN-IM denied extortion of money from vehicles, the 'receipts' they issued spoke otherwise. Between 200 to 300 passenger vehicles or goods carriers plied everyday along Imphal-Dimapur-Guwahati.

The yearly collection by underground outfits would come in terms of crores of rupees. Going by the sources, the collection of money by various underground groups was nearly 100 crores of rupees a year. Of course, the amount would vary from year to year depending on the financial position of the state government.

In a memorendum submitted to the Union Home Minister on 6 August 1996, the All Manipur Road Transport Drivers and Motor Workers Union (AMRTDMWU) and Manipur Truck Owners Welfare Association said the NSCN-IM cadres in the name of the 'Government of People's Republic of Nagaland (GPRN), were collecting 'various taxes' ranging between Rs 1000 to Rs. 10000 from vehicles plying along Imphal-Dimapur-Guwahati and Imphal-Jiribam-Silchar highways since 1990. However. NSCN-IM strongly denied 'forcible collection of money' from individuals or from vehicles carrying essential items on highways. In another memorendum to the Union Home Minister on 12 March 1999, the AMRTDMWU sought protection of road transporters and passengers on the highways alleging that the NSCN-IM members were 'demanding and extorting with receipts in the name of GPRN 'from each and every truck as goods tax in the following rates: (1) from every gas cylinder truck, Rs 2000 per trip. (2) from every oil tanker, Rs 3000 per trip. (3) all the trucks carrying different goods: (a) truck carrying iron rods and scrap irons, Rs 3000 per trip. (b) the truck carrying cement, Rs 1000 per trip; (c) the truck carrying rice from Food Corporation of India godowns; Rs 500 per trip; (d) the truck carrying essential commodities such as rice, pulses, edible oils and others, Rs 700 to Rs 800 per trip; (e) truck carrying sand, Rs. 300 per trip. The NSCN-IM, the memorendum pointed out, collected yearly road taxes from the vehicles. The rates were, according to the copy of the memorendum, Rs 12,000 from every tourist bus, Rs 7000 from every truck and Rs 1,00,000 per annum per agent of gas cylinder. However the NSCN-IM denied the charges levelled against them. The memorendum copies of which were also sent to Chief Ministers of Manipur and Nagaland urged the Union Home Minister to 'do at least something in order to lighten the heavy financial burden imposed on the transporters directly, and to the people of Manipur indirectly.' Police confirmed the 'extortion' by unknown militants but said it was not possible to deploy forces all along the national highways.

What will be the future of Manipur? Various underground organisations are locked in factional fights. Two major underground groups, UNLF and NSCN-IM are gunning for each other while NSCN-K and NSCN-IM are after each other's blood. There should not be any confusion because the two NSCN factions, although primarily based in Nagaland, also operate in some hill areas of Manipur. Cadres of UNLF and another underground outfit, Kanglei Yawol Kann Lup Oken group, KYKL-O, had been killing each other for some years till the People's Revolutionary Party of Kangleipak (PREPAK) brought a 'truce' between the two in the middle of

2001. The NSCN-IM and KNA, both of which denied the involvement in the Kuki-Naga clashes in Manipur, can not see eye to eye. A fierce factional fight was also reported within the PREPAK some years ago. The number of victims in the underground factional fights has well crossed four figures now but there is no sign yet of ending the 'fratricidal killings.' ,While the cause of factional fights among some underground groups was over the issue of leadership and 'differences' among 'senior members,' the main factor for the killings among various rebels particularly between the UNLF and NSCN-IM originated from the demand for division of Manipur. The NSCN-IM's 'Nagaland' which includes four hills districts of Manipur will never be accepted to the UNLF or other valley-based organisations. Also, the clash between the NSCN-IM and KNA was a result of the latter's demand for formation of a 'Kukiland' by incorporating Kuki settled areas of neighbouring Myanmar and some parts of Manipur where there are joint settlements of both Kukis and Nagas. The internecine fight between the NSCN-K and NSCN-IM followed the 'differences' between the leaders of the two, NSCN-K feels that NSCN-IM has 'compromised' the idea of fighting for 'an independent Nagaland' by agreeing to hold 'peace talks' alone with the representatives of the government of India while NSCN-IM, denying the charges, says the former is not working in the interests of the Nagas. It had been alleged at one point of time that Kuki militants were being 'aided, supported and armed' by some agencies to fight against the Naga militants during the Kuki-Naga ethnic feud in early nineties. When ceasefire between the government of India and NSCN-IM was extended to Manipur, some thought the government's decision would intensify the 'fight' between the Naga militants and other insurgent groups operating in Manipur. In the circumstances mentioned above, only a spark is necessary to ignite the whole prairie. Unless the government tackles the issues with extreme care,' expressed some 'seasoned' observers, the north eastern region may go up in flames in the near future.

It is not only in Manipur but also in parts of Assam particularly in Kokrajhar district where ethnic conflicts were also reported. Bodos and non-Bodos were often locked in ethnic clashes in parts of Assam. Various insurgent outfits in different parts of north eastern India have developed 'links' among 'like-minded groups.' This is not a healthy sign as the region surrounded by four foreign countries is considered 'very sensitive.'

When some Kuki groups demanded formation of 'Kukiland', some Nagas felt that Kukis were a stumbling block in their attempt to form 'south Nagaland' by tearing apart four hill districts of Manipur because the proposed 'Kukiland' included a large area of the said 'south Nagaland.' Most of the problems confronting Manipur today are connected with attempts to break up Manipur. It is now time, one should realise the futility of such attempts as these would lead to mutual destruction.

Unfortunately, people in the valley are very easygoing and pay excessive attention to every festival even at the time of difficult situation. Are they really religious people? While Manipur was being rocked by anti-ceasefire agitation, insurgency-related crimes, ethnic conflicts, underground factional fights, etc, people in the valley hardly failed to celebrate the festivals. It is really unthinkable why the people even during the peak of insurgency-connected violence or in similar circumstances took the celebration of festivals as 'compulsory.' People may celebrate festivals but there are 'certain things' which should be paid more attention than celebrating festivities before the situation gets out of hand. Meiteis are known for 'disunity' among themselves. Isn't now time to realise what is going on in the state and to understand who are those obstructing the emotional and complete integration of people in the state.

True. Every community living in the state more 'or less had made mistakes in the past but what is important is why can't these 'mistakes' be turned into historical experiences and utilised in building a strong state. Obviously. This sense seems to be lacking among the 'leaders.' Don't Meiteis have a big role to play in consolidating the ties among various communities? Shouldn't other sections of the people cooperate with the valley people in this regard? The present problems have dogged the state for several years.

The people, particularly living in the far flung and inaccessible areas have not experienced the fruit of any developmental activity. The so-called leaders and 'those one-sided authorities' are to blame for this. In fact, the developmental activity, if at all, has remained the prerogative of the privileged few both in the hills and valley. The road communications have worsened over the years resulting in the gap between those in the towns and in the interior places. It is sad to point out that those at interior areas have remained without basic amenities like medical facilities, water supply, latest means of agriculture production, education and. other developmental projects. Everyone is also aware of the 'worsening' law and order situation over the years and people are living in perpetual danger to their lives and properties. People appear to be losing faith and confidence in the government The state continues to remain adversely affected by problems mentioned above. Official sources said between 50 to 60,000 forces including police, para-military and army have been deployed in the state to contain insurgency and deal with other law and order problem. But, there is no sign of improvement of the situation. A huge amount of money is spent everyday on the maintenance and deployment of forces. What if this amount was utilised on the development works. No one on earth will come and work for a better future of Manipur except those who are living in it.

There has been unceasing inflow of outsiders in the region for some decades, and there is apprehension in the minds of the people that one day their separate identity, culture, customs, lands, etc, may be swamped.

It should not be overlooked that all communities had played major role iI1 defending and in trying to protect the state from any outside attack. Besides the well-known Anglo-Manipuri 1891 war, the history of Manipur has witnessed the courageous fight of Kukis against the British in 1917-1919 and movement of Zeliang Nagas under the leadership of Jadonang in 1930s. It is time to learn lessons from the history.

Manipur had well-defined territories which were much bigger in size than the present one. As per some old written records, neither the movement under Jadonang nor the Kukis' war (1917-1919) with the British had intended to disintegrate the state of Manipur. It may be noted that both had targeted to drive out the colonial powers from the soil of this former ancient kingdom. It may again be noted that the movement of Jadonang and Kukis' fight against the British, which had been termed as 'Kuki rebellion' as per the records, had concentrated at certain parts of hill areas of Manipur. It may be pointed out here that Jadonang was hanged on August 29, 1931, by the British on the charges of killing four Meiteis from the valley. However, he had denied the charges.

The continued control of the state by colonial powers, it had been viewed by some leaders in those days, had not only curtailed the rights of the people but also driven a wedge between the people in the hills and valley. This could be discerned from the fact that the two areas had been placed under different administrative structures.

It should be of great concern that thousands of villagers had become either displaced or homeless persons during the ethnic feuds among some major tribes in the state in the past one decade. Hundreds of women and children have become widow and orphan. What are their fault? Unfortunately, the rehabiliation work has remained far from satisfactory. The wretched condition of these people can not be described in detail because of the space problem. It is very painful to note that hundreds of helpless women have joined the 'flesh trade' to earn livelihood while the cases of robbery, crimes, looting, etc, have increased manifold. This is the result of the ethnic conflict.

Intelligence officials have received reports about the building up of arms by various underground outfits operating in the region. A point which can not be overlooked is that the tribes and Meiteis inhabiting the state are of same racial stock and have close ethnic affinity among themselves. History has also witnessed a gory past. Why have people failed to learn from the past mistakes? Some of the current problems can be tackled and solved. Increasing number of educated and unemployed youths and demand for formation of smaller states coupled with demographic change and historical background of the region are some factors that led to the birth of various problems including insurgency. Factional fights within the underground organisations recalled the warfare among clan principalities at the historic period. Should a multi-pronged strategy be required to tackle to instil confidence of the people in the government. To pull the state out of backwardness, the centre, it has been pointed out, should implement some major projects and share the income at fifty-fifty basis with the state government. 'Bankrupt' Manipur government can't improve the economy condition of the state unless the centre intervenes in the affairs of the state. What if the centre concedes to the demand for handing over of the Loktak hydro-electric project in Bishnupur district to the state government which was unable to pay salaries to its employees for months together. Hundreds of villages were affected by the project which has benefited the National Hydro-Electric Power Corporation in terms of crores of rupees apart from recovering the construction costs. The centre, it is felt, should strictly moniter the development programmes being implemented by the state government which with 'will and determination' to tackle the 'burning issues' should instil sense of security among the youths, introduce if necessary inner line permit system (it was abolished about some decades ago). Create more job opportunities by mobilising the resources, work for emotional integration of different communities, etc... The constitution, if required, may be amended to protect the territories of Manipur or other north eastern states. A drastic action must be initiated to bring about an all-round development in the state.

The problems being confronted in Manipur must not be taken lightly. First and foremost thing for the people to do is to change their mindsets, and jointly work for a 'future' Manipur. It should not be overlooked that all communities had played major role in defending and in trying to protect the state from any outside attack.

Who will listen to the woes of people? For example, there has been a series of crimes and violence perpetrated by militants on the national highways in the region for many years. On 5 September 2002, armed persons looted Manipur-bound vehicles and molested female passengers at Piphema on Imphal-Dimapur road in Nagaland. It was only after a prolonged agitation by the apex body social organisations, United Committee Manipur (UCM) that the authorities had decided to develop NH 53 and 'protect' the two highways in the state.

It is distressing to note that Manipur has not so far had (or hardly had) a government that works to fulfil the hopes and aspirations of the people, that instils confidence in the minds of the people at the time of despair, that foresees the impending problems and tackles them in time, and that sets a path, despite the prevailing odd situation, for a Manipur where everybody living in it can be proud of their motherland.

Also, are people aware of the fact that the attempts to break up the state will only lead to the 'unwanted situation' that everybody wants to avoid. Who will protect Manipur? Those who pretend to be unaware of the problems should foresee the things in store for Manipur if the present situation is allowed to go on. Is Manipur returning to prehistoric or historic period? It is obvious who will give answer to this question.

CHAPTER I

The Great Massacres

The winter was yet to set in but that misty September morning was cold in the western hills of Manipur. The chilly wind could not keep the inhabitants indoors in a remote hilly village. Everyone was awake at the dawn. They were busy, and appeared to be hurrying against time. That morning, unlike in the past, they were packing up household items and personal belongings. Barring the toddlers, who did not understand what was happening, villagers wore gloomy face as they knew that they would encounter an uncertain future. The situation in the past one and half years in Manipur hills had unsettled their lives and dislocated several tribal settlements in interior parts of the state at the close of 1993. The unceasing intra tribal clashes between Nagas and Kukis in the hills had already taken a great toll on both sides. Dwellers had been fleeing to safer places as the warring groups intensified the bloody conflict which was apparently engineered by some armed activists of both the communities.

That day, 8 September 1993. Villagers of Joupi thought their only hope of survival was to wade through the jungles and villages which now became under the control of Naga, a fellow-tribe-turned-foe, and reach Kangpokpi, a small hill town about 35 kms north of Imphal, the capital town of strife-torn Manipur state in India's north eastern region.

Joupi, an isolated Kuki village, is located in picturesque Tamenglong district in west Manipur. Surrounded on all sides by dense and oak-needled forests, locally known by different names, the area had remained inaccessible until the present squatters settled there some decades ago. The village perches on a somewhat flat hillock. On its north and west is Intuma hills at whose foothill flows Barak river which demarcates the boundary between Manipur and Nagaland state. Like other interior villages, Joupi stands isolated with the nearest Yanglenphai Kuki village situating two kilometers away in the north-east. Straggling Dulen Kuki village, Lenlong Naga settlement and Khunphung Naga village are located a few kilometres away from it in the directions of east, north and south respectively, almost encircling the remote hamlet.

As it stands out on a hillock, the lay-out of the village—its gates, paths, houses, sheds, etc.,—could be grasped easily from any nearby hill spots. Village shacks were huddled with sheds for domestic animals. Houses were of small or medium-sized, and built on posts with walls of split bamboos and thatched roofs. The path passing through the village was uneven, horrible and muddy during the rainy season. The impoverished community hall where villagers held all social functions was at the southern periphery of the village. Even children playing in the village could be seen from not-so-distant jungles. The hilly road entering the village from the north branched off two at the main gate—one passing through the middle of the village and the other half-surrounding it before going down to Barak via lower Jampi settlement. Only the torrents of the river and sounds of grasshoppers or cicadas from nearby virgin forests disturbed the calmness of the sleepy village at night. As practised in other hill villages, inhabitants bred pigs, goats and fowls for purposes of food as well as for sale besides cultivating nearby fields.

That morning nervous-looking villagers got up quite early for preparing a hazardous journey to Kuki-majority Kangpokpi, about 40 kms from the village in the east. They knew that sooner they abandoned the village the better for them. As the internecine tribal feud uprooted several villages with torching of hundreds of houses by the warring tribes almost everyday in the early nineties, thousands of villagers belonging to both the communities were rendered homeless in their own state. Everyone was worried and concerned as the government in spite of beefing up security measures at various places failed to protect the lives of people, and slayings of inhabitants in interior hills by armed activists of both communities continued unabated. Appeals to stop the carnage from public leaders, social organisations or activists went unheeded while rallies and public demonstrations across the state failed to evoke response from any involved parties. Animosity between the two communities was so deep-rooted that even travelling to a hill town or area settled by rival group was considered unsafe in those days. 'We are cats and they are rats in our area, they are cats and we are rats in their area,' said a Kuki village leader in an interview with the author while cleaning his single barrel gun before his grandson at Kangpokpi in late 1996. Sparse deployment of security forces was far stretched and of little use as they could not track down armed persons who sneaked into thick jungles after committing mayhem from one village to another throughout hill districts. Hills in Manipur had been smouldering for most part of the nineties. Villagers wondered why unarmed civilians were being killed and butchered? Why did not the armed activists of both the communities kill each other instead of taking lives of innocent dwellers. This was the situation in those days.

Villagers of Joupi planned to carry whatever materials and items they could as they were not sure of returning to their villages in the near future. The decision to leave the village forthwith was taken in haste. As two village youths, Lalchon and Letchon, brought a message from Kangpokpi that armed Naga activists had served 'quit notice' to Joupi and Yanglenphai, they realised that it was no longer safe for them to stay in the village. The 'quit notice' which had been given to some people at Kangpokpi to send it to respective villages told the inhabitants to leave their dwellings and desert the village on or before 15 September 1993. But past experiences in other villages goaded them to prepare for leaving the village a few days before the deadline. The terse message was also sent to Yanglenphai through a village youth.

While youths were speeding up things for the perilous track, elders arranged a prayer meeting' for safe journey.

As the sky was clearing up and villagers were about to set out for a risky trek that morning, about 70 well-armed Nagas sprang up from nearby jungles and swooped on Joupi at around 8 A.M. Villagers were also aware of the fact that once the 'quit notice' had been served, danger loomed large over their village. The intruders did not waste time, barged into all the houses, ransacked and destroyed household properties as panic-stricken villagers ran helter skelter for life. Gunshots were fired in the air. As the attackers wielding automatic weapons were criss-crossing and pillaging the village, there was nothing the villagers could do but to watch them helplessly.

While some armed intruders were vandalising the village, others were flocking the inhabitants into the community hall. Hapless inhabitants thought their last day had come. There was no one to protect them nor was there any means to hold out against the well-armed assailants who used abusive languages and ravaged anything they found in their way. Amid cries, pleas for lives and gunshots, some elders and womenfolks were praying for their protection. Both Kukis and Nagas are Christians though some tribes still follow animism. Fraught with anger, some village youths who attempted to resist the attackers while being taken to community hall were severely beaten up.

About three hours after the rampage, when villagers resigned themselves to fate, a man known to the assailants came running and said something to them. The, armed intruders did not bother much nor flee but they stopped depredating the village. This brought a respite for the villagers. It was later learnt that the man had told the attackers about the Assam Rifles party patrolling the nearby Khunphung Naga Village. However, unfortunately, the happenings at Joupi went 'unnoticed' by the security personnel. Angered by the arrival of security forces at Khunphung, the armed interlopers collected themselves, shot dead two pigs, sliced them and put it in their bags before slinking off to nearby jungles. This did not end the drama. What shocked villagers most was that the attackers caught hold of forty-year-old Joupi village chief Lenkhopao Haokip and took him away. This shattered and divided the villagers with god-fearing elders insisting on finding the chief while youths pressing for immediate abandoning of the village. The youths were in a dilemma because they could neither leave the village nor follow elders. Commonly known as 'Ningthou', literally meaning 'king', in many Kuki villages, the chief was respected deeply by the villagers. It was because of the chief's importance in the village that the armed attackers carried off Haokip.

It was soon getting dark. As the militants' attempts to cross Barak with Haokip did not succeed that evening, the armed assailants halted the night at lower Jampi which is located by the side of the mighty river. The barak which originates in Manipur flows through major portion of south Assam before merging in the bay of Bengal. There was nothing the villagers could do against the armed Naga activists nor the security forces, which were deployed at the subdivisional headquarters of Tamei, could detect the movement of the attackers in the remote village. It had been a long wait for about six Naga captors who woke up quite early in the next morning and, without losing a second, they crossed the river by a local-made bamboo-raft with Haokip. Some minutes after they had climbed the bank, villagers of lower Jampi heard two gun shots from the jungle before Katang Naga village on the other side of the river. They presumed Haokip was killed by the captors.

Dejected over the development in the last two days, Joupi youths insisted elders to leave the village at the earliest opportune time but the latter refused to move saying they should first find the body of the chief. However, villagers also knew that the armed Naga activists, after yesterday's incident in which the village had been ravaged and destroyed, would not come immediately to attack again though prolonging their stay at the hamlet was considered inexpedient. It may be pointed out that at some intermingled villages, common Kuki and Naga villagers know each other, are close friends, work together and help one another but they became sworn enemies only when they were 'incited' by armed militants belonging to both the communities. If any one defied 'order' of the armed activists, he or she was coerced into committing the crime either at gun point or by other ignoble means. Villagers in interior places where there had been no security protection for years were at the mercy of armed attackers who dictated their terms. They, supported by armed assailants, committed the crime either at isolated place or remote area where they would not be recognised by friends or known persons belonging to the rival group. Once they perpetrated the felony, they need not be told further. Several villagers interviewed by the author said in most cases attackers were known to them.

Some elders of Joupi went to Khunphung Naga village on 10 September 1993 and enquired whereabouts of Lenkhopao Haokip assuming that Khunphung village elders would have known the activities and movement of the armed Naga attackers who had taken away the chief. They were told that Haokip had been taken across Barak and gunshots were heard in the jungle near Katang Naga area. No further information could be obtained nor did they dare to cross the river and search for the body. Returning to their village crestfallen, they were at a loss what to do next. As there was no means to locate Haokip's body they finally decided to perform the burial process in memory of the chief without the mortal remains. And by the time they did everything including burial rites and prepared for the journey, the deadline set in the 'quit notice' was fast approaching. Their stay could no longer be extended further even if there were any other misfortune or calamity that should have generally delayed their departure. There was no other choice but to leave the village at the earliest. Developments in the past few days also unnerved the inhabitants. The delay was only because of their having faith in god and they wanted to perform burfial rites in memory of the chief so that Haokip's soul may rest in eternal peace. On the other hand, the happenings at Joupi alarmed villagers at nearby Yanglenphai where the 'quit notice' had also been as stated above served.

Heavy-hearted over the uprooting of their dwellings, and with an unknown future, between 400 to 500 villagers from the two villages carrying whatever they could started trudging the hilly road on their way to Kangpokpi. That was on 12 September 1993.

The scene was pathetic. Small babies were piggybacking on their mothers, young persons helping elders, able-bodied youths carrying whatever they could-utensils, spades, lanterns, knives, clothes, some eatable items, single barrel licensed guns, personal belongings, etc. It was like a human stream leaving their own country as refugees either because of a civil war or an external aggression. Wailing of pain, cries of starving children, anger and thirst for revenge filled the air. The nearly two-kilometre-long human stream would have been looked like a giant python moving along a snaky hilly road from western sky. There was no one to console them nor was there anyone to give them protection. Above all they were not sure whether all would reach Kangpokpi safely or not. Like in other hill districts of Manipur, several Kuki villagers including women and children had been killed in some months in Naga-majority Tamenglong district since the conflict surfaced in early 1992. Some elders who had been told by their forefathers about the intra-tribal rivalry decades ago wondered the recurrence of such a bloody conflict after the two communities have lived together for almost two centuries. For youths and womenfolks, they simply took it that armed Naga activists supported by militants were driving out Kukis from their villages located in Naga areas and Kuki militants expelling Naga villagers from Kuki areas. But in most cases, Kukis had been at the receiving end this time.

For hill inhabitants, trekking a long distance is not a new thing because they are used to it. But this particular journey for the villagers of Joupi and Yanglenphai had worried them most. The psychological fear of being attacked by armed activists bothering their minds all the way while they were passing through jungles from one segregated village to another. They knew militants were always roaming in the jungles. The Kukis felt relieved while traveling through Dulen Kuki village but panic soon struck them while approaching another settlement inhabited by rival group. Tamenglong district which borders with Nagaland and Assam is a backward area where the progress of development like in other insurgency-ravaged districts was at a snail's race. In fact, reports revealed that chunk of the money meant for development either went into the pockets of local leaders or was looted at gun point by militants in interior region. Barring at some major towns and places, there had hardly been any motorable roads in the interior hills.

As it would take about two days to reach Kangpokpi, villagers planned to halt the night at Chalwa Kuki settlement situated some kilometers away from Tamei Naga area. Though tired but with an ironic determination to live, they wanted to cross Tamei town before sunset. Everyone knew that crossing Tamei would be the most important moment in their lives as after this there was no other major Naga villages till Kangpokpi.

After tracking about 12 kms, villagers of Joupi and Yanglenphai reached Tamei that evening, completely exhausted, worn out and tired. As the sun was setting on Joupi and Intuma hills, they were rushing to cross the village but they were held up at the newly-erected gate. Like in the past, villagers thought they would have a smooth passage through Tamei because they had friends among Nagas at this village in spite of the ethnic tribal conflict. Friends turned foes overnight. None of their friends came to their rescue. After allowing 24 Kuki youths, the rest were pushed back saying the gate was closed at 6 P.M. everyday and it would be re-opened at 5 A.M. next day. There was nothing the villagers could do nor were they prepared to return again to their unsafe villages. They were virtually in between the proverbial the devil and deep blue sea and spent the frigid night at the jungles before Tamei. One can imagine how villagers slept out that discomfited night without food in the cold.

Despite living together for almost two centuries, the old tribal enmity appears to have existed in the minds of some Nagas and Kukis inhabiting in rugged hills and parts of valley in Manipur. That hostility resurrected, and was reflected in early 1990s in the form of what was described by some tribes as 'ethnic cleansing' in Manipur which witnessed extirpating hundreds of villages and killings of hundreds of Kukis and Nagas. This time Kuki victims far outnumbered Nagas in the internecine clashes.

While the cause and origin of the clashes shall be dealt at length in future chapters, some tribes and sub-tribes in spite of living cheek by jowl for the past some centuries, and education spreading among them, failed to remove abhorrence of one another from their minds. They viewed one another with suspicion, and mistrust among them together with an intention of living in seclusion at an area dominated by a particular tribe led to the tribal warfare in early 1990s. During the period of ethnic violence, it appeared, Manipur had 'temporarily returned' to the olden days of 'head hunting' in which, at some parts of the interior hill region, persons from villages other than their own were killed in tribal warfare and heads of victims taken by victors to their village. Only heads were not taken in the present clashes though warring groups adopted 'severe and brutal' manner of eliminating their enemies. The manner in which both Nagas and Kukis killed each other during the ethnic violence reflected the gory past. 'Head hunting' particularly among some Nagas was in vogue in olden days, and viewed with different opinions. 'The customs of head hunting is a very special factor in the social life of the Nagas. The fame of the Nagas rests more in the head hunting practice.[1] The practice of head hunting among the tribes in olden days was noticed in other parts of the world too. In most cases in tribal warfare in olden days. Heads were taken as trophies by the victors. Some writers viewed the feuds among tribal villages in Manipur or in the then Naga hills (now Nagaland)

[1]Genesis of the Ethnoses of Nagas and Kuki-Chin, Gangmumei Kamei p. 5.

in olden days as similar to some tribes in other parts of the world. 'The blood feud of the Naga, as with the Corsican "vendetta', is a thing to be handed down from generation to generation, an everlasting and baneful heirloom involving in its relentless course the brutal murders of helpless old men and women, innocent young girls and children, until, as often happens, mere family quarrels, generally about land or water, being taken up by their respective clansmen, break out into bitter civil wars which devastate whole villages.[2] This seems to be old tradition or custom among some tribes in the past. In some interior hill areas of Manipur in the past, the practice of head hunting or frequent tribal warfare existed among some bellicose tribes who later came to be known under the nomenclatures of 'Naga' or 'Kuki'. It was the Manipuri kings or their forces who in most cases had come to the rescue of weak tribal villages from the ferocious attack of 'more powerful' tribal villages. Protection of the villages in their territories was considered as main duty by the rulers in those days.

The present slaying among tribals or vengeance on a neighbouring tribal village was not much different from the past. Almost everything was the same except that the militants or the attrackers in these days besides other old traditional weapons used highly sophisticated and automatic rifles. Everything was well-planned before any attack. When Nagas decided to take vengeance or attack any opponent village in olden days, they would occupy a 'favourable' position in ambush surrounding the enemy's village at night. 'After taking repast they had carried, and when the cock first crows on the following morning, they rush, with great shouting, into the village, and cut up every body they meet with; sparing neither old infirm men, nor helpless women, nor children: even the cows, pigs, and poultry of the foe are slaughtered.[3]

Kukis were no less in the past and in fact known for savage attacks either in the plains of Cachar during the

[2]The Nagas in the Nineteenth Century, edited by Verrier Elwin, p. 56.

[3]Ibid.

British period or elsewhere in the region. 'They used to come down and attack the villages in the plains, massacre the inhabitants, take their heads, loot and burn their houses. These aggressions used principally to be made after the death of one of the Kookie Rajahs, when the having human heads to bury with him is in the idea of the Kookie a matter of great consideration."[4]

While Nagas live in compact areas, Kukis have been found settling at different parts of hills with both the communities keeping their age old traditions and customs intact despite their conversion to Christianity more than a century ago. There are twenty nine recognised tribes and sub-tribes in Manipur and most of them come under the headings of either 'Naga' or 'Kuki'. And there are also tribes or sub-tribes who are known by the name of the community to which they belong. While Anal, Aimol, Chothe, Lamkang, Maring, Monsang and Moyon have their concentration in Chandel district bordering with Myanmar (Burma), Mao, Maram, Puimei, Koireng, Koirao and Chiru inhabit the Senapati district which also borders with Nagaland. In Chandel district, to be precise, Marings occupy Tengoupal area whereas the Moyon, Monsang, Lamkang, Anal, Tarao, Chothe are found in Chandel proper and Chakpikarong. Tangkhuls inhabit Ukhrul district besides settling at foothills and parts of valley while Zemei, Liangmei and Rongmei together better known as Zeliangrong settle in Tamenglong district. They also inhabit parts of valley and some other areas in Nagaland and new Cachar hills in Assam. Kuki-chin-Mizo group of people inhabit Churachandpur district in south Manipur bordering with Mizoram and Myanmar besides settling side by side at several places with Nagas who outnumber them in other hill districts particularly in Ukhrul, Tamenglong and Senapati.

Some Nagas such as Kabuis (Rongmei) settle in Churachandpur district. Kukis are in majority in Sadar hills area in Senapati district. Thadou, Paite, Hmar, Vaiphei, Gangte, Simte, Zou, Beite, Mizos, etc, in Manipur fall under

[4]The North East Frontier of India, A. Mackenzie, p. 287.

the nomenclature of Kuki though some like Zou, Paite, etc, try to distance themselves from being identified as Kuki. Zemei and Liangmei were known to the British as Kacha Nagas while Rongmei was known as Kabui to the people in the valley. In short, the Naga tribes of Manipur are the Tangkhul, Zemei, Liangmei, Rongmei, Puimei, Mao, Maram, Maring, Anal, Moyon, Monsang, Lamkang, Chothe, Thangal, Koireng, etc, inhabiting across the hill districts except Churachandpur. It has been stated that Anal, Moyon, Monsang, Lamkang, Tarao, Chothe, Koireng and Kharam have linguistic affinity with the Kuki-Chin group of people but 'cultural identification' with the Naga. Tribes and sub-tribes in Manipur speak different dialects and Manipuri spoken by the valley people is the main medium of communication among them.

Going by the number of tribes, and deep-hatredness among some of them, one wonders whether they would ever patch up 'differences' and live harmoniously for forever. Nagas and Kukis together with Meiteis of the plains are inalienable parts of Manipur though attempts have been made by vested interests to identify some of them with those tribes inhabiting neighbouring states and merge with them politically and geographically. It may be relevant to point out that earlier the tribes in Manipur were known by the community they belonged to or the area they inhabited. 'The Naga tribes of Manipur are known by their tribal names.'[5] The Mao and Maram Nagas derive their names from the two most important villages in their area. While they are often associated, they are in all probability as different inter se as any two Naga tribes in such close proximity can be.[6] What is to be stressed is that Meiteis and some hill tribes have been living together in Manipur since time immemorial though some tribes migrated to the state some centuries ago. Some of the tribes were in occupation of the present habitat in the early centuries of the Christian era or even in the centuries before Christ. The Meitei historical and literary works refer

[5]See Kamei 'Genesis of the Ethnoses of Nagas and Kuki-Chin.'

[6]The Naga Tribes of Manipur, T. C. Hodson, p. 3.

to the Naga (the words 'Naga' or 'Kuki' were introduced in the state only after the advent of the British in Manipur) tribes as having been in occupation of hills of Manipur.[7] So were Kukis in occupation of parts of Manipur hills about one and half centuries ago. Like Meiteis and Nagas, they had also played big role during important historical events in the past.

Both Nagas and Kukis were strong in their respective areas in the hills. It may be noted that some Kukis were active at some hill areas surrounding valley during the 'powerful' days of Maharajas of Manipur and also during the British period. Together, the three major communities had protected the state from any foreign invasion in the remote past.

Various views have been expressed about the origin of Nagas and Kukis. While a detailed study of all aspects of origin of tribes in Manipur remains an important issue, Nagas and Kukis occupy definite areas in Manipur hills. Several attempts have been made to trace the etymological origin of the word 'Naga' with different writers giving different opinions and views. Throughout the nineteenth and early twentieth centuries, the people in Manipur were known by their tribe's names and it was the British officers who gave the generic name of 'Naga' to the present Nagas of Nagaland, Assam and Manipur.[7]

'The term Naga is said to be derived from the Assamese, Noga, applied by them to the hill-tribes in the Hinterland of the Lakhimpur and Sibsagar districts (of Assam). The term Kuki is of Assamese or Bengali origin and of some antiquity."[8] While Nagas were known to the Kacharis (in Assam) as 'Nahngra' meaning warrior or fighter, this term in Assamese became 'Nhuga' and from Nhuga,' anglicised from became Naga.[9] The first reference to the Naga in Ahom (in Assam) chronicle dates back to the ninth century A.D.[10]

[7]History of Manipur, G. Kabui, p. 23.

[8]See Hodson 'The Naga Tribes of Manipur', p. 1.

[9]Origin and Culture of Nagas, R. R. Shimray, p. 39.

[10]See Kabui 'History of Manipur', p. 22.

some writers have attributed the origin of the word to Sanskrit word 'Nag' meaning snake. However, the snake race of the vedic chronicles has nothing to do with the Nagas as they never worshipped the snake even in ancient days.[11] Some others opined that the word Naga was derived from the Sanskrit word 'Nog', meaning a mountain or inaccessible place thus meaning hillmen. An interesting view expressed by some writers was the Burmese origin of the word. A group of people with holes in ears were known to Burmese as 'Na Ka'.[12] It meant pierced ears. The anglicised word for Na Ka became Naga. But what is to be pointed out is that most of the Naga tribes did not have holes in the ears except some like Tanghuls in the olden days. It may be mentioned that the word Naga, was popularised by the British in Assam.

Whatever was the origin of the word, the tribes in Manipur as pointed out before were known by their tribal names. The origin and migration can also be traced from their traditions. 'Their migration into Manipur has been told and retold in their traditions preserved in their folk lore, hymns and songs. There are legends current among the Nagas about their origin and migration—these traditions tell more about their migration and settlement in Manipur and trans Chindwin region.'[13] They are, like Meiteis of the plains, early inhabitants of the state. Some Naga tribes claim their origin from the 'caves or holes in the earth which is a myth reminiscent of the distant echo of cave men's style of life of the Nagas.'[14] Some others claim their origin from Makhel village in Mao and Maram area in Senapati district while Naga tribes in Chandel district whose dialects are akin to Kuki-Chin group appear to have migrated there from Chin hills and Kabaw valley in upper Myanmar. Tangkhuls are found over a large area and 'the Somra group of villages (in upper Myanmar),

[11]See Shimray 'Origin and Culture of Nagas'.

[12]Ibid.

[13]See Kabui 'History of Manipur', p. 23.

[14]See Kamei, 'Genesis of the Ethnoses of Nagas and Kuki-Chin', p. 7.

which is outside the territory of the State of Manipur, is of Tangkhul origin.'[15] The Koireng and some other sub-tribes are said to be from Chin hills in present upper Myanmar. There are legends and traditions which tell different stories about origin of different tribes. Moreover, the tribes in Manipur are more akin to Meiteis in valley than those settling in neighbouring states.

While tribes like Ao, Angami, Serna, Lotha, Rengma, Chakhesang, Yimchunger, Konyak, Cheng, Sangtam, Phom, and Khiemungan mainly inhabit Nagaland, Konyak, Phom and Timchunger are also found settling in upper Myanmar areas which borders with India's north eastern states including Manipur, Nagaland, Arunachal Pradesh and Assam. It may also be stated that Rengmas also inhabit parts of Assam while Tangsha, Wancho. and Nocte tribes settle in parts of Arunachal Pradesh. In Nagaland and Arunachal Pradesh, there are numerous tribal dialects that one tribe can not undersand the dialect of his neighbouring tribe. In both the states pidgin Assamese has been adopted as language for communication among themselves. While it is known as 'Nagamese' in Nagaland, it is called as 'Nafamese' in Arunachal Pradesh. Historically, hardly any major tribe which come under the nomenclature of 'Naga' in Manipur have been found inhabiting Nagaland since time immemorial except some Zeliangrongs and some others. However, some tribes from Manipur have settled in Nagaland in the past few decades.

Kukis think they came out of the bowels of the earth or a cave called Chinlung or Sinlung or Khul, the location of which was believed by some to be somewhere in China.[16] Like Nagas in Manipur who are mostly known by their tribal names, a major section of Kukis was known as Khongjai by Meiteis in the plains. Some writers expressed that the Tibeto-Burman and other Mongolian races in south-east Asia originated from western China lying between the sources of Yangtze and the Hoang-Ho rivers in the prehistoric

[15]See Hodson, 'The Naga Tribes of Manipur', p. 2.

[16]The Kukis of Manipur, T.S. Gangte, p. 14.

times. They migrated in three waves—the Mon-Khmer (Talaing, Pa Lung, En Riang, Ma, Pale, Khais and Annimite) which included Khasis, the Tibeto-Burman comprising Pyu-Burmese-Kachin, Kuki-Chin and Lolo, and the Tai-Chinese which included Shan, Siamese and Karen.[17] They followed different routes.

While Tibeto-Burman group moved in different directions, the Mon-Khmer group followed the Mekong valley towards south into Cambodia and Thailand and then to Myanmar from where they went further westward up to Bay of Bengal and then turned north. Khasis in north east India are believed to be remnants of this group. Different routes taken by the Tibeto-Burman group may also be mentioned. It has been stated that one group reaching Tibet on the north stayed there while others moved until they reached Myanmar in three waves. The Kuki-Chin and the Pyu-Burmese-Kachin groups were these people. While the latter stopped at Myanmar, Kuki-Chin group moved further towards south-west along the lrrawady and Chindwin rivers till they reached the shores of the Bay of Bengal. And from here they turned back and fanned out along the mountains down the whole length and breadth of the hilly region, on either side of the existing Indo-Myanmarboundary lines.[18] They came to the region during different periods of the history.

Though some of them belong to the same ethnic group, the time-gap in the waves of migration among these groups contributed greatly to their present wide-range of divergence and multiplicity. 'The last great race of invaders and conquerers who entered Manipur was the Kukies or Lushais. These people seem to have taken their origin in the upper Chittagong hill tracts, but finding it necessary to immigrate, the surplus population, during the past two or three centuries at least, has kept moving to the north, or in other words into Manipur.'[19]

[17]Ibid.

[18]Ibid.

[19]See Elwin, 'The Nagas in the Nineteenth Century', p. 450.

As they arrived at different points of time, they were known by various names. One wave of these people received the name of 'Khongjai Kukies, another the Kom Kukies,' and these two having numerous clans or sub divisions poured into Manipur territory, sometimes wandering up the mountains on the western side of the valley and ultimately descended into the valley itself. Suktis or Kumhaus, who appeared to be identical with the Chins in upper Myanmar, wandered along a portion of the eastern ranges before settling in parts of south Manipur while the Chassads, who were 'an offshoot of the Haokp Kukis'[20] or a branch of Suktis occupied the hills bordering on the Manipur valley near the Kongal route to Myanmar. These groups of people seemed to have come from Myanmar into Manipur and were once known as 'raiding Kukies' for their attacks on the inhabitants and villages situated earlier before their arrival. Another great branch of these groups of people were the Lushais who are also now known as Mizos.

In the region, Kukis moved across the valleys of Cachar and Manipur, and occupied the lower slopes ofthe surrounding hill range. A point which is noteworthy is that these groups of people migrated to the region at different times and they were once identified as 'old arrivals and new arrivals, old Kukis and new'. This system of classification of these groups of people were carried out both in Cachar and Manipur. And the Manipuris, while they designate each section or clan of the old arrivals in their country by a distinctive name, give the general name of khongjai to all new arrivals.[21] It should be noted that there were other tribes falling under the nomenclature of Kuki besides Khongjai. Though they are now known as Naga—Anal, Moyon, Monsang, Lamkang, Tarao, Aimol, Chiru, Chothe were once known as 'old Kuki'.

In Manipur, the Kuki migrants of the eighteenth century were settled in the hills by Maharaja Nara Singh with the assistance of the political agent, William McCulloch.[22] The

[20]Gazetteer of Manipur, E.W. Dun, p. 34.

[21]Ibid.

[22]An Account of the Valley of Munnipore and of the Hill Tribes, W. McCulloch.

terms such as 'old Kuki' or 'new' are no longer used in Manipur. All these were parts of the history, and it has been pointed out that any community attempting to isolate themselves from others by dividing Manipur may lead to mutual destructions of one another.

Back to Tamei. While the villagers were spending the night in the jungles, those who had been let in thought they would cross the village within a few minutes since it was getting dark, and continue traversing to Chalwa Kuki village, about 15 kms from the sub-divisional headquarters, to spend the night there. Since the Kukis were allowed entry only after shedding their belongings such as knives, spades, licensed guns, scissors, etc, those who had been taken before the gate was closed did not have anything in their hands. They were let go through Tamei town only after disarming them. These people thought they would continue walking next morning after the arrival of their near and dear ones who stayed behind in the jungles, at Chalwa.

As they were hurrying up through the village, they were all of a sudden caught midway by well-armed Naga activists who tied their hands behind their backs. The village at the periphery of Tamei sloped gradually towards north-west till it finds a steep end below which flows a stream. While they were being taken to the other side of the village at the dead of night by half-pulling and pushing, they suddenly realised what was going to happen. Pleas for lives went unheard amid painful cries. Some shouted the names of known persons to save their lives, some attempted themselves to free from shackles. But all attempts went in vain.

Everything was done within a few hours. As the wailing and begging for lives filled the air, they were forcibly lined up and made to march one by one either before chopping off their head or shooting to death. Within seconds the stream locally known as Buning river turned red by the blood oozing out from falling bodies. It was the 'most shocking and horrifying' scene that anybody can imagine, a survivor told the author. Although the victims were taken by 12 September night, they were killed in the wee hours of 13 September 1993.

When their turn came, 30-year old Sehtinthang Chongloi of Joupi and 20-year old Haokhosen Doungel of Yanglenphai with hands and legs tied separately behind their backs decided to do it or die. Partly injured in the first blow, they could somehow unshackle their hands and legs, and jumped to the river in just a flick of seconds before the second deadly stroke hit them. As they disappeared in the darkness, the assailants who looked for them for a while thought the two were dead. Luckily, Chongloi and Doungel found some hand holds by the side of the river and remained motionless to avoid detection, watched for sometime the falling limbs and other lifeless bodies. Then, they moved along the stream until they found a safer place which was a bit far away from Tamei. Kamsei was another lucky person because he escaped dead by the bread of a hair under cover of darkness while he was being taken to the other side of the village. Soon after the last man had been 'finished,' and totally unaware of what has happened a few hours ago, villagers from the jungles arrived at the Tamei gate early in the morning of 13 September 1993. There was not an inkling among them of the gory scene at the village side of Tamei only a few hours ago, nor Kamsei, Chongloi or Doungel could reach a message to them. While Kamsei kept running through jungles, Chongloi and Doungel were hiding themselves in the thick forests throughout the day.

A few minutes after the gate was opened, unsuspecting Kuki villagers were thronging at the entrance. While letting off women and children, most of the men folks were held up after 'disarming' them. Those womenfolks who came late were forced into sacks and beaten up before allowing them to go. There was a quandary amid pleas to let go the detained villagers. Minutes after the women and children had left for Chalwa on way to Kangpokpi, the detained Kuki villagers were taken to the same spot and slain in the same manner as before. Altogether 87 persons were killed in that ensanguined incident. It was only after Chongloi and Doungel who finally made it to Govajang Kuki village on 14 September 1993 reported the killings that the state government and people came to know about the great pogrom. Nothing had been known before that.

While 95-year old Lunlam Singsit was the oldest person among the victims, 8-year old Haokai Hangshing was the youngest. He was followed by 14-year old Lamminal Singhsit and another 14-year old Lenkhopao Dimngel. It was a touching incident. Forty-year old Phakim Haokip did everything she could to save her two sons. With tears rolling down on her cheeks and embracing her young sons, she pleaded the armed activists to spare her siblings. She offered herself in place of her sons. But it was only for a moment. While Haokip was the lone woman victim, her sons were among those killed that day. The 13 September 1993 glaringly stands out in the black annals of modern Manipur as the gruesome slayings this day came to be ignominiously known as 'Joupi massacre' since majority of the victims were from this village.

Equally brutal, cruel, ruthless and barbarous was the retaliation. The hills were sharply divided since the Naga-Kuki clashes had broken out sometime in the early part of 1992. As the number of killings was increasing week after week, the rift between the two major tribal communities was widening. Setting ablaze of villages continued unabated with the history witnessing the worst form of human slaughters in modern Manipur. Security and police forces could not do much in the inaccessible areas and remained insipid as uncontrollable violence went on unmitigated in the interior hills.

Christmas in the hills is celebrated with pomp and gaiety but the unending tribal conflict restricted the movement of the common villagers within the districts. Imphal became the hub centre for all tribal communities with people from interior places coming down to the state capital for shopping, meeting relatives and friends at the time of the Christmas. The passenger buses travelling between Imphal and other hill districts were full-loaded most of the time during the season in spite of the unceasing feud. Even the sight of riders on top of the buses was not uncommon though the situation remained tense in the hills those days. Tribal passengers, however, felt uneasy while travelling through the village or area settled by rival group. It was also thought that the warring groups might not indulge in violence particularly at the time of Christmas. The trip between Imphal and hill districts was becoming frequent because of increasing number of passengers. And in one such trip on 19 October 1994, about 80 persons mostly Nagas boarded a Tamenglong-bound passenger bus which left Imphal in the morning. It is about 156 kms from Imphal to Tamenglong district headquarters in the north-west direction. The district is known for its deep gorges, mysterious caves, splendid waterfalls and exotic orchids. There are several tourist attracting points also in the district.

The road to Tamenglong from Imphal passes through a major portion of the Imphal-Jiribam-Silchar national highway number 53. It is a snaky road passing through several hill corners and mountainous region. Keithelmanbi is the first hill village, about 18 kms from Imphal, which will be encountered by any traveller from Imphal on this national highway. Soon after crossing this village, the bus was slowing down its speed as it started negotiating many hill corners. Both sides of the road at these points were not as thick as those in the interior places. Because of frequent lootings, robberies and hijacking of vehicles by militants along this highway, several security check points had been set upon this road. Militants belonging to various underground organisations were active in this region. It takes considerably a long time to reach any hill village, town or Tamenglong because of thorough time-consuming checking of the passenger vehicles travelling along the highway at various check posts manned by either para-military forces, army or police. Frequent clashes between militants and security forces also made the life of any traveller insecure and unsafe. In the name of tracking down militants or searching the armed activists by the security and police forces, common people traveling along the highway were subjected to sometimes extreme inconvenience or harassment. The highway also passes through several Kuki as well as Naga villages.

As this particular bus was passing 'through village after village that day, passengers inside the vehicle remained always alert. When it reached Kotlen Kuki village, about 35 kms west of Imphal, the driver apprehended some trouble because there was not a single Kuki passenger. So unlike in the past, he did not stop the vehicle there and proceeded towards Sinam without losing any time. The passengers also pressed him not to stop at any secluded and unguarded place. Life was not secure from one village to the other. Though there were several check points, security and police forces were patrolling the isolated places only when they had the full strength. And hardly the police or para-military forces had adequate strength to patrol the secluded or isolated places. They hardly moved out of their camps or posts, unless they had full strength, in view of the frequent attacks from militants wielding sometimes more highly sophisticated weapons than those of the government forces.

A short distance before Sinam, the driver saw some men in combat dress with automatic rifles moving along the road and mistook them as Manipur Rifles personnel patrolling the national highway. He was gravely wrong. Suddenly, the Kuki militants pointed the gun towards him and shouted at him to stop the vehicle. The militants pulled out the driver, and asked the Meitei passengers to get out of the vehicle immediately. Several passengers trembling with fear remained inside the bus thinking that they would be outrightly killed the moment they got out of the vehicle. While some Meiteis and dumbfounded Naga passengers thought they would be looted or shot dead after calling out, some others alighted from the vehicle. Everything was done in a few seconds. The attackers made sure that those who got out of the vehicle were not Nagas. The militants bolted the door of the vehicle from outside and pushed the bus down the hill. The vehicle turned somersault. The passengers inside the vehicle were heard screaming 'help, everybody is dying.' It overturned several times before falling into a 400-ft; ravine. While 37 persons including two pregnant Naga Women were killed, 17 others who sustained grievous injuries had providential escape. Both 40-year old Ningonliu and 20-year old Kakhangthailiu who were killed with their unborn babies were in advance stage. Of the victims, thirty were Nagas and five Meiteis. A Punjabi and a Nepali were also among those killed. An employee of the Border Road Task Force (BRTF), S. Vohra Came to Manipur from Punjab only some weeks before the fatal incident while 60-year old Gopilal was a Nepali villager of the state. Meitei victims were mostly small time traders doing business between Imphal and Jiribam. Sixteen females including 1-year old Chingthailiu and 3-year old Gaihiamli were among those killed.

"I was in the front seat,' recalled 18-year old Ch. Inaobi of Kangchup area in the outskirts of Imphal. The Meitei girl witnessed the dreaded moments. "As the bus started rolling. I heard people shouting dying, inside the vehicle,' said Inaobi who was found unconscious near the gorge down below the hills. She said only some passengers who were at the back actually got down from the vehicle when the militants stopped the bus.

The feud between two tribal communities perturbed Meiteis in the plains as the latter's repeated appeals and social mobilisation to stop killings went unheeded while the state government appeared 'helpless.' The main factor which had prolonged the clashes was that underground groups of both the communities were, according to intelligence sources, behind the killings of unarmed and innocent villagers. The hostile youths, supported by respective underground militants, were involved in the slayings of villagers mostly women and children. At one point of time, it looked as though the government and security agencies were 'concerned only' about the rehabilitation of the affected victims. It was noticed that during the crucial period at the peak of Kuki-Naga conflict attempts were made by some militants to involve majority Meiteis in the tribal conflict. In fact, some Meitei underground activists were sceptical about the killings of five Meiteis on 19 October 1994 by Kuki militants by pushing the passenger bus down the hill. What if Meiteis became involved in the ethnic tribal clashes, asked a senior underground leader who in an exclusive interview with the author in early 2001 refused to answer when asked what Meiteis would do if tribal militants of various factions intensified activities to divide Manipur. On condition of anonymity, the leader said the territorial integrity of Manipur must be protected at all times and at all costs, and every community must realise 'disastrous consequences' when any section attempted to break up the state. It may be noted that the 19 October 1994 incident was not the only happening in which attempts had been made to drag in Meiteis in the tribal warfare.

On 20 and 21 February 1996, at a time when the Naga-Kuki feud was at its zenith, five Meitei wood cutters were shot dead by some unknown gunmen at Yangnoi area under Saikul police station in Senapati district. In this connection, two 'regular' cases were registered at the Saikul Police Station, The attackers used highly advanced weapons and automatic arms including what officials described as 7.62 self-loading and M-16 Rifles as this was evident from the empty cases recovered from the place of occurrence by police during the course of investigation. By chance, an ex-serviceman named, Nipamacha Singh was present on the second day near the place where the killings had taken place on 20 and 21 February. Singh who escaped unhurt through the jungles helped the investigators to some extent. Angered by the two incidents, people from different parts of the state particularly from Yangnoi and surrounding areas launched a series of agitations demanding immediate arrest of the culprits and investigation into the incidents to find out the reasons or 'intention' for killing of poor villagers who earned livelihood by cutting woods in the jungles. It provoked the majority community but because of the self-restraint imposed upon themselves, the situation was saved from turning to worst.

Forced by the people's pressure and wrath, the state government ordered an investigation and it came to the 'light' that both the crimes on 20 and 21 February 1996 were committed by a 'particular militant group' (the government knew the group but refused to disclose their identity). It also 'very well knew' the motive behind what was later termed 'Yangnoi killings'. The incident nearly brought some sections of the people in the then ongoing tribal conflict. Finding of the investigation said, 'identity of some of the culprits have been established but they are concealing themselves at different locations to evade arrest. It is improper to disclose the identity of the culprits and their organisation at this juncture as it will affect further investigation.' An official statement on 1 April 1996 said' there is likelihood of creating misunderstanding between various communities in the area which may lead to serious breach of peace affecting public order.' The statement asked the 'public to remain calm and not to interpret the events in a communal fashion. The unfortunate incidents which have occurred are against the mankind as a whole and are a crime against the state. The lives of all its citizens, whichever community they belong to or whichever place they hail from, are equally precious to the state. The government is taking all possible steps to book the culprits and no person, whoever he or she may be, involved in this crime against humanity will be spared.' The statement was good for public consumption and to some extent subsided the public anger by those in the powers that be, at that time but one thing is clear. The issue was soon forgotten by both the public and the government. And in spite of 'known identity' of the culprits and a cash reward of Rs 20,000 to those persons who could throw any light or give a tip about the where about of the 'hiding culprits,' the killers had never been arrested nor any action initiated further to apprehend them.

The ethnic clash posed a 'serious law and order problem as the militants of both tribes take an active part in the fight,' said a Manipur government report on the Naga-Kuki feud. 'While the National Socialist Council of Nagaland (NSCN) is recruiting, training and providing arms to Nagas in the garb of village volunteers, the same is true of Kuki militants who are all out to avenge the atrocities committed by the members of the Naga Lim Guard (guards of Naga's land) on their people,' the report pointed out. While NSCN broke into two—NSCN (Isac-Muivah), NSCN-IM and NSCN (Khaplang), NSCN-K, in 1988, Naga Lim Guard (NLG) was formed in many Naga villages during the ethnic feud. The NLG was allegedly involved in the bloody clashes while Kuki militants belonging to different outfits were behind the attacks on Naga villages. The allegations that some 'important persons' of both communities were behind the unending conflict had appeared to have given credence when a former Governor of the state in his report to the central government in 1993, according to an intelligence report, 'hinted the involvement of certain political leaders of the state' in the Naga-Kuki clash. The enmity between the two was so antagonistic that the leaders turned a blind eye to the violence that continued uninterruptedly despite the fact that they have lived together for centuries. To have a deeper knowledge and understanding of the crisis with the armed struggle by various underground organisations for an 'independent Manipur,' one can not overlook the history of this tiny state which had witnessed a turbulent past.

CHAPTER II

Tumultuous Manipur in Remote Past and British Subjugation

Slightly bigger in area than the state of Israel or almost the size of little-known central American Republic of Belize[23] land-locked Manipur was an ancient kingdom. With an area of 22,327 sq kms, it shares about 350 km-long international boundary with Myanmar in the east and parts of south, and is bounded by India's other north eastern states of Nagaland and Assam on the north and west, and Mizoram on the south. A charming mountainous state which had once separated Assam and Myanmar before the creation of Nagaland, Arunachal Pradesh, Meghalaya and Mizoram out of Assam, Manipur had witnessed fortune and glory in the past and experienced vicissitudes of her long history. It saw the transformation from a primitive tribal state to an independent kingdom, and later from a British-controlled native state to a state of the Indian Union. Manipur lies on beautiful mountain ranges and is somewhat between the valleys of Cachar in Assam and Kabaw in upper Myanmar. Nature has given Manipur an elegant look with its unique natural setting comprising of eye-catching waterfalls, lakes, streams and evergreen forests. With hills surrounding a fertile valley of about 2,238 sq kms in the middle of it. Manipur is a gate way of India to south-east Asia and was an important route of the Japanese forces under the Indian National Army (INA) of Subhas Chandra Bose during the second world war from neighbouring Myanmar side to India. It had been less known earlier because of its isolated geographical location.

[23]Malayalam Manorama Year Book.

Endowed with a large number of rivers and streams which traverse mountains and valleys, and flow from north to the south, Manipur has a large number of lakes with well-known Loktak being the biggest fresh water lake in the entire north eastern region of India. The state's climate is salubrious. Three major ethnic groups inhabit the state-the Meiteis in the valley, and the Nagas and Kuki-Chin group of people at the surrounding hills. The people predominantly belong to Mongoloid racial stock and speak Tibeto-Burman Languages.

Called by different indigenous names such as 'Kangleipak', 'Meitrabak' or 'Poireipak' in the olden days, the word 'Manipur' for the state was introduced sometime in the early eighteenth century during the reign of Garibaniwaj who was also known as king Pamheiba (1709-48).[24] Its old names seemed to have denoted certain portions or areas of the present state during various phases in the early period. It had been a long march for Manipur in her historical development from a small clan principality at Kangla in the heart of Imphal to a 'powerful kingdom' comprising the surrounding hills. It once extended its territories to present Kabaw valley in upper Myanmar. For the greater part of the eighteenth century, Kabaw valley 'unquestionably'[25] belonged to Manipur. In the past, Manipur's size extended or contracted according to the fluctuating fortunes and powers of her monarchs.[26] The present boundary of Manipur with an area of 22,327 sq kms remained fixed since the controversial transfer of Kabaw valley to Burma (Myanmar) in 1834.[27]

As one looks back over the history of Manipur, like elsewhere in some parts of the world, it is hard to find a time when the early inhabitants were not killing one another, grabbing each other's lands and properties, indulging in bloody tribal warfare, burning and raiding villages. In one way or the other in the historic period, occurrences were more or less similar whether it was in Europe, Africa, Asia,

[24]Sanamahi Laikan (in Manipuri) by O. Bhogeshwar Singh quoted in 'History of Manipur'.

[25]Manipur and the Naga Hills, James Johnstone, p. 81.

[26]Report on the Eastern Frontier of british India, R.B. Pemberton.

[27]See Kabui, 'History of Manipur', p. 7.

Arab countries, America or elsewhere in the world. History of even today's some advanced nations reveals a gory past. There were several small states ruled variously by counts, dukes and bishops at different places of Europe at different points of time. These small states were frequently locked in wars, made forays into each other's territories, burned churches, ravaged, pillaged and attacked one another's properties.[28] There were internecine clashes among warlike Germanic tribes, Franks, Saxons, Celts, Romans, Phoenicians, Greeks, Helvetians, Lombards, the Latins, the Picts, Goths, the Illyrians, the Etruscans, etc, at historic or pre-historic times. At some historic period, they assimilated into several societies or formed various nations incorporating diverse cultures, languages, races and communities. The present Germans, French, Italians, British and some other European nationals are descendents of these people. Most of these nations had witnessed turbulent past in early period.

In no way, Manipur can be compared with these nations but an interesting question has come up. Have various tribes and Meiteis in such a very small state whose total population is far less than that of a major district of Uttar Pradesh or any other big state, in spite of living together for centuries, failed to assimilate into a society in which all can dwell in harmoniously? 'Sharp differences' among them are palpable. It may be stated that almost all the communities or tribes in the state are having their so-called 'armed outfits'. While some insurgent organisations are separately fighting for an 'independent Manipur', there are some other underground outfits demanding formation of 'smaller states' by dividing the state's territories. Some of the tribal underground groups had also been formed to what was termed 'protect' themselves from 'rival tribes'.

To some extent, it seems, the problem and situation in Manipur are somewhat similar to that of its neighbouring country, Myanmar, where various ethnic tribes like Chins, Kachins, Shans, Karens, Kayahs (red Karens), Arakanese, Mons or Wa are fighting for 'separation' of their respective

[28]Cities of Europe: A Berlitz publication printed in Switzerland in 1986.

regions from the union of Myanmar. Only the magnitude of the problem is different because of geographical location, size of the population and number or' warring tribes. There are at least five or more tribal underground outfits fighting for division of Manipur along the ethnic lines.

Various ethnic tribes who had been at loggerheads with one another inhabited the Manipur valley at the pre-historic or historic times and these people (Meiteis) were later divided into seven class (or lineages)-Ningthouja (Mangang), Luwang, Angom, Khuman, Moirang, Kha-nganba (Khaba and Nganba) and Sarang-Leisangthem (Chenglei). At the same time, different tribes who are presently known by various names also inhabited the hills surrounding the valley. And both the tribes have lived together since time immemorial. In the valley, these ethnic tribes spread across area with each tribe having their own principality. The chief of each tribe exercised full power in his respective area. Each clan had territory of their domination. Roughly, Luwangs inhabited parts of Imphal west and Khumans who had lived together with Luwangs, after separation from the later, occupied a large tract of land in central and south east Imphal. Angoms lived in the east extending even to foothills while Khabas and Mangangs who had both occupied and ruled over Kangla at different times inhabited central territory and foothills of nearby surrounding mole hills in the valley. While Moirang clan lived in south-West Manipur near the Loktak lake, Mangang territory formed the major area of the Ningthouja kingdom of the later period. It has also been stated that in spite of some political autonomy, there was social and cultural contacts among these ethnic tribes at the historic period. At times, they fought among themselves for supremacy but one thing was clear. The one who ruled at Kangla was considered more powerful than others and became the central point.

Several rulers including Khabas and Mangangs (Ningthoujas) had reigned at Kangla before the establishment of the Meitei kingdom under Nongda Lairen Pakhangba who ascended the throne in 33 A.D.[29] It was not a smooth transition of power. At one point of time, there was anarchy, chaos and 'political vacuum' at Kangla with every potential ruler vying for power at Kangla. Ultimately, Pakhangba who was a great warrior subdued all his opponents and emerged as the new king. During the conflict for supremacy, Pakhangba received support from the Angoms. It was also stated that Luwangs and some other tribes also extended their support to Pakhangba who, in the early struggle, had once been defeated by the Khabas and was forced to take refuge in Moirang principality where he lived for many years before conquering the Kangla later. The emergence of the Meitei kingdom was an outcome of the struggle between various ethnic groups and clan chiefdoms in the valley.[30] Some Khabas were said to have fled to hills and became hill people. The rivalry between Khaba and Pakhangba continued throughout the reign of the latter.

The origin of Pakhangba was not clearly given in the Royal Chronicle but history-mythology of the state mentioned that he was a 'descendent of the creator'. Some referred to Pakhangba as a 'divine personality' who was a mythical figure but Nongda Lairen Pakhangba was a historical king as proved by the Royal Chronicle locally known as 'Chietharol Kumbaba' in Manipur. 'He used to assume the form of god by the day and by the night he used to be a man.'[31] At this nature, his wife Laisana suspected him of keeping a consort and told him that she would also assume the form of god. Pakhangba said to her that she could not assume the form of god since she was a relative of Poireiton who along with his horde were said to have migrated from somewhere in upper Myanmar to Manipur during the pre-historic or historic times. Pakhangba said he could assume the form of god or a man since he was the incarnation.[32] The point that

[29]Cheitharol Kumbaba (Royal Chronicle), L. Ibungohal Singh and N. Khelchandra Singh and Diary of Manipur (Manipur State Archives).

[30]See Kabui, 'History of Manipur', p, 70.

[31]See Singh and Singh, 'Chetharol Kumbaba' and Dairy of Manipur (Archives), p. 1.

[32]See Singh and Singh, 'Cheitharol Kumbaba'.

Pakhangba was a 'divine personality' was interpreted by some writers in many ways. This means that during the day Pakhangba attended to his royal duties and administered justice with such excellence that he was like a god. But at night, he was available to the members of his family, friends and relatives and at that time, he was a good husband, a father, a friend and a relative.[33] Some writers point out that the chief of a clan was given the responsibility of performing rituals for the clan or the principality. 'And the Chief's control over the land and people was legitimised by the creation of myth associating or adducing divinity status to the chief. This happened among the Ninghthouja and Moirang rulers.[34] With his horde, Pakhangba came along the Iril river and then along the range of Heingang hill in the outskirts of Imphal. After conquering all his enemies, the new king consolidated his position with an ironic determination to build a powerful kingdom by integrating various ethnic tribes. Pakhangba was the first maker of Manipur, and his reign was long and successful.[35]

After ascending the throne at Kangla, and with the support from some ethnic tribes, Pakhangba also held sway over other clan territories. Thus the history witnessed the gradual integration of various ethnic tribes during the periods of different rulers of the Ningthouja dynasty founded by the first ruler. And slowly Manipur turned from the primitive tribal state, and a feudal state to a small kingdom with various ethnic tribes evolving themselves into Meitei society.

Who are Meiteis? Mystery shrouded over the origin of the word 'Meitei' with ethnologists giving different ,views and opinions. The name, Meitei, was a 'combined appellations of the Siamese "Tai" and Kochin Chinese "Moy" (Moy Tai = Moytai = Meitei) and the Meiteis belong to the Moi section of the great tribe called Tai.[36] It was also suggested that the

[33]A Short History of Manipur, R.K. Jhaljit Singh, p. 40.

[34]See Kabui, 'History of Manipur', p. 7l.

[35]See Singh, 'A Short History of Manipur', p. 40.

[36]The Meitheis, T.C. Hodson.

'meithei' (Meitei) was derived from mi=man or people.[37] The suggestion that Meitei originated from Moy Tai was rejected on the ground of Meitei being a Tibeto-Burman language and the Tai of Siamese-Chinese lingustic family. 'It is difficult, especially on the linguistic grounds, to group the Meitheis with the Tai races when the structure and vocabulary of the meithei language alike agree with those of the Tibeto-Burman races.[38]

Some others viewed the origin of the word differently. It has been explained that Mitei (not Meitei) was derived from the creation of man by god in his image: Mi = image, Tei = modelled. Thus, Mitei = modelled after god's image.[39] This was somewhat like writings in some old Meitei scripts which said god created man from his image (image = Mee) and this 'Mee' is 'Atei' = other. That is other than god himself. Mee and Atei = Meeatei = Meetei = Meitei (now both Meetei and Meitei are used). Meitei, as the language spoken by the people of the same name, was grouped in the Kuki-Chin sub-family of the Tibeto-Burman languages in the report of the Linguistic Survey of India by G. A. Grierson.[40] While the etymological origin of the word 'Meitei' needs a thorough research and remains an academic interest, the people are in majority in the state. The language they speak, as stated earlier, is also known as Manipuri. 'The origin of the Manipuris is obscure, and the written records, having been mostly composed since they became Hindus, are not worthy of much interest.[41] Though the British and some other writers had meant 'Manipuri' only 'Meitei', it may be noted that Manipuri means anyone who was born, brought up and lives permanently in the state. Some writers, under the influence of Hinduism, attempted to depict Hindu origin of Manipuris which has been out rightly rejected by other non-partisan authors, saying the people (Meiteis) are the original

[37]Ibid.

[38]Ibid.

[39]Journal of Manipur University quoted by Kabui in 'History of Manipur', p. 14.

[40]Linguistic Survey of India by Grierson quoted in 'History of Manipur'.

[41]See Dun 'Gazetter of Manipur'.

inhabitants who appeared to have migrated from either surrounding hills or from different directions long before the prehistoric period. Others viewed that the Tibeto Burman and other Mongoloid people in south and south-East Asia inhabited the upper courses of the Yangtze and Hoang-Ho rivers in China and migrated to the region thousands of years ago. They believed Meiteis, like Kuki-Chin, might have been one of the tribes who had migrated to the region some thousands of years ago but there was no historical evidence to prove this point. While the origin of the people again needs to be thoroughly researched, it should be pointed out that Hinduism became a state religion during the reign of king Pamheiba,

As mentioned before, various ethnic tribes inhabited across the valley in Manipur. 'From the most credible traditions, the valley appears originally to have been occupied by several tribes, the principal of which were named Koomul (Khuman), Looang (Luwang), Moirang and Meithei, all of whom came from different directions. For a time the Koomul appears to have been the most powerful, and after its declension, the Moirang tribe. But by degree the Meithei subdued the whole, and the name Meithei has become applicable to all.'[42] There are close linguistic and cultural affinities between various ethnic tribes in the valley and tribes in the surrounding hills. 'Tradition brings the Moirang tribe from the south, the direction of the Kookies (Kukis), the Koomul (Khuman) from the east, the direction of the Murrings (Marings), and the Meithei and Looang (Luwang) from the north-west, the direction of the Koupooees (Kabuis). The languages of the Murrings, Kookies, and Koupooees, are all very similar, and as the Koomul, etc, the offshoots of these tribes were, as before said, at different periods the dominant tribes in the valley, it might be expected that the present language of the people, united under the name of Meithei, would have a very apparent likeness to these languages, and such is the case. All these

[42]See McCulloch 'Account of the Valley of Munnipore and of the Hill Tribes'.

tribes have also traditions amongst themselves that the Munnimporees are offshoots from them.'[43]

Some writers opine the same origin of both valley and the hill people in Manipur. At one time, the valley was devastated by flood with the early settlers fleeing to surrounding hills. It was probable that only a small portion of the valley was arable those days with some hill people borderirig it, cultivating the area. As lands increased, it was thought, some of them settled permanently in the valley, gradually increasing in numbers. Thus various tribes settled in different parts of the valley and came into contact with one another, and 'amalgamated'[44] after a struggle for supremacy. However, some others disagreed with this point. Whatever had been the case, one thing is certain that languages of Meitei and surrounding hill tribes belong to Tibeto-Burman group of languages.

Though various tribes were off and on at wars for chieftancy over the other and domination of the area, it should also be noted that successive foreign invasions in the past left permanent marks on the civilisation of the people turning from primitive culture to somewhat comparative civilisation. It was only after the ascension of Nongda Lairen Pakhangba at Kangla that different ethnic groups and tribes, particularly in the valley, were brought under the seven clans as stated above, and this laid the solid foundation of forming a powerful kingdom.

Today's Manipur can not be compared at all with the period of those turbulent and distant past. But a point which should be borne in mind is that killings of persons either in insurgency-related crimes or other forms of violence, intermittent clashes of militants with security and police forces, bloody factional fights within the underground groups, 'armed struggle' for 'an independent Manipur' by some insurgent organisations, frequent intra-tribal conflicts, etc. are some of the 'routine happenings' in present day Manipur which are somewhat like the situation in the olden days.

[43]See Hodson 'The Meitheis', p. 7.

[44]Ibid.

There has been no sign of ending the unceasing violence as different outfits are locked in internecine clashes.

While social and cultural integration was taking place vis-a-vis formation of a kingdom, Manipur was witnessing an unpleasant past like in other parts of the world in early period. Though the social and cultural integration brought the tribes together, there were unwholesome relations among chiefs of various ethnic tribes in the historic period and they were often locked in tribal warfare in the olden days.

About 518 A.D., Sameirang, a descendant of Pakhangba, ascended the throne and defeated, according to the Royal Chronicle and Diary of Manipur (records of royal events in English version), chief of Angom principality, Kwakpa Thawanthaba, and took possession of his territory after killing him. Konthouba, who succeeded his father, defeated the tribal chiefs and possessed their villages, Shelloi and Longmai, near the present Nongmaiching. It was during the reign of Khongtekcha, who ascended the throne sometime in 762 A.D., that the king of Moirang attacked the ruler at Kangla but Khongtekcha defeated the invaders[45] and took sixty three captives. Yaraba, a grandson of Khongtekcha, conquered the tribal villages of Howkip Chingshang, near the present Langol Ching, while his son, Ayangba who succeeded the father subjugated the village of Howbatok. What should be noted is that the names and places mentioned either in the Royal Chronicle or the Diary of Manipur were ones called by the people in those days. For instance, Senloi Langmai (Shelloi and Longmai in Diary of Manipur) and Haokap Chingshang Khunpham Ngangcheng (Howkip Chingshang in Diary of Manipur) were villages near today's Nongmaiching and Langol Ching in the heart of the valley.

In 1247, Puranthaba became the king at kangla and fought the battle of Poeroo (Poirou) with Khumans and brought lots of captives after defeating them. His son, Khumomba who ascended the throne after him took possession of the village of Thanga, and brought two of its

[45]Diary of Manipur (Manipur State Archives), p. 2.

headmen as captives. It was during Thangbi Lanthaba, a grandson of Puranthaba, that a war was fought with Moirangs and took possession of the village of Loktak and brought lots of Moirangs as captives. History and the Royal Chronicle point out frequent clashes with Moirang. In 1432, Ningthoukhomba ascended the throne and fought the 'great battle of Moirang, defeated the Moirang principality and took possession of his kingdom.'[46] This together with similar instances showed that Manipur had a turbulent period in the historic times but, as happened elsewhere in various parts of the world in early period, it formed parts of the great history of this once 'powerful' kingdom.

During the reign of Loyumba who ascended the throne in 1074, 'it was clear that the domain of the Ningthouja kings included most of the hills as king or his officers went to the hills to realise tributes.'[47] Tributes were paid in terms of cloths and other products of the hills.[48] It was also the policy and dreams of the rulers at Kangla to conquer and absorb neighbouring principalities and territories of different clans to make a strong Manipur. What should be mentioned is that sometimes a principality was subdued or they fought back and restored their former position again. By 12th century most of the principalities and villages in the surrounding hills were either absorbed or dependent of the kingdom, Moirang later became a part of the kingdom. After integrating the whole of the state, the rulers from 1263 looked beyond the surrounding hills.

It may be pointed out that the book is not a history book. The remote past is depicted sketchily to help understand what was the situation, condition or position of the state in the past. What is again necessary to note is that inspite of its turbulent past and small in size, it became a powerful kingdom having rich culture and its own civilisation.

[46]See Singh and Singh 'Cheitharol Kumbaba', p. 19 and Diary of Manipur, p. 4.

[47]Ningthourol Lambuba (in Manipuri) quoted by Jhaljit Singh in A Short History of Manipur, p. 70.

[48]Ibid.

In 1443, Ningthoukhomba, a powerful ruler with a determination to expand the territorial limits of the kingdom, raided Akla inhabited by Shans of Kabaw valley (present Tamu) in Chindwin basin of upper Myanmar and conquered it. It Was an early attack on Shan principality of Kabaw valley by a Manipuri king. Before this there had earlier been a hostile incursion of the Shan to the then Khuman principality in valley during the reign of Khumomba at Kangla. Interaction with the Shans of different principalities even dated back to centuries ago. A Shan prince named Samlung, Younger brother of King Sukanpha of Shan Kingdom of Pong in upper Myanmar, after conquering some eastern and western kingdoms in the region, 'visited' Meitei Kingdom in 698 A.D.,[49] and stayed for ten years at Apong Inqkhol (homestead of the Pongs), a place in the present Imphal east district. While the Royal Chronicle does not record of any fight between Meiteis and Pongs, Some writers believed that Pongs 'invaded' the Meitei kingdom though they did not commit any atrocities. Some old texts also mentioned the intermittent contacts between Meiteis and Pongs from early period. Who were these Pongs? The Shan kingdom of Pong was formerly bounded on the north by the range of hills dividing Myanmar and Assam: in south it extended to Khanpat; in west to the yoma range; in east to the Yunan. The capital was Mogoung. After varying fortunes, it was annexed to Burma (Myanmar) in 1752.[50] Pong rulers were once powerful having considerable influence in the region in early period.

While Ningthoukhomba was away at Akla, queen Linthoingambi and other female members of the pala.ce were taking shelter at a remote village called Langkham. Taking the opportunity, Tangkhul chief attacked the palace of Meitei kingdom but they were defeated and taken captives by the Manipuris. Linthoingambi, who dressed herself as king and her maids as male soldiers, defeated the attackers without much difficulty. After Ningthoukhomba, his elder son

[49]See Singh and Singh 'Cheitharol Kumbaba', p. 6.

[50]See Dun 'Gazetteer of Manipur', p. 88.

Thangwai Ningthouba succeeded him in 1467 at the age of 24 years. As his father, the new king also wanted to conquer territories in upper Myanmar. It may be noted that different principalities of Shans had reigned in that region. While Shans of upper Myanmar or Shans of Chindwin basin were called Kabaws, Kabaw was the name of an ethnic group and the valley inhabited by them. In his effort to attack the Kabaw, Ningthouba made friendship with Pong king, Choupha Khekhomba, and combined forces of Meiteis and Pongs in 1470 invaded Kyang, a Shan principality in the Kabaw valley, and conquered it.[51] Since he conquered Kyang, the Meitei king was known as Kyamba, the conquerer of Kyang and the two kings celebrated their victory with great pomp, and 'demarcated' their boundaries under the treaty of 1470 concluded between the two rulers. This was the first ever treaty Manipur had entered into with a foreign country. The Royal Chronicle and the Diary of Manipur give the boundary in very clear terms in the north (in the area) Manipur boundary extended up to Mungkhong Muwai and the land of the dwarf mango groves was for Pong: in the east, it was upto Loijiri hills, in the south upto Miyatong hill. It was pointed out that regarding Samjok (Thaungdut), the eastern portion was for Pong and the western portion was for Manipur.[52] With the conclusion of this treaty, and demarcation of the boundaries thereafter, a major portion of Kabaw valley was 'made over'[53] to Manipur. It was stated that the kingdom of Kyang was 'handed over'[54] to Manipur after the battle with the latter getting the greater share. The treaty and demarcation of boundary showed international recognition of Meitei kingdom by a power in upper Myanmar as the former exercised full fledged sovereign power having internal and external independence in the true sense of the term.

[51]See 'Cheitharol Kumbaba', p. 19. and Diary of Manipur, p. 4.
[52]See Singh 'A Short History of Manipur', p. 90.
[53]See Pemberton 'Report on the Eastern Frontier of British India'.
[54]Statistical Account of Manipur, R. Brown.

Great warriors, brave and courageous, the rulers tamed the jungles or forests infested by wild animals, set up a civilisation, made a kingdom and expanded the territory. Only their unflinching determination to consolidate and make a strong motherland subdued the affliction and hardships they faced in their way.

After raiding and defeating several other villages in the surrounding hills in the north, west and east, Kyamba's reign also marked further consolidation of the kingdom with more and more territories integrating to the kingdom. In 1504, Kyamba's kingdom was invaded for the first time by a group of people known to the Meiteis as 'Mayangs' from the direction of Cachar district of Assam. As the invaders came fully equipped, Meitei forces under the leadership of Angom chief were defeated. The king then sent reinforcements under the command of his son, Nongthonba who together with Angom chief routed and drove out the attackers. The invaders were thought to be Kacharis, a tribe of Assam considered to be early inhabitants of that state. In 1505, Nongthonba pre-deceased his father.

During Kyamba's regime, several persons including Brahmins and Hindus migrated to Manipur and were allowed to settle in the state by the king. Brahmins were also employed to look after the Hindu temples set up by the Hindus. The immigrants of all kinds of people were later integrated into Meitei society with Manipuri language becoming their mother tongue. Considered as one of the greatest kings of Manipur, Kyamaba continued to be the follower of the old Meitei religion in spite of the beginning of Vishnu worshipping by some people particularly Brahmins. After a reign of about 40 years, Kyamba who was a valiant warrior and a good statesman whose conquest of Kabaw valley greatly enhanced the power and prestige of Manipur died in 1508 at the age of sixty.

More or less the first half of the sixteenth century, after the death of Kyamba, witnessed a lull period in Manipur though there were frequent minor attacks or counter attacks between Meitei kings and nearby hill tribes or sometimes with some villages in neighbouring countries including Cachar. Contact with Ahoms of Assam was also started during the reign of Kabomba, who ascended the throne in 1524, and a trade route to upper Assam was also 'opened'[55] in 1536. But another remarkable period began with the ascension of Thangwai Ningthou Kiyamba who later assumed the name of Mungyamba in 1562 A.D. The period was considered the beginning of yet a series of military expeditions by him and his successors to neighbouring countries particularly in the present Kabaw valley.

It was with Myanmar that Manipur had intermittent clashes in the past. As mentioned above, its boundaries extended upto the present Kabaw valley and attempts had been made to drive out Manipuries from Shan principalities in upper Myanmar. In the ensuing clashes, Manipur sometimes suffered heavy casualties and while trying to understand the past history of this state, the history of its big neighbour can not be isolated also. For better understanding, it may be stated that Myanmar is broadly divided into three regions with fertile valley of Irrawady, Sittang and Salween rivers forming upper Myanmar while coastal region around fertile Irrawady and Sittang river deltas are considered lower Myanmar. The Tenasserim and Arakan coasts are also generally taken as parts of lower Myanmar though they are not exactly in the lower portion of the country. Up in the north, north east or north west of the country are thickly forested mountainous region, rugged tracts and high plateaus covering about four per cent of the total area, and is inhabited by various ethnic minorities, what is noteworthy is that these areas have been witnessing different kinds of conflicts, violence, insurgency movements and other forms of unrest for some decades as various ethnic tribes are, as stated before, fighting for separation of their respective areas from the country. The central government has also been unable to effectively contain the violence perpetrated by these tribes though none of the

[55]See Kabui 'History of Manipur', p. 126.

group has so far succeeded in seceding from the union of Myanmar.

One of the most important factors that has caused the present situation in Myanmar is because of the extremely large number of ethnic minorities with diverse cultures and customs, and their unceasing fight for independence of their respective region where access by the forces has often been found difficult on various occasions. Of about 4.6 crore population[56], approximately sixty per cent of them are majority Burmans settling in lower and upper Myanmar while the rest, mostly numerous ethnic tribes, inhabit rugged and inaccessible mountainous regions and high plateaus. However, some ethnic minorities such as Mons are also found in large number to have settled in the city like Moulmein. Myanmar has been divided into seven union states—Rakhine, Chin, Kachin, Karen, Kayah (or Karenni), Mon and Shan. Again upper and lower portions, where burmans are in majority, have been divided into seven divisions—Rangoon (Now Yangon), Irrawaddy, Tenasserim, Pegu, Magwe, Mandalay and Sagaing.

Myanmar's ethnic situation is very complex and confusing since the number of minorities may well go upto two hundred. Over a hundred different languages have been identified apart from Burmese. Some important ethnic groups are Karen, Pa-O, Karenni, Shan, Chin, Mon, Kachin, Palaung-Wa, Chinese, etc. There are also many smaller ethnic groups such as Naga, lahu, Akha, etc. Besides some of those which have been mentioned earlier. Like its small neighbour, it had also witnessed a turbulent past with different principalities either ravaging or plundering one another at the prehistoric or historic times.

Formerly known as Burma, Myanmar was a 'fragmented' country with majority Burmans at the centre, surrounded by different tribes who had come from different directions years ago. Even Burmans, who are also known as Mramma, were believed to have come originally from China-Tibet border, and they later moved down the Irrawady, overran the

[56]Malayala Manorama (1998).

Kyaukse plain, and established themselves as the major power in the rice-cultivating region of the north sometimes in the ninth century. It has been stated that upper Myanmar was once inhabited by the Pyu tribes who were believed to have migrated from the Tibetan plateau. During the historic period, Pyus later 'disappeared' or assimilated into various other ethnic groups. The Mons whose language belongs to Mon-Khmer family, were the first group to reach Myanmar several centuries before Christ, and settled on the estuaries of Salween and Sittang rivers.[57] They were said to have 'established' the Buddhist tradition in Myanmar. Historically, Mons once set up their first capital at Sri Ksetra, a place near the present-day Prome. Though not certain, mentions were made in some historical records that the next groups to pass into central Myanmar after the Mon and Pyu were Karen and Chin. About the same time as the main group of Burmans arrived, or a little earlier, the Shans seemed to have entered Myanmar as part of the major Tai migration into south-east Asia. Around the same time, the Tai people were 'pressing' south-ward from their ancestral home in Yunan. 'As a part of the powerful Nan-ch' ao dynasty, they subjugated upper Myanmar in the Nineth century, attacking Hahn (once controlled by Pyus) in 832, and carrying the population off into slavery,[58] The Shans (descendants of Tais) migrations were followed by several Tribes, mainly Tibeto-Burman in origin, and spread to different parts of the country including mountain areas of the north east region. And various other tribes including Kachins who probably arrived from different directions settled at the frontier areas whereas the Burmans with Shans or Mons spread to both upper and lower portions of the country. It should be noted that the migrations went on for centuries.

The first Burmese empire, after conquering the Mon capital of Thaton was established by Anawrahtra (of Pagan dynasty) in 1.057.[59] The Pagan dynasty, founded by

[57]Burma, published by Apa Productions (HK) Ltd 1982.
[58]Ibid.
[59]Ibid.

Anawrahtra, flourished very well lasting from the eleventh century to the Mongol invasion in the thirteenth century.[60] It was he who brought both lower and upper Myanmar into one united kingdom for the first time, somewhat like unification of different principalities and tribal villages in Manipur under the kings at Kangla. Anawrahtra also overpowered and conquered the neighbouring principalities of the Irrawady valley.

After conquering the Mon capital, king Anawrahtra returned to Pagan with Mon king, thousands of captives, skilled craftsmen, Theravada Buddhist monks and master builders. Ironically, despite the Mons' defeat, their culture became supreme in the Burmans' capital with Theravada Buddhist religion becoming predominant. In other words highly developed Mon culture, art, lifestyle, etc, assimilated with Burmans who were considered primitive in their ways. It was said that the mixture of Mon culture, Burman hegemony, and Buddhism were frequently called 'golden age of Burma (Myanmar)' in those days. Along with these developments, efforts were on to preserve the unity of the Burmese empire. With a view to cement the empire further, Kyanzittha (1084-1113) who ruled the country gave his daughter in marriage to a Mon prince and chose their son, Alaungsithu as his successor. But it was not for a long time.

Sometime in the middle of 13th century, the Burmese empire began to crumble with Shans threatening from northern Myanmar. Burman kings continued to rule from Ava, near the present Mandalay, though upper Myanmar virtually came under the control of the Shans. Around the same time, the Mongol army of Kublai Khan became powerful expanding beyond their territory. Originally from central Asia, the Khan and his forces had once occupied the Nan-ch' ao empire in Yunan,[61] Following the expansion of their territorial control, they wanted the smaller and weaker neighbours to pay tribute to-them. But, their superiority was not readily accepted by some. As king Naranthihapate of

[60]Burma, Ethnicity and Insurgency by Michael Fredholm, p. 21.

[61]See Burma published by Apa Productions (HK) Ltd 1982.

Myanmar who overestimated the strength of his own forces, ignored the Mongol forces and refused to pay any tribute. Soon a bloody war ensued with Burmese forces being 'annihilated' in the battle of Vochan, and the subsequent conquest of Pagan by the Mongols in 1287. After this, Burma (Myanmar) became a devastated country with the Mons, supported by Shan leader Wareru withdrawing from the first Burmese empire. It was followed by the Arakanese on the bay of Bengal. Myanmar, after the fall of the Pagan, was divided into several states of varying sizes for almost three centuries. While the Mons founded a new kingdom in the town of Pegu in lower Myanmar, Wareru even established a kingdom in lower Myanmar in Martaban. With these developments, the centre of power and culture shifted to south again. Arakan in the west along the bay of Bengal spread north to Chittagong in the present-day Bangladesh.

As the states disintegrated after the fall of the empire, conflicts among them 'destroyed' Myanmar for several years with the Mons and Shans engaging in a long war between about 1385 and 1425, but in spite of the internal clashes the Theravada Buddhism underwent a revival in the court of Pegu. It was around this time that the king of Manipur, Ningthoukhomba raided the village of Akla under Kabaw Shan principality in 1443 (1445 according to the Diary of Manipur). Upper Myanmar came virtually under the control of Shans of different principalities and other mountain tribes. In 1527, even Ava where Burmans had reigned for years was attacked, burned down and captured. After this the burman population withdrew to the town of Toungoo, where Tabinshwehti, the ruler of Toungoo dynasty, had consecrated him self as King of Burma (Myanmar) in 1546 at Toungoo before moving the capital at Pegu. It was he who controlled a large portion of the country. Although his reign was not long, Tabinshwehti extended his control down the Tenasserim coast to Tavoy after his victory over Martaban, and west to Prome on the central Irrawady. Bayinnaung (1551-1581) who succeeded him overwhelmed the Shans and conquered the Tai kingdom of Chiengmai and Ayutthia, thus extending Myanmar's boundaries to their maximum limits. He united upper and lower Myanmar.

The country witnessed unceasing warfare and conflicts among different regions and ultimately disintegrated into various states with none of them powerful enough to reunite the country for a long time. It may be mentioned that the Dutch, British and French set up trading companies in ports along the coasts of Myanmar during 17th century. When the country's capital was transferred back to Ava, it was retaken in 1752 again by Mons who eventually deposed of the last remnant of the Toungoo dynasty with the help of the French arms. As a result, the second Burmese empire foundered and dissolved. However, the empire was to be rebuilt again under another leadership.

A new Burman leader named Maung Aung Zeya, by then, had already emerged. Not long after the collapse of the second empire, Maung Aung Zeya proclaimed himself as king of Burma and assumed the title Alaungpaya and founded the third Burmese empire. He was from Shwebo, Soon after establishing the third Burmese empire under Konbaung dynasty, Alaungpaya defeated and ousted the Mons of lower Myanmar, which prompted an insurrection at Pegu, the ancient Mon capital, deported the French to Bayingi, and burned down the British trading posts. It was because of the fierce attack from Alaungpaya that Mon insurrection at Pegu ceased entirely, and the Mon people either fled to Siam or assimilated with the Burmans. Alaungpaya also laid siege to Ayutthia, the capital of Siam, but it was his successor Hsinbushin who later attacked Ayutthia in 1767 and returned to Ava with artists and craftsmen after completely destroying the Siamese capital. The artists and craftsmen taken as prisoners later gave a fresh cultural impetus to the Burmese kingdom. It was during the reign of Bodawpaya who ascended the throne in 1782, that Arakan was conquered, bringing the borders of the country to Indian province of Bengal which was ruled by the British East India company. He moved his capital to Amarapur, not far from Ava, As British India and Burma

(Myanmar) now shared a common boundary, the number of border incidents increased with Royal Burmese troops frequently pursuing rebels over the border and often penetrating the Indian territory. Konbaung dynasty, founded by Alaungpaya, was the last royal dynasty in Burma which had ruled the country until the first Anglo-Burmese war.

The Manipuri Royal Chronicle and the Diary of Manipur mentioned mostly about the achievements and successful expeditions of the Kings or the Rulers of those days and it hardly contained the setbacks or defeats in the hands of the enemies. On several occasions, according to historical records, the Kings and his forces suffered humiliating defeats in the hands of the enemies. The state was sometimes ravaged or devastated by the enemies. In 1540, the king of Kabaw valley invaded Manipur but Kabomba repulsed them. This was not considered an important event as the state with its not-so-powerful rulers remained somewhat, as pointed out earlier, inactive during the first half of the sixteenth century. As a result its control over others including parts of Kabaw valley had loosened. During the reign of Mungyamba there had been repeated military expeditions into Kabaw valley and a major portion of the territory was under the control of Manipuris. No doubt, Manipur produced many famous rulers in those days.

Considered as one of the most illustrious rulers of medieval Manipur, Ningthouhanba, also known as Khagemba (1597-1552) who had acquired a proper training in the fields of military warfare, statecraft and diplomatic skills from his father Mungyamba, conquered more areas and expanded the state territory further besides consolidating his sway over the whole hill areas and Kabaw valley. During his reign, he successfully defended the state from several foreign incursions and invasions by the Muslims, Kacharis and Shans of Kabaw valley. Besides, he also strengthened the internal political control, and made frequent military expeditions and raids over recalcitrant hill tribes or villages.

Sometimes, the territories which had been brought under Manipur kingdom were lost again owing to driving out of

Manipuri forces by the leaders of those principalities which the Manipuri kings had conquered. During the reign of Kyamba, some Shan principalities of Kabaw valley such as Kabaw (Tamu), Kyang, Khampat, Samjok, etc, were conquered, according to the Royal Chronicle. However, as the successive rulers after him remained inactive for some decades, the influence and grip over these areas were fast loosening. These tributary principalities were physically far away from the capital, and this caused an unfavourable condition for the kingdom to maintain its influence over these territories. As a result, the Shans or the tribes in these areas attempted to unshackle themselves from the political control of Manipur. It should be pointed out that these tribes were also encouraged by bigger states in upper Myanmar and the central political power at Ava. Besides, these tribes were more akin to the people in neighbouring Shan states with whom they had close economic and cultural ties. However, in the second half of the sixteenth century, king Mungyamba re-established his firm rule and control over these areas. It was further consolidated by his son, Khagemba who made frequent military expeditions to this region. In order to keep these places under control, the rulers in those days were sometimes very harsh and tyrannical. Officials from Manipur were also posted at strategic locations in Kabaw valley including Tamu and Angoching, on the western bank of Chindwin river. This was done mainly to help integration of Kabaw valley to mainland Manipur.

But in later part of his reign, Khagemba came into conflict with Burmese who under the Toungoo dynasty were trying to capture nearby Shan principalities and control over them. The Royal Chronicle records two invasions in 1648 and 1651 from Burma (the name of Burma and Burmese were changed to Myanmar and Myanmarese some years ago. There must not be any confusion while mentioning Burma, Burmese of Myanmar). It may be mentioned that the invasion was in the eastern frontier of Kabaw valley and in both the cases, Burmese forces were successfully driven out. In the 1648 invasion, the Manipuri forces chased the enemy right upto the frontier portion and drove them out. But in the second attack, though they expelled from the country, some important army officials including Pheida Hidang Monnai were killed. The Meitei 'military control' over Kabaw valley was quite strong though there 'was no administrative integration of the valley with mainland Manipur.'[62]

In 1608, a brother of the king, Sanongba who had fallen out earlier with Khagemba over the wreckage of a boat with the support from forces in Cachar invaded Manipur but Khagemba defeated them and took '1000 captives including their leaders, 30 elephants and 1000 guns'. He made these captives settle in different parts of Manipur and appointed them to work as Bugler, Drummer, etc, and were given jobs according to their skills.[63] The captives also included Muslims. They were early Muslim settlers in the state.

Known as a gifted administrator and for his broad social policy under which people from outside the state including captives or immigrants were settled in different parts of the state, Khagemba introduced Meitei script throughout the kingdom in 1608 on a large scale.[64] It may, however, be pointed out that Meitei script had already existed much before this. It can be adjudged from writings on stones during the reign of Kyamba.[65] The reign of Khagemba was marked by developments in different fields. After strengthening the internal position of the kingdom, he introduced new methods of agriculture, constructed marketing centres and set up new villages to bring about all round development. During his period, the practice of the old Meitei religion was at its peak and the king was a deeply religious person.

After a colourful and glorious reign of Khagemba, no significant events had taken place during reigns of his immediate successors though there was some military campaigns in Kabaw valley. In February 1692, Burmese

[62]See Kabui 'History of Manipur', p. 225.

[63]See Singh and Singh 'Cheitharol Kumbaba', p. 33 and Diary of Manipur, p. 10.

[64]Diary of Manipur (Archieves), p. 36.

[65]See Kabui 'History of Manipur', p. 276.

troops encamped at the Manipur frontier and invaded the country during Paikhomba's time (1666-1697) in which two Manipuri soldiers were killed. This was recorded as an important event of that time. After a brief skirmish, the enemy was later driven out of the country. During the reign of Charairongba (1677-1709), there had been a regular inflow of Brahmin immigrants and scholars to Manipur and they tried to 'exert Sanskrit influence on Manipur's court life specially in the field of astrology.'[66] Known for his statesmanship, Charairongba further consolidated his rule in the state and there had been considerable peace in the Kabaw valley in the eastern frontier during his reign. As he had developed frequent contacts with Burma, he also engaged Burmese artisans and skilled persons in the construction of several temples. With the influence of the growing Hinduism, the visiting Brahmins used to get aquaintance with the king and other members of the Royal family. What was recorded is that upto the period of Charairongba, the royal succession was 'fairly regular' though the direct line was sometimes broken by some strong princes or intruders attempting to usurp power. After Charairongba, Manipur witnessed power struggle among succeeding princes and it often led to unwanted violence.

A new era set in with the ascension of Pamheiba at the throne in 1709. He succeeded Charairongba and assumed the name of Garibaniwaj. With the fortunes of Manipur reaching pinnacle and attaining power like the Ahoms of the neighbouring Assam, the period of Garibaniwaj as remarkable with full of developments taking place in various fields. The state also witnessed conversion of people to Hinduism. During this revolutionary change, Garibaniwaj who was a brilliant ruler and one of the greatest kings Manipur had ever had, played a significant role in shaping the future of Manipur. Having a deep political insight and military prowess, Garibaniwaj launched military expeditions towards the hill tribes for internal consolidation and it was followed by wars against Burma and later against Tripura. As stated

[66]See Kabui 'Histolry of Manipur', p. 276.

earlier, both hill and valley people were also locked, as elsewhere in other parts of the world in the historic and formative period of the state, sometimes in tribal warfare and skirmishes. Sometimes both sides suffered heavy casualties. Meitei forces attacked Tokpa and Naongphow (Anal villages) in 1712 but the hill men killed 19 Meitei soldiers including prominent warriers—Chingkhwam Kiyamba, Haodeijam Khomma and Khoitongbam Chaoba.[67] Soon after this, king Garibaniwaj with a large number of forces defeated and took possession of the villages because the intention of the rulers was to build up a strong state. Following reports of restless of people in the eastern hills, the king sent military expedition to Hundung side where both people were engaged in bloody conflict in which 'sixty six Meitei soldiers were killed in 1733' but the defeat of the Hundung and some nearby villages was an important event in consolidating the internal position and building a strong state. In the later period, after complete integration of various tribal villages with the rest of the state, both hill and valley people joined together and became one force, and fought against invasions by foreign countries such as Burma and Tripura.

Frequent wars between Manipur and Burma occurred during the reign of Garibaniwaj, Sometimes in late 1724, the Manipuri king attacked and defeated a Burmese force at the mouth of Maglang river in the region and in 1725 'repulsed a strong army of 30,000 men'[68] who had penetrated into the valley at Manipur frontier. The entire force was defeated. Pamheiba, as he was popularly known, also crossed Chindwin river (in upper Burma) in 1735, attacked and ravaged Myedoo on the banks of Mu river within Shwebo Province of the kingdom and carried off numerous captives. The invasion was a major one carried out by any Manipuri king on Burma. It was a hectic period of active military expedition to Burma during which Garibaniwaj successfully invaded that country on different occasions. The Manipuri king also led a

[67]See Singh and Singh 'Cheitharol Kumbaba', p. 74.

[68]See Dun 'Gazetteer of Manipur', p. 37.

strong force of 20,000 army and crossed Chindwin again in 1738, attacked and dispersed a Burmese army. And in the same year at the termination of the rainy season, he and his forces marched between the Burmese army, 'three divisions of which occupied the towns of Matsen, Dabayen, and Myedu, and, to use the language of the Burmese historians, 'without stopping' attacked and carried the stockaded positions around the ancient capital of again (a city near Ava), of which he obtained possession.'[69] A fierce fight between Manipuri and Burmese forces accrued as the Meitei forces stationed at Thalunbyu to the west of Sagaing destroyed or set afire houses and monasteries in that area in addition to heavy casualties on both sides. He planted the standard of Manipur at Sagaing. Garibaniwaj again invaded Ava in 1739 but later retreated to Myedu where he was deserted by some of his allies. After suffering much loss, he retired to the stronghold of his frontier border. And a friendship between the two countries followed. For sometime, both Garibaniwaj and the Burmese King reconciled with the latter requesting a matrimonial alliance by seeking the hand of a princess. After giving a careful thought and scrutinising the proposal, the Manipuri king gave a daughter to the king of Ava. On way back home, the king and his party were attacked by a fierce tribe known as Koi who were, with some Burmese help, defeated and subdued. It was pointed out that the reasons for frequent attacks on Burma were because of Manipur's attempts to expand territory.

Manipur had adopted different military tactics to defeat her enemies in the past. In 1723, both Burma and Tripura invaded Manipur more or less simultaneously. In an apparent attempt to buy time while some Manipuri forces were fighting with Burma at Wangjing area (now in Thoubal district), the king sent representatives to negotiate with Tripuri forces in the south-west part of the country. However, the negotiation could not be achieved and Manipuri forces who successfully defeated and drove out the Burmese forces, came back and dispersed the Tripuri forces who later fled to

[69]Dun, p. 38.

their country. Patriotic Manipuri soldiers were always at the fore front to defend the country whenever their services were required. Frequent incursions between Manipur and its neighbouring countries occurred in the olden days.

The long and glorious 40-year reign of Garibaniwaj was ended by the 'black tragedy of the murder of the old king'[70] by his son Chitsai. Some different versions were given on this issue. The king was upbraided by Chitsai and his party for his incomplete expedition to Burma and for tendering submission to the king of Ava by giving a daughter. Supporters of the king, it was pointed out, deserted him after he gave his daughter to Burmese king. Garibaniwaj had several wives and eighteen princes. This put the king in a very delicate situation with who would succeed him though he favoured his eldest son, Shyam Shai who was also the natural successor. However, king's third wife, Gomati Devi upon an alleged promise made by the king earlier wanted her son to be the successor. While this portion remained a mysterious part of the history, Garibaniwaj with a hope of getting help from the king of Ava countered against his rebellious son Chitsai resided for a short period at Tsingain in Burma until Toungoo dynasty at Ava was subdued by the latter's opponents. As all hopes of reviving his forces were shattered, he attempted to re-enter Manipur and was murdered by emissaries of Chitsai who were also known as Ajit Shai. His devoted eldest son Shyam Shai was either killed along with him or drowned by jumping into the Chindwin river as he could not bear the scene of slaughter of his father.[71] But the parricide (1748-1752) could not retain the throne for long as he was driven out by Bharat Shai (1752-1753) who reigned for two years. People were shocked at these developments, and whole country raised against Chitsai for committing parricide. Bharat Shai was succeeded by Maramba who was also known as Gour Shyam, the eldest son of Shyam Shai. 'This Gouroo Sham (Gour Shyam) was a cripple, and it is related that considering himself from his

[70]See Hodson 'The Meitheis', p. 80.

[71]See Dun 'Gazetteer of Manipur', p. 38.

infirmity unfit to be sole ruler, he associated himself with his brother Jai Singh or Chingthang Khomba, and that they ruled alternatively. This arrangement lasted until Gouroo Sham's death, about 1764, when the sole authority fell to Chingthang Khomba who also became known as Bheigyachandra), who held it up to 1798.'[72]

It should be understood that Manipur had attained considerable power following the triumphant achievements of Garibaniwaj as this could, some writers pointed out, also be confirmed from Burmese historical works. Neighbouring Burma also underwent a change since the collapse of Toungoo dynasty. About this time, Alaungpaya set up the third Burmese empire and ascended the throne of Burmese kingdom at Ava after driving away rebellious Mons as well as Shans. He brought a change in the political situation in Burma as was the case in its neighbouring countries. After the death of Garibaniwaj, Manipur also witnessed a series of upheavals as numerous sons of the great king scrambled for power at Kangla and this resulted in bloodshed and series of fratricidal killings. Ultimately, the situation led to the downfall of this ancient kingdom. The internal conflict of princes and attempts to usurp the throne among them gradually made Manipur vulnerable to any foreign invasion. 'The early history of Manipur was barbarous in the extreme. It was not only marked by constant raids of the Manipuris into Burma, and of Burmese into Manipur, but by internal wars of the most savage and revolting type, in which sons murdered fathers and brothers murdered brothers, without a single trait of heroism to relieve the dark scene of blood and treachery.'[73]

By the time Alaungpaya set up the third empire, Burmese army became a considerable force as they were now acquainted with the use of more advanced weapons and firearms than the primitive spear, lance, and bow and arrow. After consolidating his position in his own country, the Burmese king wanted to revenge Manipur for the latter's

[72]See Hodson 'The Meitheis', p. 80

[73]See Mackenzie 'The North East Frontier of India', p. 149.

earlier agressions. In 1758, Alaungpaya commanded a strong Burmese force with modern arms, and proceeding up the Chindwin with a fleet of boats ravaged the Kabaw valley, a Shan tributary to Manipur. After marching through Kabaw valley, the Burmese forces then crossed the Angoching, entered Manipur valley by the Aimol pass and defeated the Manipuri forces at Pallel (now in Chandel district). It was a great invasion by the Burmese forces as they routed the Manipuris after a fierce sanguinary conflict. According to the Royal Chronicle, the Manipuri forces retreated to Kakching, near pallel, under the command of the king's younger brother, Chingthang Khomba to fight the battle there. Soon Burmese forces ravaged and devastated the country 'occupying the capital for nine days'[74] after which Alaungpaya and his forces returned to Ava following news of revolt of people at Pegu there.

Dejected over the recent developments, the Manipuri king and general people who had earlier gone to nearby hills came down to occupy the throne again. While returning home the Burmese forces took as much booty as they could besides a large number of Manipuri prisoners. It was a great concern for Jai Singh over the rising power of neighbouring Burma who used more advanced firearms than Manipuri forces. His main concern was to get more advanced weapons. At the same time, he was also aware of the fact that dethroned Chitsai who had been expelled from Manipur was trying to elicit support from the Bengal government with the help of king of Tripura to capture the throne of Manipur.

Relations with the British

Concerned over Chitsai's attempts to capture power again and frequent attacks from Burma, Gour Shyam looked for ways to defend the country. And Manipur's search for more advanced weapons led the king to come into contact with the British government in India. His brother Jai Singh (Chingthang Khomba) sent a confidential messenger named Haridas Gossain with a letter to Henry Verelst, chief at

[74]See Singh and Singh 'Cheitharol Kumbaba', p. 120.

Chittagong factory for acquiring British help against Burma. Through this messenger, the real character of Chitsai and the ignoble crimes he had committed were also exposed to the British. As a result, the Tripura king and the British authorities, who both wanted to help Chits ai, stopped further communications with the latter.

After reaching a negotiation, a treaty favourable to the British was concluded on 14 September 1762 between Haridas Gossain and Henry Verelst. Some other Manipuris including important functionaries like Ananta Shai, Podullo Singh and Chitton Singh were also involved in the negotiation. It may be noted that this was the first treaty with the British signed by Haridas Gossain, on behalf of Gour Shyam who had become the king again because of his turn, and Verelst. Approved by the Bengal government on 4 October 1762, under the 'treaty'[75] between Manipur and the British, the latter promised the former to help in its attempt to recover its territory which had been wrested by Burmese. There was, however, no further communication between the two though the British troops who came upto Khaspur, the then capital of Cachar, returned to Bengal again owing to bad weather condition and English war against Mir Kasim, the Nawab of Bengal. Jai Singh was informed of the treaty. Gour Shyam, however, sent three-accredited agents including Ananta Shai to Chittagong to convey his inability to pay the expense (as mentioned in the treaty) incurred by the English troops. However, he gave 500 Manipur gold bars. The treaty then ceased to exist. Very soon followed the death of Gour Shyam, and Jai Singh became the king again.'

Around 1765, Manipur was again conquered by the Burmese forces. The country was devastated after the bloody conflict which prompted the Manipuri king to flee to Cachar. The Burmese also carried a large number of Manipuri prisoners who were later settled at Ava. The Burmese returned to their country after raising the king of Moirang, Khellemba, to the vacant throne of Manipur. With the assistance from Ahom (Assam) king, Jai singh who came

[75]See appendix.

back from Assam and was supported by the people, regained the throne in Manipur and expelled Khellemba. The Burmese again invaded Manipur in 1769 but were driven away by Jai Singh. From 1775 to 1782, the Manipuri king had made successfully drive away Burmese forces for at least four times though at times he was compelled to flee to Cachar by fresh Burmese invasion. However, by 1782 peace prevailed for sometime, and Jai Singh remained in power reconstructing the devastated country. It may be mentioned that for about four decades Jai Singh had valiantly fought against Burmese invasion and did his best to defend Manipur from the foreign rule. Known for his tireless fights against the enemies, Jai Singh also paid attention to develop arts and culture in the state during his reign. In early 1798, the king handed over Manipur to his eldest son, Labanyachandra who administered the country very efficiently. In his last days, Jai Singh devoted to the propagation of Vaishnavism and died in October 1799 in Bengal. With his demise dawned a period of unvarying scene of disgusting treachery and fratricidal killings among numerous sons of Jai Singh in their fight for power and supremacy in Manipur. In short, Manipur was thrown into political instability and turmoil, and this ultimately led to foreign intervention and conquest of the country by the Burmese forces.

Labanyachandra, the eldest son who had ruled the state efficiently in the absence of his father, was murdered in November 1800 by a hired hand engaged by some of his brothers. Modhuchandra, the next in succession, was thrown out by his half brother Chaurajit Singh who was supported by another brother Marjit Singh. Marjit Singh was the *Senapati* (Commander in chief) at that time. Modhuchandra who invaded Manipur to regain the throne with the assistance from king of Cachar was killed by the Manipuri forces under the command of Chaurajit Singh who was also joined by Marjit Singh at the battle of Shamupan village in June 1804 according to the Royal Chronicle. When Chaurajit Singh ascended the throne, his brother Marjit Singh whom he made the *Yubaraj* (next successor) for supporting him against Modhuchandra conspired to dethrone the new king. However, having failed in an attack, Marjit Singh fled to Burma where he sought the assistance from the king of Ava. This was a golden opportunity for the Burmese forces who had been waiting to attack and defeat Manipur. With the help of Burmese forces, Marjit Singh then invaded Manipur from Tamu and reached the capital where there was fierce fight between the invading and Manipuri forces. Chaurajit Singh drove out his rebellious brother who then fled to Cachar where his plea for assistance was turned down by Cachar king Krishnachandra and his brother Govindchandra. Humiliated, Marjit Singh with a few followers made his way to Ava through the province of Arakan and sought help from Burmese emperor Bawdawpaya to overthrow his brother Chaurajit Singh from the seat of power in Manipur. He thought with the Burmese help, he could easily dethrone his brother this time.

After staying at Ava for six or seven years, and making friendship with the Burmese, the Burmese king after a long persuasion agreed to help Marjit Singh and sent a large number of Burmese forces along with Manipuri prince for a major attack on Manipur. It was said Marjit Singh 'agreed to renounce all claim on the Kabaw valley, and to acknowledge his dependence on the king of Burma.'[76] The Royal Chronicle records that Burmese king provided about one lakh army. Finally in 1813, a considerable number of forces marched from Burmese territory to instal Marjit Singh as the ruler of Manipur. At Tamu, two divisions were formed. While one division including Marjit Singh proceeded to Kakching Khulel by Aimol pass, another division including Marjit Singh proceeded to Kakching Khulel by Aimol pass, another division led by the Raja of Samjok entered the state via Machi route and encamped near Heirok (now in Thoubal district). It may be noted that the second division was completely defeated by Pitambar Singh, a nephew of Marjit Singh at Heirok but Maharaja Chaurajit Singh and his forces were routed by well-equipped Burmese forces at

[76]See Dun 'Gazetteer of Manipur'.

Kakching. This forced king Chaurajit Singh and Gambhir Singh, another brother, to flee to Cachar,

Though Marjit Singh became the new ruler of Manipur in 1813, his popularity plummeted for accepting Burmese suzerainty and ceding Kabaw valley to Burma. For some years, he reigned in Manipur. Not content with the present territory, Marjit Singh in 1818 invaded Cachar penetrating the hills in three divisions with a large number of forces. But king of Cachar, Govindchandra, knowing enmity between Chaurajit Singh and the Manipuri king, enlisted the support of the former. On hearing that Chaurajit Singh was on the side of the Cachar king, and knowing reluctance of Manipuri forces to fight against Chaurajit Singh, Marjit Singh rushed back to Manipur. Around this time, Gambhir Singh and Chaurajit Singh jointly became a considerable force and they occupied a portion of Cachar much to the disgruntlement of the king of Cachar.

When Bagyidaw ascended the throne of Ava in 1819, it was decided to celebrate the coronation in a big way by summoning tributary princes including Marjit Singh. The relation between the Manipur and Burma had become somewhat strain. Some earlier action of the Manipuri king such as cutting of timber in Kabaw valley without permission or construction of a gilded palace had annoyed and angered the Burmese who saw a Vassal ruler as asserting his independence in this manner. It was customary for any Vassal ruler on such occasion to pay homage to the new Burmese king. Apprehending retribution and reprisal, Marjit Singh defied the order and absented himself at the installation ceremony of the new Burmese king on the pretext that he expected some troubles from his brothers, Chaurajit Singh and Gambhir Singh if he was away from Manipur. Soon followed the Burmese invasion. A powerful Burmese army under the command of General Mingi Maha Bandula routed, defeated and ravaged the Manipuris forcing Marjit Singh and his supporters to flee to Cachar. A large portion of the population after having been vanquished and were unable to bear the torture and harassment by the foreign invaders fled to

Cachar, marking a dark period in the history of this once powerful tiny independent kingdom. This time, the Burmese who also invaded other parts of the north eastern India, put their puppet ruler at the throne of Manipur bringing the kingdom under their rule for seven years (1819-1826) which are known in Manipur's history as 'seven years' devastation" (chahi taret khuntakpa in Manipuri). As the Burmese forces were occupying the capital, the people were fleeing to nearby hills. However, on some pretext that a royal prince would be made the king, they were asked to come down. Later the people were entrapped in 1820 by the invading forces under the commands of Generals—Pakhan Woon and Kane Woon. Never before Manipuris had faced such atrocities and cruelties as in the hands of the Burmese forces who took not only thousands of the population to Burma but also massacred a large number of inhabitants. It was one of the worst periods that saw atrocities, savagery and oppression of the people in an unusual high degree by the Burmese forces. This ultimately led to the depopulation of the country. The Burmese atrocities in the countries they conquered were well known as they indulged in genocide in Assam, Manipur and other areas. While bulk of the Burmese left for their country with thousands of entrapped Manipuris, Kane Woon remained with about 2000 troops at the capital, according to the Royal Chronicle. At one time, the population of Imphal valley was said to be about 10,000.

At Cachar, Marjit Singh submitted the regal authority to Chaurajit Singh and three brothers, Marjit Singh, Chaurajit Singh and Gambhir Singh were reconciled for sometime. They joined hands together and 'unjustly' deprived Govindchandra of power. Govindchandra's appeal to the government of British India to annex Cachar went unheeded. Though Cachar was divided among the three Manipuri princes, they could not pull on long. While Chaurajit Singh retired to Sylhet, Marjit Singh and Gambhir Singh occupied a large portion of the Cachar territory.

Around this time, Burma attained the zenith of its power over running Manipur and Assam. And were at the frontier border of British India. When the frontier was threatened by the expanding Burmese forces through Cachar, negotiations between the Manipuri princes and the British India were on for a joint operation against the Burmese. After Marjit Singh was thrown out of power by the Burmese, Herachandra, a son of Labanyachandra, started a guerilla warfare with some supporters against the Burmese occupation. A highly patriotic prince, Herachandra's heroic action against the Burmese forcesis still regarded by the people in the state. More and more patriotic Manipuris joined the fight against the atrocities and Burmese occupation. The first attack of the Manipuris under the leadership of Herachandra on the Burmese forces, as recorded in the Royal Chronicle, was a shattering blow to the latter as the Manipuris slew about 200 of 500 Burmese troops while the enemies were going to Moirang side for gathering food in early 1820. More encounters followed between two sides with both suffering heavy casualties. As Burmese decided to strengthen its grip, more reinforcements arrived in Manipur sometime in November 1820. While the state was in turmoil and chaos with Burmese forces ransacking, ravaging and devastating the country, Gambhir Singh with whom the British government had negotiated an agreement, raised among his supporters a body of 500 men. They contributed to the British troops in driving out the Burmese forces from Cachar. The strength of this force then rose to 2000 in 1825, and it came to be known as Manipur Levy under the command of a British officer, Captain Grant. It was paid, accounted and supplied with ammunition by the British government.[77]

The Burmese overestimated its strength and power when General Bandula reported to the king that his forces could easily conquer Bengal impressing upon the king and his nobbles that the Burmese were superior to the British. Was this their miscalculation? It may be noted that the earlier policy of non-interference by the British on eastern frontier led to the occupation of Assam by the Burmese forces. At the

[77]See Mackenzie 'The North East Frontier of British India', p. 150.

same time, Govindchandra's petition for help in Cachar against Manipuri princes was not given proper attention by the British. Accordingly, as the situation took a different turn, Govindchandra sought Burmese help, which was obliged. Three Burmese army divisions from Jaintia, Assam and Manipur converged on Cachar sometime in 1824. The Burmese army planned to invade the British district of Sylhet and this caused panic among the British subjects. The situation demanded the Governor General of India Lord Amherst to declare war on Burma on 5 March 1824. It may, however, be noted that there were clashes between the British and Burmese forces with the Burmese commander saying, before the battle of Jatrapur, that their object was to capture the three Manipuri princes, Chaurajit Singh, Marjit Singh and Gambhir Singh.[78] Soon after the declaration of the war, the Burmese suffered heavy casualties with over 3000 dead in Cachar alone. A simultaneous operation was then launched by the British against Burma with the former attacking the enemy by land at Assam and Arakan, and by sea in Yangon front. The British forces to some extent were successful in keeping their enemy at bay at Assam and Arakan front but they failed to make much headway owing to lack of supplies and geographical barriers. However, Burma was weakened following attacks at different fronts. General Bandula was also faced with a grave situation because of shortage of supplies. He returned to Burma from Assam front and it was at this time that Gambhir Singh entered Manipur with his men accompanied by British officer Lt. R B Pemberton. After crossing innumerable hurdles, Gambhir Singh and his men ultimately reached Manipur valley on 10 June 1825. An exemplary action against the Burmese forces by Gambhir Singh was shown in the 'battle of Tilain'[79] supported by the British. With an ironic determination to liberate Manipur, Gambhir Singh with soldiers of his Manipur Levy armed by the British came to Manipur from Sylhet on 17 May 1825. A war broke out

[78]See Singh 'A Short History of Manipur', pp. 240.
[79]Ibid.

with the Burmese forces. After the first encounter with Gambhir Singh, the Burmese forces fell back to Andro, about 20 kms east of Imphal. When he marched to Andro along with his troops, Burmese retracted. Gambhir Singh returned to Sylhet again leaving behind only 300 soldiers to defend Manipur. During his absence, Nara Singh who was commander in Chief looked after the state. There at Sylhet, Gambhir Singh who was praised by the British government for his recent action against the Burmese got an additional aid of 1,500 muskets. Since he raised the requisite number of men, he came back to Manipur capital after about six months. He was accompanied by Captain Grant and a new reinforcement. No one could stop the Manipuri forces now. Following his arrival, about 400 Burmese soldiers in the Kabaw valley left the valley while the chief of Samjok (appointed by the Burmese king), a Burmese general and 22 privates were caught alive. It was pointed out that by now the local Manipuri forces who were not accustomed to using advanced weapons such as good muskets with sufficient ammunitions, helped those trained forces from outside Manipur to a great extent in expelling the invaders. Manipuri forces overcame the Burmese troops at Tamu, and took over the Samjok prince and others as prisoners. After Tamu, the Manipuris ravaged the capital of Samjok, planted a standard on the bank of the Chindwin (which Manipuris called Ningthee) thus completing the liberation of Kabaw valley. Ningthee was the eastern boundary of Manipur's dominion.

As it turned out, Gambhir Singh emerged as a powerful leader in Manipur. On 1 February 1826, he arrived on the western bank of Chindwin and found the entire area deserted. The inhabitants had made a hurried retreat leaving their cattle behind and allowing the Manipuri prisoners to escape. By this time, the Burmese had realised their weakness, and defeat and death of dynamic leader Bandula in April 1825 during the battle at Donabew with a British officer, Archibald Campbell, shocked, upset and shattered emperor Bagyidaw. It was now, he thought, time for peace. However, he first could not accept the terms and conditions put forward by the British.

Around this time, some Burmese forces were still roaming in Assam, Manipur and north Burma. The fighting continued unabated as the conditions were not acceptable to Bagyidaw. By now, Manipur was under the control of Gambhir Singh and his forces. 'Campbell also advancing northward, occupied Yandaboo, a town within 45 miles of Ava. As the chances of defence diminished, the war came to a close by the treaty of Yandaboo signed on 24th February 1826.'[80] Under the treaty, the British and Burmese agreed for 'perpetual peace and friendship' with the king of Ava (Burma) renouncing 'all claims upon and will abstain from all future interference with the principality of Assam and its dependencies and also with the continuous petty states of Cachar and Jaintia.'

'With regard to Munnipore, it is stipulated that should Gambhir Singh desire to return to that country, he shall be recognised by the king of Ava as *Rajah* thereof.' Thus, Gambhir Singh was recognised by the treaty as *Maharaja* of Manipur. The confusion whether Gambhir Singh should be treated as the sovereign ruler of Manipur or vassal king under Burma was well settled after the treaty. It was Gambhir Singh who restored independence of Manipur with the help of the British. It must not, however, be construed that Gambhir Singh accepted the throne of Manipur as a vassal of the British. There was a sort of political relation between Manipur and the British government after the Anglo-Burmese war.

By the treaty of 1833, the second such treaty between Manipur and the British, the British ceded the line of Jiri river in perpetuity and western bend of Barak as a boundary to Manipur while 'the 1834 agreement'[81] transferred the Kabaw valley from Manipur to Burma. A money compensation for parting Kabaw valley was awarded to the Maharaja of Manipur by the British government in the shape of a stipend of Rs 6,000 per annum. It was the view of some writers that

[80]See appendix.

[81]Ibid.

the lack of any provision about Kabaw valley in the Yandaboo treaty led to the loss of the valley. The Kabaw valley issue will be dealt again in future chapter. The British, it was pointed out, wanted to please Burma by transferring Kabaw valley to them so that the latter did not make any further aggression.

It should be pointed out that there was also not a clause showing the curtailment of sovereignty of Manipur in any way in the 'the 1833 treaty'[82] between the Manipur king and the British government. According to the Statistical Account of Manipur by a former British official, R. Brown in 1873, 'on the conclusion of the Burmese war by the treaty of the Yandaboo in 1826, Manipur was declared independent.' 'Thus by the end of 1826. Manipur which had become a subordinate of Burma, now regained her independence and despite the British agency, she enjoyed greater elbow room in deciding her policies than she had done in the late eighteen and early nineteen century.'[83] It was now clear that Manipur which had lost her independence during war with Burma restored her independent kingdom after the Yandaboo treaty.

Closer Relations with the British and British Subjugation

An important step which would shape the future of Manipur was the appointment of a British political agent for what was considered 'preservation of a friendly intercourse, and as a medium of communication with the Manipur government. And, as occasion may require, with the Burmese authorities on the frontier, and more especially to prevent border feuds and disturbances which might lead to hostilities between the Manipuris and the Burmese.'[84] The role of the political agent, it can be pointed out, was like that of an ambassador, and a British officer, Captain Gordon who was somewhat

[82]Ibid.

[83]Bulletin of the division of History (1874-75) published by the Centre of post-graduate studies. Imphal Centre (now Manipur University).

[84]Political Correspondence quoted by Mackenzie in the North East Frontier of British India.

thorough with Manipur affairs and its people was first appointed for the post in 1835. Till the reign of Nara Singh (1844-1850), the political agent maintained strict political neutrality in the internal political affairs of Manipur though there was political instability as Manipuri princes on several occasions scrambled for supremacy and power among themselves. It was also considered an advantage for the British to keep an independent country between the territories of the British empire and Burmese government. Perhaps it was because of these reasons that the British secured an independent status for Manipur by making some concessions to the Burmese, pointed out some historians.

After the death of Gambhir Singh in 1834, his infant son Chandrakirti Singh was placed upon the throne with Nara Singh becoming regent of the king. Frequent attempts were made by different princes to seize the throne but none of them succeeded. As it happened, the mother of the young king, fearing that his son would be murdered by the regent, in collusion with some bad elements made an abortive attempt on the life of Nara Singh. It misfired. She along with Chandrakirti Singh and some supporters fled to Cachar in 1844 and their flight was taken as abdication of the throne. It made the regent the real king soon. After the death of Nara Singh, there was political instability as some princes fought for supremacy but Chandrakirti Singh with some British help emerged victorious and ascended to the throne again. In the beginning relations between Chandrakirti Singh and the British political agent was not good though the 'differences' were patched up in the later period with the king helping the agent on different occasions. .After the retirement of W. McCulloch as political agent in Manipur in 1867, the political agents who came to Manipur were considered 'inefficient and failed to maintain 'friendly relationship' with the government of Manipur till the appointment of James Johnstone. F.St. C. Grimwood, a junior officer of Sylhet, was sent to Manipur as political agent, but was suddenly transferred to Shillong and again . called upon to become the political agent in Manipur in 1889.

After the death of Maharaja Chandrakirti Singh, Manipur began facing a series of problems following dissension among his eight sons. Although his eldest son, Surachandra Singh succeeded him with his brother Kulachandra Singh and Tikendrajit Singh as heir-successor and commander-in-chief respectively, the new ruler was not a powerful one. Moreover, they were of different mothers. Sharp differences had cropped up among the princes particularly between the Commander-in-Chief *(senapati)* and Paka Sana, another prince. And this dissension among royal brothers brought about a demonstration against the Maharaja. This hostile movement resulted in the resignation of Maharaja from the throne and, expecting help from Grimwood to restore his position, Surachandra Singh rushed to the residency (residence of the political agent) located near his palace. The immediate cause of the problem was when a young prince Jila Singh owing to some misunderstanding and quarrel among the princes, scaled the wall of Maharaja's residence with his brother Angou Sana and some followers, and began firing on the night of 21 September 1890. Though it was begun by two younger brothers of the Maharaja, it was said they could not have taken this 'extreme step' without the active support of Tikendrajit Singh.[85] The brothers were divided into groups-one group under Surachandra Singh who was trying to remain in power and the other led by Tikendrajit Singh trying to seize the power.

After Surachandra Singh, Kulachandra Singh who was the heir successor to Manipur throne and had kept himself aloof from either side during the commotion at the palace and the events of the following day, became the king since Surachandra Singh 'abdicated' the throne. At this stage, it may be noted, the British started interfering in the internal affairs of Manipur, and they knew very well that without their active support any ruler, in view of the opposition or attempt to usurp power either by a royal member or anyone, could not remain in power. They were also aware of the fact

[85]Documents/political correspondence etc. (Enclosure 10 in No.3 dated 21, 1891), Manipur Archives.

that thousands of able-bodied Manipuris were killed or taken as prisoners during the 'seven years devastation period' by the Burmese. The British did not recognise Kulachandra Singh as Maharaja of Manipur. They knew that removal of Tikendrajit Singh and Paka Sana from Manipur would be an advantage for furtherance of British interests in this kingdom. Maharaja Kulachandra Singh, they thought, was a puppet in the hands of these princes. It was because of these things that the British did not recognise Kulachandra Singh as Maharaja but as a regent. They knew that the real power was in the hands of Tikendrajit Singh. After a careful study of the situation, they set some conditions which Kulachandra Singh should fulfil if he wanted to be recognised as a 'Maharaja' by the British. The conditions placed upon him were. (1) He should allow the political agent to keep 300 soldiers in the residency. (2) He should administer the country according to the advice of the political agent, and (3) He should agree to the banishment of Tikendrajit Singh from Manipur and help the British government in achieving these conditions. Interestingly, without informing Kulachandra Singh about these conditions, the Chief Commissioner of Assam J. W. Quinton with about 400 soldiers from 42nd and 44th Gorkha regiments arrived in Manipur on 22 March 1891.

A warm welcome was given to the British officer as he was received with usual guard of honour and salute. Already around 100 soldiers of the 43rd Gorkha regiment had been shifted to Manipur this time. The Assistant Commissioner of Assam Lt. P. R. Gordon had already been sent to Manipur to study the situation but he was told by the Political Agent, Grimwood that the arrest of Tikendrajit Singh would not be an easy task. It appeared haughtiness on the part of the British that they had planned to arrest the Commander-in-Chief in the latter's own palace and kingdom.

Soon after his arrival, Quinton instructed Grimwood to arrange for a conference of the *Durbar,* the highest administrative body in Manipur with Maharaja as its president. The Political Agent, on learning that Tikendrajit Singh would be arrested during the conference, opposed the idea but he had to submit to the will of the supper officer. Most of the Durbar members were Princes and important persons of those days, and a member can be said to be an equivalent of a cabinet minister now-a-days. During the Durbar, Quinton was to announce the conditions which were placed upon Kulachandra Singh. Grimwood visited the palace to convey the plan of the British government but without result, and Quinton then sent written ultimatum to Kulachandra Singh warning him that, unless Tikendrajit Singh was surrendered, he (Tikendrajit Singh) would be arrested. Kulachandra Singh was told that his recognition as Maharaja by the British government depended on the surrender of Tikendrajit Singh. At this point, Tikendrajit Singh got a hint of the plot and did not attend the conference of the Durbar. Quinton declined to receive Kulachandra Singh who came to attend the Durbar at the residency. The domineering attitude of the British provoked some patriotic Manipuris and in spite of all unfavourable conditions, the Chief Commissioner of Assam who had discussed the issues with Kulachandra Singh in the afternoon of 22 March 1891 without producing any result, was determined to arrest Tikendrajit Singh in the latter's palace. Was it an undoing on the part of the British officer or a destiny which would have faltered the history of Manipur.

As the information about the plan to arrest Tikendrajit Singh and banish him outside the state spread like a wild fire, his supporters collected arms, troops and stationed them at his house. Already people in Manipur, including high officials, were angry against the British because Kulachandra Singh and his brothers were kept waiting outside the residency before holding the conference of the Durbar on 22 March. 'It is very strange that the person whom the government of India decided to recognise as the head of a state, was kept waiting for an indefmite period at the gate of the Political Agent's house in his own kingdom. In this respect, the chief commissioner, Quinton displayed his utter lack of courtesy and tactlessness.'[86]

[86]Insurgency Movement in North Eastern India, P. Tarapot quoting History of Manipur by J. Roy.

The atmosphere was thick and heavy as the tension between the British and Manipuris was mounting because of the former's insistence to nab a patriotic, Manipuri leader. It was evident that the people were becoming restless and were full of avenging spirit against the foreigners. They could no longer suppress their anger and tolerate the action of the British empire but the burning spirit of patriotism made them prepare for any eventuality. The people were already alarmed at the disposition of the British forces about the Durbar area and residency. The night of 22 March 1891, in spite of some tension during the day because of the insistence of the British for the presence of Tikendrajit Singh during the Durbar, was quiet. The Durbar was again ordered to meet at 8 a.m. on 23 March, and again at 1 p.m. but nobody appeared for the conference, and suspicion arose among the British since the Manipuri troops marched into the Maharaja's palace. On these developments, Captain Boileau of the 44th Gorkha learnt that an attack on the residency was probable and reported this to Col. C.McD. Skene who instructed Lt. Brackenbury with 30 men and Captain Butcher of 42nd Gorkha with 70 men to march out at dawn to surround Tikendrajit Singh's palace and seize him. They were to be supported by Lt. Lugard with 50 men and the movement was carried out at 5 a.m. on 24 March.

It was natural that the Manipuri forces, irked at the high-handed behaviour of the foreigners, were all out to defend and protect Tikendrajit Singh. Determined to save their leader and with a vigour to fight for their motherland, the Manipuri forces collected themselves and stood solidly against the foreign forces in spite of inferior weapons. Their only strength was that their forces outnumbered the British troops whose arrogant attitude had already provoked the Manipuris. The British officials very well knew that their action and behaviour were not proper but they did this after knowing the sharp divisions among the princes.

After the failure of the political negotiations, Col. Skene who was the commander of the Chief Commissioner's escort with about 250 soldiers entered the extensive palaces enclosure at dawn on 24 March 1891 and besieged the house of Tikendrajit Singh. It was well-planned, and both sides were prepared. The firing began at around 6 a.m. and the fierce encounter between the two caused several casualties on both sides. Lt. Brackenbury, about 20 of his men and several Manipuris were wounded in the firing that lasted upto 4 p.m. The British official later succumbed to the wounds in the night. The British soldiers could not, however, capture Tikendrajit Singh in spite of using force as he had already left for some other place. This incident increased the determination of the Manipuris to fight against the foreign forces. By now both sides were concerned over the growing tension, and in an attempt to stave off the situation, an armistice was arranged at around 8 p. m. through exchange of messages during which Quinton, Col. Skene, Grimwood, Lt. W.H. Simpson of the 43rd Gorkhas, and W.H. Cossins, the Assistant Secretary to the Chief Commissioner, went to meet Kulachandra Singh. As the ceasefire was declared, Manipuri forces asked the British troops to 'fall in and assemble,' and discussions between the two began during which the Manipuri leaders asked the British for 'unconditional surrender' including the arms. Instead the British officials insisted discussions directly with Kulachandra Singh and Tikendrajit Singh.

At the palace, they were led into the courtyard inside the fort where the Durbar hall was situated. The Durbar was held, and the discussions went on for half an hour during which Tikendrajit Singh insisted on the British officers to surrender all the arms. Sticking to implement the government of India's plan, Quinton expressed his desire to carry on further talks since no decision could be arrived. At this time, many people were waiting outside the Durbar hall to know the result. Some of them who had lost close relatives in the encounter with the British demanded the punishment of the British officers. There was complete chaos and disorder. The B:citish officers, who had left the Durbar hall, were chased by the Manipuris after they had come out. Grimwood requested the minister. Angou Sana to send an escort with them. They were given escort but they were attacked by the Manipuris at the main gate. Lt. Simpson was struck on his head by a sword and was severely wounded. He was, however, rescued by a Manipuri official. Grimwood was' also struck by a spear hurled from the mob and died on the spot. The remaining officers were hurriedly taken into Durbar hall to save their lives by a Manipuri prince. After hearing about the mob's fury, Tikendrajit Singh came out and instructed the posting of guards around the hall for their protection. He did try to control the situation.

The last Durbar was also attended by General Thangal (popularly known as Thangal General) who was a great patriotic leader. He was already much agitated by the behaviour of British officers. General Thangal was pressurised by the people who lost their relatives in the firing incident to give orders for execution of the British officers. The situation was quite alarming and Tikendrajit Singh told General Thangal to desist from such an action. However, owing to a communication gap, the British officers were later executed. On the other hand at the residency, the remaining British officers Mrs. Grimwood, Capt. Butcher, Capt. Boileau, Capt. Woods, Lugard and Calver, thinking that all chances of peace had gone, stealthily left the residency with about 200 Gorkha soldiers and later arrived safely at Lakhimpur, Cachar. They thought the Chief Commissioner and his party must have been arrested. Also the residency was later seen under fire.

Anglo-Manipuri War

Soon after learning about the trouble in Manipur, the British launched a full scale invasion of Manipur with about 8000 soldiers marching into Manipur from three sides—Kohima, Silchar and Tamu. While Major General H. Collect, who led Silchar column, was given overall command of the whole operation, the Kohima and Burma (Tamu) columns were led by Col. R. H. F. Rennick and Brigadier General T. Graham respectively. Both sides were prepared and determined for any eventuality and outcome. At this time, Manipuris inside and outside the state were very much agitated and greatly concerned about the fate of the Manipur state. Nearly 35,000 Manipuris were in Cachar. The Manipuris inhabiting Sylhet, Dhaka, Shillong, Golaghat, Nabadwip and other places also became very agitated over the British move because they considered Manipur as their motherland. At home, every able bodied person was prepared for the worst and defence of their motherland in spite of unpropitious situation .

General Thangal wanted full preparation as the Manipuri ruler was determined to fight unto last. Following the call from Maharaja Kulachandra Singh, the last king of independent Manipur, hundreds of people came forward to defend the country. Some leaders were given specific instruction to command at certain battle fields. The information was also received at the capital that the British forces had entered the northern side. As the war began, patriotic Manipuri forces despite the inferior arms and unsophisticated weapons showed their ironic determination to defend their motherland. The historic battle was fought at Khongjom, about 35 kms south-east of Imphal. Led by Paona Brajabashi and Major Chongtha, about 400 Manipuri forces put up a strong and spirited opposition to the British column from Tamu at Khongjom. How spirited and courageous were the Meiteis in those days. 'Fellow countrymen, enemy's shell can land in our camp whereas ours can not reach theirs,' Brajabashi told the patriotic soldiers at the peak of the battle. 'Our field guns too have not arrived. There is sure death for us now; however, we will never retreat.'[87] The Manipuri leader thundered inspiring the soldiers and charged the enemy with his sword. Both sides were locked in fierce and deadly hand-to-hand fight. Both sides suffered heavy casualties. The battle of Khongjom was not only decisive but most remembered as valiant Manipuris fight unto the last. Brajabashi and other leaders did not give away so long they were alive and their courage and heroism received 'admiration' from their enemy.

On 27 April 1891, the Union Jack was hoisted over Imphal. Manipur lost its independence and sovereignty and became under the British paramountcy. General Collet, who

[87]See Singh and Singh 'Cheitharol Kumbaba', p. 492.

encamped at the palace, announced the occupation of Manipur. Tikendrajit Singh and General Thangal who had valiantly fought against the enemy were tried and executed. It was said that the accused were not allowed the usual facilities to defend themselves. Kulachandra Singh and Angou Sana were sent to Alipur jail in Kolkata. Later they were transported to the island of Andaman for life. While the Manipuris called the British action 'treachery' because they interfered in the internal affairs of an independent kingdom, the latter termed the events of 1891 as 'rebellion'.

After the conclusion of the war, two questions raised in the minds ofthe British authorities about the future of Manipur-either to annex the state or to restore the native rule under their control. Various arguments for and against were put forward among senior officials. They minutely studied the political, financial and administrative advantages particularly in view of the strategic location of the state between India and Burma. While the Chief Commissioner of Assam, W. E. Ward who replaced Quinton favoured annexation giving opinion that this would among other things enhance the prestige of the British and a warning to other native states, the then Viceroy Lord Landsdowne unfavoured annexation though the state, he said, had 'forfeited its right to exist' after what he termed 'rebellion' during which some British officials were killed. According to a note prepared by the Viceroy on the future of Manipur, he said he wanted infliction of a 'punishment' on the state. He said he would 'regrant to a new ruler whom we shall select a carefully limited amount of authority under conditions which would for all time render it impossible for any Manipuri to contend that the state is one enjoying sovereign rights.' Finally, the government of India decided to permit re-establishment of native rule under their control. Manipur's charge that the British interfered in its internal affairs had never been clarified.

On 21 August 1891, the Governor-General in Council issued the proclamation, 'Whereas the State of Manipur has recently been in armed rebellion against the authority of Her Majesty the Queen, Empress of India; and whereas, during such rebellion, Her Majesty's representative and other officers were murdered at Imphal on the 24th of March last; and whereas by proclamation bearing date the 19th April 1891 the authority of the Regent, Kulachandra Singh, was declared to be at an end, and the administration of the State was assumed by the General Officer Commanding Her Majesty's forces in Manipur territory: It is hereby notified that the Manipur State has become liable to the penalty of annexation, and is now at the disposal of the Crown. It is further notified that Her Majesty the Queen, Empress of India, has been pleased to forego Her right to annex to Her Indian Dominions the territories of Manipur State; and has graciously assented to the re-establishment of Native rule under such conditions as the Governor-General in Council may consider desirable, and in the person of such ruler as the Governor-General in Council may select.'[88]

After a careful search, Governor-General in Council selected a five-year old boy, a great grandson of former Maharaja Nara Singh, as the next ruler. 'Governor-General in Council has been pleased to select you, Chura Chand, son of Chowbi Yaima, to be the chief of the Manipur State; and you are hereby granted the title of Raja of Manipur, and a salute of eleven guns,' said the 18 September 1891 notification signed by H. M. Durand, secretary to the government of India. 'The chiefship of the Manipur State and the title and salute will be hereditary in your family; and will descend in the direct line by primogeniture, provided that in each case the succession is approved by the Government of India.' It said 'further you are informed that the permanence of the grant conveyed by this *Sanad* (Edict) will depend upon the ready fulfilment by you and your successors of all orders given by the British government with regard to the administration of your territories, the control of the hill tribes, dependent upon Manipur, the composition of the armed forces of the State, and any other matters in which the British government may be pleased to intervene.'[89] Thus, Manipur came to be under the full control of the British.

[88]Foreign Department Secret (E) October 1891, Nos. 123-147 (Manipur Archives).

[89]Ibid.

CHAPTER III

Early Prodrome of Ethnic Feuds and Formation of Various Underground Organisations

Some of the problems that Manipur is confronting today have its roots in the past. Notwithstanding the installation of a native rule, common people had been feeling the pinch of restrictive measures imposed by the regime for years. Unable to challenge suppression, there had been simmering discontentment among the general inhabitants who were also utterly sick of unsettled rule, and pined for some government which would permit them of carrying on their daily avocation in peace. But, uncertainty persisted for years in spite of having the native rule. Seeds of hatredness were also sown and wedges driven between some ethnic tribes or people in the hills and valley sometimes in the early or middle part of the nineteenth century by the colonial power. The hills and valley were placed under different administrative controls after the native rule. On the other hand, it may not be wrong to say that the history of Manipur would have been totally different had not the fratricidal killings taken place among the royal brothers or princes. In any case, it would be amiss to ignore the history while attempting solution to any of the present day problems.

It was now obvious that no Manipuri ruler could remain in power without the patronage of the British who selected the Raja according to their choice. The notification conferring the Chiefship on Churachand Singh provided for 'complete subordination' of Manipur state as the right of the new ruler 'depended solely' upon his selection by the government of India, which never allowed that right to be called in question on any ground. It was also made known that the 'Chiefship of the Manipur state and title and salute will be hereditary' provided the succession, in each case, was approved by the government of India, which never allowed that right to be called in question on any ground. It was also made known that the 'Chiefship of the Manipur state and title and salute will be hereditary' provided the succession, in each case, was approved by the government of India. An annual tribute of Rs 50,000 was to be paid with effect from 21 August 1891 to the British. And a war compensation of Rs 2,50,000 was also imposed upon the state. The Political Agent, Maj, H. St. P. Maxwell who was also appointed the Superintendent of the state became the virtual ruler during the minority of the young Raja. Empowered with full authority to introduce any reforms, Maxwell who conducted the investiture ceremony of the Raja on 29 April 1892 had also been told to regard the customs and traditions of the Manipuris while discharging his duties. At the investiture ceremony, Maxwell announced doing away of slavery and the 'lallup' system of forced labour whereby every adult male was required to work for the Raja (later Maharaja) for ten days after everyone month. It brought some relief and unburdened a section of people who unschackled themselves from cultivating royal lands and working for the Raja round the year. The 'lallup' system was substituted by a yearly house tax.

Despite the abolition of slavery or 'lallup' system, the British rule was unwelcome, and people were hostile to it in the beginning. To protest against the British, people set ablaze some bungalows occupied by British officers. First the bungalows of Captain Nuttall, tutor to Raja and his assistant, J. G. Dunlop, were burnt to the ground on 16 March 1904 by some unknown persons. Again, over 28 sheds with seats for over 3,000 market women of Khwairamband Bazar (present Imphal market complex) were set afire on 6 July 1904. The way it was set on fire showed involvement of several persons who either opposed the British rule and the latter's day to day involvement in important affairs of Manipur. In August that year, the new bungalow of Nuttall and

Dunlop which were purchased by the state from another British official, Mitchell (an executive engineer in those days) was also set ablaze, and the Political Agent took it as a 'positive proof of incendiarism' in this case. He then announced a reward of Rs 500 to any person giving information which could give clue to detect the guilty persons but it failed. At times, when an unpalatable order was issued, people mobilised meetings which were often suppressed by the force. As an order was promulgated by the Political Agent to rebuild the last bungalow burnt by unknown persons at the expense of the local inhabitants, people objected to it. Some of the British officials viewed the incidents of setting ablaze of bungalows and other public properties of which similar cases were also reported in 1891-92 as the 'national manner of showing ill-feeling, opposition or disrespect to foreign rule.'

Soon after the order for rebuilding the bungalow was issued, people stepped up their protests and launched different types of agitations including demonstrations and public rallies in September and October 1904. Besides, they also picketed at public places, closed down shops and markets. As the Political Agent refused to revoke the order, about 5000 women launched a demonstration on 5 October 1904. Ultimately, the issue was settled through negotiation. Six persons who were relatives of royal family and had led the protests were 'banished'[90] from Manipur. However, the people of Imphal did not rebuild the bungalow. Though the direct British administration produced some good results such as improvement of road communication ordevelopment in some other fields, people in general were opposed to the British rule in early stage.

As the Raja who had been sent for schooling at Mayo College (Ajmer) attained adulthood, the administration of the state was made over to him on 15 May 1907. The post of the Superintendent of the State was abolished. The administration was carried out mainly by the 'Manipur State Durbar' (MSD) formed under the 'Rules for the General Administration of

[90]See Singh 'A History of Manipur', p. 312.

the State' (RFGAS). Framed by the Government of Assam and introduced in 1907 when the power was handed over to Maharaja Churachand Singh, the RFGAS was amended in 1919 to include the administration of hill areas. It was again amended on 14 September 1935. Though Maharaja Churachand Singh's approval was required for almost all the MSD resolutions, the Manipuri ruler did not involve in the daily affairs of the highest administrative body, the MSD. Under the RFGAS, the Governor of Assam appointed an officer as the President of the MSD to replace and assist the Maharaja. The President of the MSD was to attend all meetings of the MSD and exercised a general supervision over all departments of the state. The President of the MSD was also in direct charge of finance, land revenue, fisheries and the administration of the hill tribes. There were at least three Manipuri members of the MSD who held charges of different departments and were known as ordinary members.

It may be pointed out that the British Indian Empire comprised of the British India and Indian India with the provinces forming the former and native states making the latter. While the British India portion was ruled directly by the Government of India, the Indian India which was protectorate of native states was governed through native rulers. While the native states dealt with the Government of India through the Viceroy who was known as the Crown Representative, the same Viceroy was Governor General when he was dealing with provinces ruled by the Governors. It meant the same person was the Viceroy for the native states, and the Governor General for the provinces. Maharajas or Rajas under the native states had a good deal of control over the internal administration. Maharaja of Manipur was no exception though the state was remotely controlled by Governor of Assam. Regarding the external affairs, defence and communication, these subjects were left with the Government of India as native states did not enjoy any international status.

In Manipur, the MSD being the supreme administrative body with Maharaja as its president earlier, Churachand Singh exercised considerable executive, judicial and legislative powers. As the system of administration in the state underwent changes from time to time, the valley and hills were put under different sections of the RFGAS. To be able to understand more, the territories of Manipur as mentioned earlier consisted of hills, valley and the British reserve area. While different tribes inhabit the hills, Meiteis live in the valley. The present Kangla, Babupara, Kangchup hills, etc, were parts of the British reserve area which was administered by the Political Agent.

Did placing of hills and valley under different sections of the RFGAS create a chasm among inhabitants after the state came under the native rule? Moreover, it was not a difficult task to set a wedge between 'strict Hindus' (there are now many who follow the pre-Vaishnavite religion) of the valley and different hill tribes in those days. Though the Maharaja exercised a considerable power over the internal administration in the valley, the hills area was administered by the President of the MSD in the name of the Maharaja with a very few people of the state associating with the hill administration. To be precise, the hills area was ruled more or less by the government of Assam. 'By far the most important restriction on the powers of Maharaja and MSD was in the administration of the hill tribes. They were, in fact, administered by the government of Assam (meaning officers involved in the administration were from government of Assam and any major issue of the hills was referred to the Governor of Assam) on behalf of the Maharaja.'[91] The direct charge of the hills administration was in the hands of the President of the MSD who was an Indian Civil Service officer of Assam cadre. His two British assistants were also of Assam Civil Service. Maharaja Churachand Singh was earlier the President of the MSD. A Manipuri was appointed as assistant at the headquarters. The President of the MSD was primarily responsible for the hills administration though it was subjected to political control of the Political Agent whose duties were not clearly defined but whose powers were

[91]Letter of Political Agent C. Gimson dated 23 December, 1934 to Chief Secty. to the Government of Assam (Manipur Archives).

considered 'wide'. It may be pointed out that the Maharaja could veto any resolution adopted by the MSD but the Political Agent was to be informed who would later refer the matter to the Governor of Assam. The decision of the Governor of Assam was binding on the Maharaja and the MSD. As a matter of fact, the MSD also functioned as the highest original and appellate court both civil and criminal which, as a capacity of the judicial court, passed sentences for imprisonment. If the sentence for imprisonment was for five years or above, it was subjected to confirmation by the Maharaja. For the death sentence, the approval of the Governor of Assam was necessary. But it must be stressed that the Maharaja with his powers could pardon any accused in criminal in preliminary stages provided that such cases did not affect the British interests. The Maharaja also had the revisionary powers in both civil and criminal cases though approval of the Political Agent was necessary. Since the hills and the British reserve area were placed under different sections of the RFGAS, the MSD's civil and criminal jurisdiction limited in the valley only. Below the MSD, there were some lower courts for different purposes. Cheirap court had a criminal powers of imprisoning the accused upto two years and a fine of Rs 1000, and civil powers upto any amount. Criminal power for Sadar Panchayat was upto three months and civil upto Rs 300 while Rural Panchayat exercised criminal as well as civil power upto Rs 50. Appeal against the ruling of any of the lower court could be made to upper courts while judicial section of the MSD was the highest court in the state. A state force known as State Military Police (later to be called Manipur Rifles) had also been raised earlier. Revenue collection, improvement of road communication and other development work were looked after by the respective departments.

For the hills, the British officials were appointed as sub-divisional officers to aid the President of the MSD in the hills administration. The hills area had earlier been divided into four sub-divisions though the arrangements further underwent changes. And in 1933, Sadar sub-division was created. Tamenglong sub-division which had earlier been abolished was reopened again in October 1932. It was mainly because of the fact that when the sub-division was abolished and control of the area loosened, war between the Kukis and Nagas was started within a few months and the hills were soon in a turmoil as it led to head-hunting and tribal conflict.[92] The system further underwent changes and finally three sub divisions were created: (a) Sadar sub-division comprising all the hill men living in the valley and in the hills bordering on the valley besides certain other areas, such as the Mao and Maram groups, and this sub-division was under the direct control of the President of the MSD; (b) the Tamenglong sub-division covered the hills on the western side of the state, and was inhabited mainly by Kabuis, some other Nagas and Kukis; and (c) the Ukhrul subdivision covered the hills on the eastern side of the state and was inhabited mainly by Tangkhuls, Kukis, and others.[93] Churachandpur was once a sub-divisional headquarters. Appeals against the orders of the sub-divisional officers could be made to the President of the MSD while that of the President to the Political Agent. It should be pointed out that Tamenglong was considered as a troublesome area because of the frequent hostility between the Kukis and Nagas. The President of the MSD and sub divisional officers were to deal with all cases of both civil and criminal as far as hill people were concerned. All major hills-related cases were tackled by the hills bench of the MSD and was always presided over by the President of the MSD. While the Maharaja had the right to be consulted in all important matters, any imprisonment exceeding seven years needed the permission or confirmation from the Governor of Assam.

There used to be some people who acted as intermediaries between the British officers and hill subjects and were locally known as 'Iambus'. They were entrusted to arrange everything

[92]Correspondence of J.P. Mills, Secretary to the Governor of Assam to the Secretary to His Excellency the Crown Representative dated 22 April, 1937 (Manipur Archives).

[93]Letter of C. Gimson to Secretary to Governor of Assam dated 1 June 1937.

for touring British officials. They also delivered messages or summons to hill people. And were considered 'powerful' by hill inhabitants. There were some British officials who included a civil surgeon in charge of the civil hospital and a state engineer who was in charge of works department. All these showed a semblance of proper administration in the state. But, separate sections of the rules for administration coupled with 'communication gap' had been slowly drifting the people in the hills and valley apart as direct contact between the two was becoming infrequent. At the same time, different tribes settling in the hills had been nurturing deep hatredness and animosity over the years which ultimately resulted in perpetual tribal warfare. And hostilities between the people in the valley and hills were also not uncommon in those days.

As one looks back over the history in the stormy past in Manipur, Kukis settled at the exposed frontiers of the state were constantly locked in deadly clashes with Nagas. In 1892, 'some 286 persons were massacred'[94] when a band of Kukis raided Chingjaroi Naga village in the eastern Manipur. In the series of intra-tribal conflict, a Kabui Naga village in the western part of the state in one of the retaliatory attacks of a previous foray on their village wiped out a small Kuki settlement in 1918 slaying the inhabitants[95]. A leader of the same Kuki settlement, in yet another revengeful act, collected supporters and destroyed 20 Kabui villages besides taking 76 heads.[96] It was often a difficult task to control the standing hostilities between the two different tribes in Manipur though any warring tribe was frequently suppressed and punished by the authorities. The main reasons for frequent clashes were because of attempts by different tribes to dominate over the other. Kukis from Burma borders also made forays on some frontier Naga villages to extract their allegiance and pay tribute to them. The attack and counter attack continued. Having superior firearms, Kukis marauded

[94]History of the Frontier Areas bordering Assam, Robert Reid, p. 77.
[95]Ibid.
[96]Ibid.

most of the Naga villages. Nagas also ravaged and destroyed Kuki villages in the same manner. In February 1880. Chingsao Tangkhul Naga village in east Manipur was attacked by well-armed Kukis from nearby Chassad Kuki village. It was stated that their arms including guns and other weapons had been supplied by a chief of Samjok area, which was a tributary of Burma, and 'when the people of Chingsao reckoned up their losses, they found that 20 men, 7 boys and 25 women and girls had been killed, and one man, one woman, and one girl were missing.'[97] Kukis from Chassad had earlier demanded tribute from the inhabitants of Chingsao, and asked them to become the subjects of Samjok. The inhabitants of Chingsao refused this, saying they were subjects of Manipur, and the attack on the village prompted the establishment of a Manipuri police post at Chattik, a Tangkhul village south of Chingsao. The animosity between the two tribes was so deep-rooted that whenever any chance arose, they killed each other. Thus, unfortunately. Manipur had an unhealthy past, witnessing violence of one kind or the other. But that was part of the history which the denizens should take as experiences while building a strong Manipur.

When the British planned to draft labourers from Manipur hills for the employment with the army in France, some Kukis objected to it and rebelled against them. The British officers took action and launched operations against those who opposed the British plan. For some months owing to bad weather conditions, the operations were slackened during which the Kukis in between 1917 and 1918 'seized the opportunity to payoff old scores, against Naga villages, the Kabuis and Tangkhuls being the chief sufferers. Upwards of 200 heads were taken by the raiders, and several village destroyed.'[98] Some political leaders in the state feel that these were some of the examples of Kuki-Naga clashes of a remote past which, with the education spreading far and wide in interior places and people yearning for living together as no

[97]See Mackenzie 'The North East Frontier of British India'.

[98]See Reid 'History of the Fronteir Areas Bordering Assam', p. 80.

single community can live in isolation, should not be repeated. Did the recurrence of similar violence in the early nineteen nineties indicate what would be the situation in Manipur in future, or were some vested interests working to divide the common people for personal gains.

Though the attempt to conscript labourers from the hills was considered as primary and immediate cause of rebellion by some Kukis, the administrative system had, in fact, kept apart the hill and valley subjects for years. Hill people had also been nurturing ill-will against the authorities since they felt ignored. It was, on the other hand, not possible for the President of the MSD to cover in his annual tours the whole of about 20,000 sq kms of impassable mountains and give adequate attention to the tribes. Loose administration and dealing of hill people mostly through intermediary persons caused extreme discontentment and unrest among hill subjects. The inexperience of the President of the MSD, want of staff, bad means of communication and lack of funds also added to the problems faced by the hill people. Outwardly the British emphasised the need for good governance in hills but no welfare schemes or other development programmes had been implemented there. Since the British assumed a major role in the state administration, some sections of Kukis mostly Khongiais viewed the foreigners with suspicion and were not satisfied with the then prevailing system. In fact, the rules for the general administration of the State were further amended after the 'Kuki rebellion' of 1917 to 1919.

Among the Kukis the most important tribe Was that of Thadous which were divided into several sub-tribes such as Doungel clan and those connected with it (also known as Aishan Kukis, ... Sitlou and connected clans, Chassad Kukis and Haokips—all having some influences in their respective areas. While the Haokip Thadou Chief under the leadership of their seniormost clan, known as the Chassad Haokip, exercised influence at hills in the east and over the border in the Somra Tract' and Burma, the Aishan Kukis were influential at hills in the north-eastern part of the state and to unadministered areas of Somra. Also known as Chief of Jampi, the Sitlou Thadou Chief held sway in the west and north-west of the state while Haokip made their active presence felt in parts of the western hills.

When the demand for labourers for employment with the army in France was made in 1917, opposition from the Kukis had not been anticipated neither by the Maharaja nor by the British officers. However, soon after the demand was communicated to the Maharaja through the Political Agent, Lt. Col. H. W. G. Cole, Churachand Singh lost no time in offering to raise at once 2000 labourers and another 2000 later on. It was not smooth sailing. As the recruiting began, some of the Kuki chiefs in the outlying hills obstructed the government action. Chief of Aishan, Chengjapao who was considered head of all Thadou Kukis had earlier asked the leading Thadou chiefs to resist recruiting with force, if necessary, which were complied by other influential chiefs. As they defied government orders, 'a small force was sent from Aizawl'[99] (capital of present Mizoram which was then a part of Assam) at the request of the Political Agent in March 1917 to prevent some local Kuki chiefs from interfering with recruiting, and this step to some extent overcame the opposition among the Nagas and certain sections of the Kukis. After completion of the recruitment, the first labour corps of about 2000 hillmen with some 30 'Iambus' as interpreters and their leaders was despatched to France under the command of Lt. Col. Cole in May 1917. J.C. Higgins who was the President of the MSD, became the Political Agent.

When attempts were made to raise the second labour corps, some Kukis strongly opposed the move, resisted the enrolment and rebelled openly against the British. Interestingly, it was also an early opposition to the British presence by Manipur subjects. Historically, the 'different phases'[100] of the rebellion can be stated as follows: the trouble

[99]A note on Kuki Rebellion prepared by J.E. Webster, Chief Secretary to the Chief Commissioner of Assam to Secretary to the Government of India No. 6310 dated 27 June 1919 (Manipur Archives).

[100]Extract from the proceedings of the Chief Commissioner of Assam in the political department No. 8856, p. dated 27 September, 1920. (Manipur Archives).

was brewing from April to December 1917, the first attempt and suppression of the rebellion was made during December 1917 to mid April 1918, the Kukis raided and harried tribesmen who did not join the rebellion besides interrupting traffic during April to October 1918, and military operations following attacks and counter-attacks during November 1918, and military operations following attacks and counter-attacks during November 1918 to April 1919.

Though the trouble had been brewing quite for sometime, the insurrection broke out when some Kukis from Ukha, Henglep and neighbouring villages 'headed by four or five Manipuris (Meiteis) raided and looted the Manipur State forest toll station at Ithai (now in Bishnupur district) on 19 December 1917.'[101] This raid was 'planned'[102] by Chingakham Sanajaoba, a Meitei who claimed to have 'some magic powers and instigated' the Kukis to fight against the British. This was the first major attack by the Kukis. Already, several Kuki chiefs had decided to fight following the 17 October 1917 incident in which Higgins and his party set ablaze and destroyed the Mombi village while searching for the Chief of Mombi, Ngulkhup who had earlier threatened some tribes around Manvum village to burn their village and kill women and children if they sent coolies for labour corps.

As the situation was worsening, Higgins and J.H. Hutton were placed on special duty to tackle the Kuki rebellion while W.A. Cosgrave took over as the political agent on 27 December 1917. Columns of Assam Rifle marched against the rebellious tribes who put up a good deal of opposition. Several hostile villages were burnt and casualties increased on both sides. The rebellion was confined almost entirely to a section of the 'new' Kukis comprising most of the Thadous, with the Manhlun Kamhao clans of the southern hills and a few Baite villages among the Mangvum Haokip clan in the south-east of the Manipur state, leaving out the several other non-Thadou and old Kuki tribes and Nagas. The British intensified their operations by using more forces. They

[101]Same as 99.

[102]Ibid.

divided the tribes and made sure that other tribes did not join the rebellion. 'The plan of the operations was to prevent a combination of the Kukis by dividing the area into sub-areas and enclosing the latter by chains of small fortified posts, and to overrun the country and harass the Kukis by small mobile columns and active patrols band on the posts.'[103] In spite of inferior arms, Kukis put up a strong fight against the mighty force.

There was, however, no means to stand up against the superior forces and the British eventually subjugated the rebellion. One of the eleven rebellious Kuki chiefs, Ngulbul of Longya, was killed in action while the remaining ten either surrendered or were captured. The ten chiefs—Chengjapao of Aishan, Khuthinthang of Jampi, ... Pachei of Chassad, Pakhang of Henglep. Tintong of Laiyong, Semchung of Ukha, Ngulkhup of Mombi, Leothang of Godok, Helijashon of Loibol and Mangkoon of Tingkai Mangkoon-were first put in Kohima jail. While Semchung died in Kohima jail, the nine others were later taken to a place in Sadiya on the northern bank of Brahmaputra in Assam. Three others whose cases were considered more serious than the above were sent to Dibrugarh jail in Assam. They were Ngulkhukhai of Chassad, Enjakhup of Thenjol of Naga hills (present Nagaland) and Chingakham Sanajaoba of Imphal. It was later stated that Sanajaoba had earlier impressed upon some Kukis that the British rule was coming to an end and that he was fighting against the government with his supporters. He also made them believe that if everything went according to the plan, the house tax imposed on hill villages would also be reduced.[104]

What stands out in the history is how courageously the Kukis, in spite of their inferior arms, had fought against the British who, at one point of time being concerned about the stiff opposition, had requisitioned more forces and prevented the rebellion from spreading to other Kuki-settled areas in Myanmar. The determination to fight against the presence of

[103]Ibid.

[104]Ibid.

foreign powers in Manipur by its subjects was welt appreciated even by the enemies.

About a decade after the Kuki rebellion, a movement which resisted the British rule in the northwestern hills of Manipur was launched sometime in 1931 to set up a '(Kabui) Naga Raj' under the leadership of Jadonang who lived at village Kambiron on Imphal-Cachar road in Tamenglong district. He claimed to have 'mystical and spiritual powers', and was viewed by his fellow superstitious Zeliangrong Nagas (Kabui and Kacha Nagas) as the 'messiah' whom they had been waiting for. Claiming to have 'miraculous powers', Jadonang revived the old Naga tradition that a 'king' would arise from his sleep under the mountains and reign over all Nagas. Sometimes locally termed as 'Makam Gwangdi'[105] (the kingdom of Makam meaning Zeliangrong) among the Zeliangrong Nagas. The concept of the 'Naga Raj'. As propounded by Jadonang and later pursued by his follower and successor, Gaidinliu, was new and attractive to Zeliangrong tribes. Though it was short-lived, the movement at one point of time caused serious concern among the authorities in the state because a large section of the people in the north-western hills supported Jadonang.

Resentful of burdens such as imposition of house tax of Rs 3 per year, role of 'Iambus' (intermediary persons) preceding the local tribal chiefs and 'encroachment' of lands by the Kukis among other things, Jadonang's call; 'Makam people will be the rulers.'[106] evoked wide response among the Kabui and Kacha Nagas. It was first a sort of religious and social reform campaign but Jadonang's movement as it later unfolded became political spreading from Tamenglong district to nearby Zeliangrong-settled areas in Nagaland and Cachar (Assam), some oppressive rules which were also in force acted as catalyst to the movement. Under what was locally known as 'pothang bekari', compulsory labour was provided by the villagers for the repairs of roads or carrying of luggages of officials touring the hill villages without payment.

[105]Jadonang, a mystic Naga leader by G. Kamei, p. 22.

[106]Ibid.

The villagers were also forced to provide the best food or accommodation for the officials or employees of the government touring the hill villages under 'pothang senkhai' system. Those who refused the order were punished mostly by whipping.

As the movement was gaining momentum, Jadonang sent followers to different villages to enlist recruits, impart them military training, engage them in armed struggle against the enemy and to regard him as the 'messiah king' who would overthrow the British rule. The main objective of the movement, according to the Annual District Administration Report (1930-31), was to make war, first on the Kukis and secondly on the government (the British rule) though Jadonang in a statement later denied this. To achieve their goal, funds were raised to purchase arms like guns, spears, shields and other weapons, his idea of bringing people through religious congregation worked as he assured large gatherings and his followers that the new kingdom which he would head would be 'free from diseases, famines, taxes and forced labour of the British.'[107] With these objective in mind, his followers mostly Lurungpu of Mukti village, Gaidinliu of Nungkao, Takhenang of Cachar (Silchar), Machungang and Mudunang of Kambiron, Namdichung of Okoklong, Siphai of Nungba and others were sent to different villages to spread that Jadonang was the 'messiah king' of Kabui and Kacha Nagas. The movement launched under the leadership of Jadonang was also a major opposition to the British rule in parts of Manipur.

As the people believed in what was preached by Jadonang, villagers in large numbers assembled at various places where the leader was well-received, and paid tributes and gifts. Villages which sent him tributes in Tamenglong in the beginning were Kekru, Mukti Khulen, Punsang Chingmei, Mongjarong Khulen, Mongjarong Khunou, Bolongdai, Okoklong, Keihao, Charoi Pantongba and Khoupum. They also looked on him as a 'maiba' (a Manipuri word meaning medicine man), or a 'sadhu' (priest) 'rather than a temporal

[107]Ibid.

leader; but that they (villagers) were quite ready to take any opportunity of making war if they found a suitable excuse.'[108] There were several smaller villages which supported him but prominent among big ones in Cachar were Paisa, Thingje, Punji, Heiaichak, Nenglo, etc, while Lalongni, Peremi, Khonoma, Henima, etc, were those villages which gave help to Jadonang in Nagaland. The villagers also thought contribution to their leader would bring good crops, improved health, and keep off sickness. However, with the movement gaining popularity, Kukis settling either in north-west of Manipur, Cachar or in Nagaland became panic. They thought Nagas might attack them anytime since the latter had collected guns, spears, shields or other weapons in recent times. Frequent gatherings of Nagas at several villages also disrupted the cultivation of Kukis who on several occasions abandoned their fields, stayed away from cutting crops and took refuge in jungles for days for fear of attack. An alarming 'letter'[109] from the Political Agent of Manipur to the Deputy Commissioner of Cachar caused serious concern among the senior government authorities in early 1931 since it said there was 'concentration of Nagas at Tampilong (Kambiron) to attack the Kukis.' What concerned the Kukis, who were viewed as 'new comers and trespassers'[110] on their lands by the Nagas those days, was that their neighbours might do the samething they did on them before or during the Kuki rebellion.

In his 'report'[111] to the Commissioner, Surma Valley and Hill Division, Silchar, the Deputy Commissioner of Naga Hills, J.P. Mills who had interviewed the headmen of several villages of Kacha Nagas stated that nine villages paid tributes to Jadonang while seventeen others did not in his

[108]Tour report of C. Gimson (Deputy Commissioner of Cacher dated 20 March, 1931 (Manipur Archives).

[109]Letter of Political Agent Higgins to C. Gimson dated 24 February, 1931 (Manipur Archives).

[110]A note prepared. by C. Gimson dated 19 March, 1931 (Manipur Archives).

[111]Letter of J.P. Mills, Deputy Commissioner of Nagas Hills to the Commissioner, Surma Valley and Hill Division, Silchar dated 24 March, 1931 (Manipur Archives).

area (Naga hills which later became Nagaland). Mills in his report wrote, 'it is clear from the statements of the four men who saw Jadonang and of various headmen that he (Jadonang) claimed to be not only a miraculous healer but the king whom tradition said was to come. The day of government (the British), the Manipuris, and the Kukis had departed and his day had come. By his story of the torture of Naga girls (in an earlier report Mills had stated that Jadonang told his supporters that through his miraculous powers he came to know that two Naga girls were captured by the Kukis saying one was brutally murdered and the other was buried alive) by Kukis during the rebellion, he deliberately fanned the flame of the old feud, Nagas were not to strike the first blow, but the first act of aggression by Kukis was to be the signal for a massacre. He must have known that an incident was always possible in such a big area, and that if his orders were obeyed it would have appalling results. Tension was very great and friendly relations between Nagas and Kukis ceased almost everywhere. Only a spark was needed to set the whole country ablaze,' concluded Mills. Obviously, how was the relation between Nagas and Kukis can be judged from the contents of the letter.

As the movement spread to interior smaller villages, various Naga villages which had earlier differences of opinion and were locked in tribal warfare made peace with one another. To some extent Jadonang brought together mutually quarrelling and 'independent' Kacha Naga villages. Notably, there were also villages either in Tamenglong or neighbouring areas of Naga Hills or Cachar which did not subscribe to the ideas of Jadonang. Several Angami Naga villages which Jadonang attempted to incorporate in his plan did not lend much support. On the other hand, with the movement becoming popular, Kukis' concern was noticed when some leaders of Kuki villages of Tamenglong moved an application to the President of the MSD on 1 March, 1931 seeking action to 'protect villagers from being attacked.' Leaders from Laikot, Songtun, T. Waichong, Songjang, Phailengkot, Kanjang, Kotlen and Makui said they might be attacked suddenly by night or any other time since their neighbours particularly Kabuis and Kacha Nagas started repairing their fences, preparing bows and arrows and practising them always. Their lives compounded with fear particularly after the recent assembly of Nagas at Thongland village in Tamenglong district. The Kuki village leaders also claimed in their application that all other N agas had agreed to make war except a few villages near Kohima cart road which would not make war but will lend their spears and shields.

Security measures were stepped up with instructions to officer commanding the outpost at Tamenglong. However, the officer commanding the outpost was told that military operations must not be commenced without the orders from the Political Agent or the President of the MSD unless an attack was made on the outpost, on a rationing column or on any force detailed from the post. Detailed 'instructions'[112] were given to the officer in case there was outbreak of active rebellion by the Nagas. And how to deal with the involved villages. These were the views expressed by the authorities in those days on the movement launched by Jadonang who was seen as a threat to the administration and maintenance of peace in the region. However, villagers who supported the movement took Jadonang as their leader who would alleviate their problems. Soon, the government started acting.

Attempts to arrest Jadonang and suppress the movement began in early 1931 when an Assam Rifles column marched to Kambiron and other places to track them down. The government officials thought it would be a difficult task to arrest Jadonang because villages wherever he resided would not cooperate with the forces. When the forces reached Kambiron, the Naga leader and his followers had gone to Cachar. The security personnel followed up to Cachar where, to a great surprise to everybody, the leader 'without much problem and resistance' was arrested on 19 February, 1931. His arrest was easy as he was unsuspectingly led into one of

[112]Instruction to the officer commanding the outpost at Tamenglong by the Political Agent dated 20 March, 1931 (Manipur Archives).

the traps of a police officer, and as the information spread like a wild fire, the once-popular movement of the 'Naga Raj' soon died down. The idea of setting up a 'Naga Raj' fizzled out dramatically with most of his supporters, greatly shaken and dejected after Jadonang's arrest, dissociated themselves from the movement.

Jadonang was brought from Silchar jail to Imphal where he was kept for sometime during the trial for the murder of four Manipuri traders who 'disappeared' in March 1930. Following the mysterious disappearance of four Manipuris— Thounaojam Here Singh, Waikhom Thambou Singh, Waikhom Pheijao Singh and Waikhom Sajor, warrants of arrest were issued against 23 persons including Jadonang and Gaidinliu. This was done following a complaint from one Thounaojam Tomba of Khagempali area in Imphal on 23 November, 1930 to the judicial member of the MSD for tracing the whereabouts of the four persons. According to the Manipur Administrative Report (1931-32). 'Jadonang was wanted not only as the leader of the new movement but also as a murderer.'[113] And 23 accused were charged with being concerned directly or indirectly, in the murder of the four Manipuri traders under various sections of the Indian Penal Code.[114] It was stated that the murder had taken place in March 1930 at Kambiron area when four Manipuri traders were attacked by a mob at 'the instigation of Jadonang.' Jadonang denied the charges.

A noteworthy statement given to the Political Agent in Manipur on 23 March, 1931, Jadonang stated that he had never asked the Nagas to 'make war on the Kukis and exterminate them.' He said people who wanted him to die must have 'invented this.' He said he had never stated that Kabuis' day had come nor was he the king they had waited for. He said he told them to worship the god, in order to get rich, so that they would pay their revenue to the government, not to him. Was Jadonang aware of a communication between the political Agent in Manipur and the Chief Secretary to the Government of Assam on 14 February, 1931

[113]See Kamei 'Jadonang, a mystic naga leader', p. 40.
[114]Ibid.

in which the political Agent said the Naga leader had asked 'his people to pay the revenue from 1931-32 to him (Jadonang).' And in May 1931, the Government of Assam following Naga leader's arrest reported. 'Normal conditions now prevail again and the idea of a Naga Raj has dissipated. Jadonang, the instigator of all the troubles, is now under trial in the court of the Political Agent in Manipur, with a number of men of Kambiron and neighbouring villages, for the murder of four Manipuri traders who disappeared about March 1930.' Jadonang, who had always been 'guarded' by about 100 men, was sentenced to death on 13 June, 1931 and hanged on 29 August, 1931.

In spite of the unfavourable conditions, Gaidinliu who took the mantle of the movement after the death of their leader, kept it alive for quite sometime. However, she could not sustain it in the wake of intensified measures of the government to apprehend her. Gaidinliu was ultimately captured at Kenoma (Pulomi) in Nagaland on 17 October, 1932 by Captain N. Macdonald, Commandant of the Assam Rifles. How was Gaidinliu, who did everything to intensify the movement, was arrested? For the greater part of the one year before her arrest, Gaidinliu had been in hiding in the north Cachar hills sub-division with the support of villages which had adopted her 'cult'. She had been spending a hard life before her capture.

When she escaped arrest in 1931 (Gaidinliu as mentioned before was one of the accused in the murder of four Manipuri traders), she went straight from her village Nungkao in Tamenglong to Atengba in new Cachar hills. After an arduous journey with her supporters through jungles to avoid notice of security patrol, she made Hajaichak in north Cachar as her headquarters for sometime and visited Binnakandi Naga village. But she could not remain there long owing to unfavourable situation and left very soon, passing through Lalongrm, Injaona, Insung, Bopungwemi, Phuilomi, Thuyeng. And finally she arrived at Kenoma in the then Naga hills. At some villages, she and her followers were unwelcome and 'unwanted quests'[115]. They were threatened with death if they revealed the villages which helped them. Because the moment the government came to know this the villages would be severely punished either by burning or by arresting the inhabitants. Desperate and cornered, she was at the end of Zeliangrong-settled territory and had nowhere else to go. Gaidinliu told her supporters that in the 'next two months either she or the government would win'. She had spent about ten days at Pulomi before her capture after a brief encounter with the forces. She felt secured at Pulomi and thought no one would be able to arrest her. Virtually the village was fortified with thousands of tree trunks and palisades surrounding it. Reinforcements were also obtained from nearby villages to protect their leader. As forces under the command of Captain Macdonald of Assam Rifles entered the village all of a sudden, the guards armed with spears and other weapons were taken by surprise and posed a threatening attitude. But that was only for some minutes.

Soon the forces located the particular house where the leader was staying. Everything happened within a few minutes. There was not much resistance from the side of the Nagas. Interestingly, Gaidinliu inspired her followers saying 'whoever strikes the first blow to the enemy, would become the 'king'.' She said she would strike the British dead with magic. Of course, it did not happen. However, her courage to fight against the enemy was noteworthy. Many people including the late Prime Minister Jawaharlal Nehru had appreciated her determination to fight against the British. Gaidinliu remained in different jails for about 15 years, and she later became a freedom fighter after India attained independence. For her heroic fight against the British, she was given the title of 'Rani' Gaidinliu by Nehru.

Even after the capture of Gaidinliu and some of his prominent supporters, the tension between the Kukis and Nagas continued for sometime following an incident in which a Kuki woman and three children were killed on 4 December, 1932 at Lakema in Naga hills by some Nagas led by one

[115]Note of Deputy Commissioner, Naga Hills dated 22 October, 1932 (Manipur Archives).

Jinongpui of Leng village. Many thought the bloodshed would spread to other neighbouring villages. But it didn't following the punishment meted out to the killers.

Formation of Nikhil Hindu Manipuri Mahasabha

When the idea of convening a meeting of all Manipuris including those settled at different places knocked up the minds of some prominent persons in the state, no one had realised that it would ultimately lead to a political movement in this small kingdom. It was a crucial period in early nineteen thirties in Manipur as people were subjected to various kinds of oppressive measures either in the name of practising Hinduism or helping officials of the government touring interior villages. It seemed the prevailing situation at that time acted as a catalyst in the growth of a political movement in the state.

As mentioned before, there were frequent and intermittent wars between Manipur and its neighbouring states including Burma. This had resulted in the exodus of Manipuris to Tripura, Assam, Bangladesh, etc, while several Manipuris were taken as captives to Burma during the bloody conflicts in the past. To develop contact with these people and bring them together through regular meetings, a few intellectuals requested Maharaja Churachand Singh to permit them to set up an organisation which could act as a platform for all the scattered Manipuris. Thus the first session of the 'Nikhil Hindu Manipuri Mahasabha' (NHMM) was held on 30 May, 1934 at Imphal with Maharaja Churachand Singh and Hijam Irabot as the President and Vice-President respectively, of the session. Second session of the NHMM was held on 30 January, 1936 at Silchar in Assam and the third on 28 February, 1937 at Mandalay in Burma.

It was during the historic fourth session at Chingalampak in Imphal on 29 and 30 December, 1938 that the seeds of the political movement were sown. The session also brought a great upheaval in the structure and activities of the NHMM. At the fourth session, the words 'Hindu Manipuri' were deleted from the NHMM and it was renamed as 'Nikhil Manipur Mahasabha' (NMM). The birth of the NMM played a significant role in bringing about a change in the socio-political history of Manipur. Presiding over the fourth session in the absence of Maharaja Churachand Singh, Hijam Irabot who had been gradually leading the NHMM to the political line called for changes in the structure of the state administration. Irabot, who later became a great Manipuri leader revered by all sections of the people particularly down-trodden, said that members of the MSD were hand-picked and appointed by the Maharaja. Since the members were not the people's representatives, he said, it would be difficult for them to understand the problems faced by the people. Moreover, they would not work in the interests of the common people, he said, 'Welfare of the people can be brought only when the elected representatives handle the administrative affairs in the state. When the present high officials lose the power one day,' Irabot said, 'the power will be in the hands of the people.'[116] And he tacitly and tactfully set the political movement in motion against the ills of the society and other oppressive measures of the government. Some of the important resolutions adopted in the session irked the government of Manipur. These included the demands for a 'full administrative unit, holding of elections on universal adult franchise, setting up of schools at villages, free compulsory primary education, establishment of health centres at villages, reduction of land tax, farmers to own lands they cultivated, release of Gaidinliu from jail, etc. It became clear that after the fourth session, the NMM transformed itself to a strong political organisation. The government moved swiftly and kept a strict watch on the further activities of the NMM.

The president of the MSD, A.R.H. Macdonald issued an order on 21 March, 1939 stating that the government employees involved in the NMM should either give up the posts they held or dissociate themselves from the NMM since the latter became a political organisation. Maharaja and several members immediately dissociated themselves and resigned from the NMM.[117] All eyes were set now on Irabot

[116]Manipuri Itihasta Irabot (in Manipuri), Soyam Chhatradhari, p. 47.
[117]Ibid.

who was holding a highly-respected post of the member of Sadar Panchayat court, and everybody was curiously watching his next step. He was married to a daughter of one of the brothers of the Maharaja and a very influential figure by being a relative of the royal family. Without any hesitation and with a determination to devote himself to the cause of the people, Irabot gave up the post of Sadar Panchayat member and also all facilities provided to a relative of the royal family, and started spending the life of a common person. His popularity soared as more and more people respected and supported him. A senior government official and friend, Elagbam Tompok Singh also resigned from his post and followed the great Manipuri leader.

During the British-controlled native rule, there was hardly anyone to whom the people could turn to unshackle them from various hardships. In order to remain in power, the successive rulers tried to please the British even at the cost of the general public who suffered most at the hands of the regime. They could not even raise their voice against the suppressive measures imposed upon them. It was a normal practice in those days for the people to bow down or fold their umbrellas before the white men or the King at the public places or roads. There was no other alternative but to tacitly writhe under the burdens.[118] No one could speak against the King. The new religion also played a havoc making the life of common people hard. The practice of Hinduism was at its peak since it became a state religion. 'At first the decrees of the King received but little obedience, and opposition to the change centre mainly round the numerous members of the royal family who were supported, not unnaturally, by the Maibas, the priests of the older religion. Religious dissent was treated with the same ruthless severity as was meted out to the political opponents, and wholesale banishment and execution drove the people into acceptance of the tenets of Hinduism.'[119]

An organisation called Brahmasabha was set up under the patronage of the Maharaja to 'effectively' enforce the people

[118]See Tarapot 'Insurgency Movement in North Eastern India'.

[119]See Hodson 'The Meitheis', p. 95.

Manipur Legislative Assembly secretariat was up in flames on 18 June, 2001. Photo: Laimayum Kheda Sharma.

Angry Manipuri womenfolks take out a torch rally during the month-long anti-ceasefire agitation in June/July 2001 against the extension of the centre-NSCN (I-M) ceasefire to territories of Manipur beyond Nagaland. Photo : Ph. Santosh.

Manipuri womenfolks protesting against the ceasefire extension confront with police at Imphal market during a rally in June 2001.

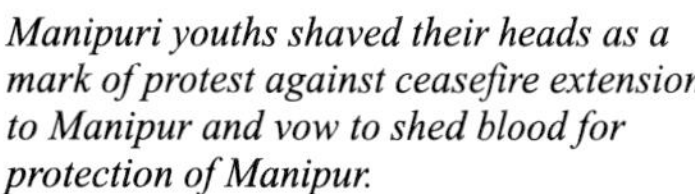

Manipuri youths shaved their heads as a mark of protest against ceasefire extension to Manipur and vow to shed blood for protection of Manipur.

Para-military forces particularly Central Reserve Police force personnel opened fire at the angry youths protesting the ceasefire extension in Imphal town.

Manipuri Muslims and different tribes opposed the Centre-NSCN (I-M) ceasefire extension to Manipur. Photo: Santosh.

Manipuri Muslims and different tribes opposed the Centre-NSCN (I-M) ceasefire extension to Manipur. Photo: Santosh.

Mass-sit-in protests, rallies etc, during the anti-ceasefire agitation across Manipur in June/July 2001. Ph. Santosh.

Mass-sit-in protests, rallies etc, during the anti-ceasefire agitation across Manipur in June/July 2001. Ph. Santosh.

Villagers guarding a remote Kuki village from rival tribe during the about one-decade old ethnic Naga-Kuki clashes in Manipur hills from 1992. Source: village youths.

A mass grave in a part of interior hills for the victims of Kuki-Naga ethnic feud in Manipur hills. Ph. Santosh

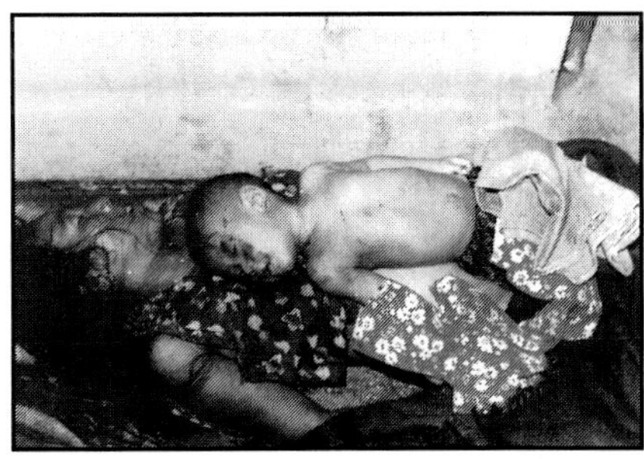

A Kuki mother and her child (killed in one of the many incidents during the Naga-Kuki clashes). Photo: Ph. Santosh.

Relatives / friends grieving at the killings of their close ones during the Naga-Kuki clashes in Manipur hills. Photos: Santosh.

Many children and women became orphans and widows during the Kuki-Naga ethnic violence. They are attending a prayer session. Source: village youths.

Photos of different weapons of Manipur People's Army (MPA), armed wing of the oldest Manipur insurgent organisation. United National Liberation Front (UNLF) circulated to Manipur press by the banned outfit in November 2001.

MPA cadres.

to imbibe Hinduism though the impact of the religion on hill people was, however, practically nil. In the name of Brahmasabha, the common people were harassed by imposing levy. The main duty of the organisation was to decide and finalise on the issue of 'untouchability and purity' of the persons in regard to the practice of the religion. It is true that the new religion was widely acclaimed by a large section of the people at the instance or initiative of the ruler. But, how far the new converts were aware of the true and sacred teachings of the great religion were questionable in those days and even now. 'The adherence of the people to the Vaishanavite doctrines which originated in Bengal, is maintained by the constant intercourse with the leaders of that community at Nadia. It is difficult to estimate the precise effect of Hinduism on the civilisation of the people, for to the outward observer they seem to have adopted only the festivals. The outward ritual. The caste marks, and the exclusiveness of Hinduism. While all unmindful of its spirit and inward eserrtials.'[120]

If a family incurred the wrath of Brahmasabha, in those days, a normal practice was that the funeral of the deceased person or the religious ceremonies connected with it were not allowed unless the family concerned paid money to the Brahmasabha.[121] if anyone dared to challenge the Brahmasabha, he would not only be ostracised but also treated as an 'untouchable or unclean'. Persons who had rejected Vaishnavism attracted the wrath of the King and were treated as 'outcasts.' People had to put 'chandan' (a kind of dry mud which is rubbed with water) on the forehead to prove that he or she was a Vaishnavite. They had to pay money to Brahmasabha for this. Brahmasabha appointed several persons known as *ratans* at different places to inspect whether people applied 'chandan' or not. Those who had disobeyed the Brahmasabha's instructions were, on the spot, declared as 'untouchables' (or unclean) by the *ratans*. They could again become a 'pure person' or 'touchable' (or clean) by a declaration of Brahmasabha. Of course, they had to pay

[120]Ibid., p. 96.

[121]Miyamgi Luchingba Irabot (in Manipuri) Mongjam Ritichandra.

money to the Brahmasabha for this and money never went into the government coffers and there was no place for poor people. Whatever the Maharaja did was 'right' and his order taken as 'precept.' For government officials touring the villages either for revenue collection or other work, the villagers should look after them by providing good food or places for stay. The villagers should also guard the official (s) while they were sleeping and supply anything they demanded. Even good looking girl in the village was called and asked to serve food to touring officials. Those who disobeyed the orders were severely punished. These repressive measures coupled with the worsening condition of farmers greatly pained the revered leader who sacrificed all luxurious life and pioneered in different fields to arouse the people and fight for their rights.

Born on 30 September, 1896 in a poor family at Pisum at the outskirts of Imphal, Irabot lost his father at an early age. Owing to some unfavourable condition at home after the demise of his father, he and his mother stayed with his aunt at Moirangkhom in Imphal. But, that was not the end of misfortunes which fell on this great patriot who faced every problem with cool mind. His mother died a few months after leaving the parental home. It, of course, shocked him greatly losing both parents at a young age but he took it as a destiny. Braving all odds, Irabot aided by his aunt went to Dhaka and studied upto class nine at Pragoj High School after completing class seven in Manipur. During his stay at Dhaka, Irabot transformed himself to a great revolutionary with increasing determination to fight against the British. At Dhaka he learnt about the students' unrest at different parts of the world. He discontinued studies and left Dhaka in 1915. After returning home, he started seeking ways to liberate Manipur from the shackles of foreign domination as the Dhaka experience helped Irabot see into the problems the common people in Manipur were facing more acutely than before. Expert in many fields, he coined different patriotic songs to arouse the minds of the people and awaken them against the British and ills of the society in those days. His aim, according to some biographers, was to 'achieve a free and welfare Manipur'. The political movement to solve the problems in those days in Manipur was quite a new thing. Everything depended on the whims of the king, and those persons who received the patronage of the king were considered as 'lucky people'. So Irabot was considered a 'senseless' person by some of the ruling members for giving up all the royal facilities. But the great Manipuri will always remain in the minds of the people for his sacrificial and unselfish deeds for his people and motherland.[122]

Though hailing from a backward state, which is buried amongst hills, irabot had a very wide vision and kept himself informed about what was happening around the world. The Non-Cooperation Movement launched by Mahatama Gandhi in different parts of India had a tremendous impact on. the life of Hijam Irabot. Under the guidance of Mahatama Gandhi, nonviolence and non-cooperation movements were launched at several parts of India against the British. Thousands of Indians were arrested and put behind the bars for participating in the freedom movement. Several innocent citizens including women and children were also gunned down without warning at Jalianwala bagh. During this crucial period. Irabot vigorously launched the movement for a 'full responsible government' in Manipur. Like the great national leader, he also appealed to the people not to use the foreign goods and set on fire all his foreign items in front of the court in Imphal to protest against the British regime. He had realised that only a large-scale movement would bring freedom in Manipur.

His active participation in NMM earlier helped him to a large extent in organising people and other things. As a part of his plan, he went to Dhaka, Burma and Assam to organise people against the British dominion. Wherever he went, he was received well by friends and people whose cooperation was needed to intensify his movement. At home, he started extensive work and travelled every nook and corner of the state to meet people and arouse their opinion against the foreign occupation, slept only three hours a day and

[122]See Tarapot 'Insurgency Movement in North Eastern India'.

campaigned for 'freedom of Manipur'. Along with the campaign, he was also alive to the worsening economic condition of the people. Manipur is an agrarian society, and barring a few, people lived on agriculture and its produce. But the life of a farmer was extremely miserable as the farmers had to work in the fields throughout the year while their share of profit was almost nil.

It was the royal family, its members, the government employees and businessmen who took the lion's share of the agricultural produce, Sometimes it became unbearable for the farmers because the exploitation was so severe that they had to remain and work in the fields as a labourer throughout his lifetime without improving his condition, However, there was no other way for them to earn livelihood other than cultivating and working in the fields. The crops they produced were to be bought again from the businessmen who enjoyed the patronage of the government officials. One can well imagine what would have been the condition of the common people in such circumstances. Moreover, the farmers did not own lands and if they disobeyed, the landlords would engage another farmer to cultivate his fields, There was no alternative but to follow what the landlords wanted, and submit to the demands of the rich people. The situation was worst. On the other hand, the communication system was also so bad that during the rainy season, it was horrible to travel from one village to another.

Greatly concerned about the downtrodden people, Irabot who lived and ate with farmers was utterly shocked to see their condition. In 1935, under his initiative, an organisation called 'Manipur Krishi Sammelan' (MKS) was set up to work for the welfare of the poor farmers. The MKS worked for removal of several constraints imposed on the farmers. It also joined the movement launched by Irabot against Brahmasabha for imposing fees on poor people in the name of religious practice. In December 1939, there was a man-made scarcity of rice in Imphal. Rice was not available in most shops of the capital. It was mainly because of the fact that the businessmen had hoarded the rice and were selling them outside Manipur at an exorbitant rate. Interestingly, Manipur in spite of the primitive method of cultivation, produced high-quality rice and was liked much by people outside the state. Situation became worst as rice was not freely available. The women folk could not meet the demands of their starving children. It must be pointed out that it had been the policy of some wealthy people supported by ruling members to earn profit by their ignoble business deals. In the history of Manipur, women had played an important role and were always in the forefront whenever a general issue or problem struck the state. On 12 December, 1939, the women folks from different parts of Manipur gathered at Imphal and demanded the immediate halt of export of rice. However, they were told that only Maharaja who was at Nabadwip in Bengal could prevent the export of rice. The protesters then brought the President of the MSD, Sharp and all members of the MSD to the telegraph office to wire to the Maharaja to immediately come to Manipur. Situation became tense, and the Assam Rifles personnel were called out to disperse the crowd. As the security men appeared, the people became restless and angry. The protester didn't move. One Laisram Kanhai addressed the gathering, 'we should not be afraid of the security men. We are unarmed innocent civilians, They can not open fire at us for our demand of rice.' More determined after the stubborn attitude of the authorities, people continued the agitation with shouting slogans, 'stop exporting rice. Give us rice. Security men go back.'

At first their plea was ignored. Instead the security men were ordered to attack the demonstrators. Despite injuring over twenty women folks in bayonet charge, the spirit of the woman agitators did not die down. They braved the security action and relentlessly continued the stir, and finally as there was no sign of withdrawing, the government within twenty four hours issued order banning the export of rice. The Maharaja also returned to Manipur within a few days. This day, 12 December, 1939, glaringly stands out in Manipur's history as *'Nupi Lal'* (literally meaning Women's war).

During 'Nupi Lal', Irabot was away at Cachar. After his return, he was asked to lead the movement against the export of rice in future and he along with some of his close associates actively supported the women's demand. Vigorous campaign was started to ban further export of rice and this gave a chance to the MSD which had been looking for a loophole and excuse to arrest the leader. A tireless person, Irabot in spite of the government threat vigorously campaigned against the export of rice by addressing public meetings at Khurai, Lamlong, Kongba, Wangkhei, Nambol, Sawombung and other places in the valley to arouse the public opinion. As he stepped up the campaign he was also aware of the fact that his enemies were on the prowl to report on his activities. In one such meeting at 'Police bazar (now Yaiskul area) in Imphal, he said, 'let us remember the incident at telegraph office, when we demanded rice, we were given gun butt. For a small quantity of rice, we had to give blood. Men should not fear the jail walls.' Was it a good opportunity for the authorities to swoop on him. The MSD charged Irabot with inciting people against the government saying that his speech on 7 January, 1940 was inflammatory and decided on 21 March, 1940 to arrest him under section 124 (A) of the Indian Penal Code. He was sent to jail for three years. But, a leader could not be suppressed wherever he was. While in Imphal jail, he spearheaded a movement for reforms of jail rules. Viewed as a troublemaker by the authorities, he was shifted and transported to Sylhet jail now in Bangladesh for his agitation in Imphal jail.

It was a sheer luck, Irabot thought, that he was shifted and imprisoned in Sylhet jail which turned out to be a training centre for the Manipuri leader. He exposed himself thoroughly to Marxism through Marxist and other communist leaders who had already been lodged there. With a determined and firm idea to launch freedom movement in Manipur, he read books extensively an Communism and the freedom struggle in different parts of the world. The agitation for achieving welfare of the farmers, the criticism of torture and exploitation of man by man, the suffering under the colonial powers, movement against the oppression of poor people under feudal system et al turned Irabot into a resolute leader of the poor people in Manipur. Mainly concerned over condition of poor people and oppressive measures of the government under colonial powers, he thought socialism was suited to Manipur.

All along the way, authorities in the state were keeping a track on all his activities. Now, the state government realised that Irabot's presence in the state would pose a great threat to the administration. Even after his jail term in 1943, Irabot was denied entry into Manipur by an order passed by the MSD. It was a humiliating castigation for him. As the government had apprehended a series of movements under his leadership, a warrant was issued to arrest him. Who could challenge the government order in those days? Owing to un favourable circumstances, Irabot was forced to go underground. At this time, one of his close friends, Longjam Bijoy who worked with him went to Cachar for a rendevous with the leader. A revolt was thus prepared in collusion with the Indian National Army of Netaji Subhas Bose against the British rule. As this was announced in the national papers, the government of India started rounding up several persons at various places including Manipur.

The underground life gave Irabot wide experiences. In spite of odds, he continued to organise the people who were very much impressed by his skill and cleverness to avoid arrest. However, as the luck would have it, he was nabbed by the police when he was sick and unable to move, and kept in Silchar jail for eight months. Towards the end of 1944, the Manipuri leader was freed but again he was refused entry. It may be pointed out that Maharaja Churachand Singh had earlier abdicated the throne in favour of his son, Bodhchandra Singh because of failing health. Churachand Singh later died at Nabadwip in Bengal in November 1941.

A few months after the accession of Maharaja Bodhachandra Singh to the throne in September 1941 in Manipur, Japan joined the axis power and declared war against the British and the Americans. As it developed, the Japanese forces bombed Pearl Harbour on 7 December, 1941 and landed their troops at Kotabaru (Thailand) simultaneously spreading their supremacy right to the eastern border of British India. In the early stages, the Japanese forces were much ahead of their enemies. Soon it overcame the Philippines Islands, Indonesia, Indo-China, Thailand, Singapore, Burma, etc, Around this time, there was hectic movement of troops in Manipur sector, and Imphal-Tamu (Burma) road. As the Japanese advanced at the frontier, the British apprehended the enemy's attack both from the land and sea. There were two land routes, it was thought, by which the invading forces could enter. One via Arakan and the other through Manipur. Subsequently, Japanese bombed Imphal on 10 May, 1942 forcing the government to stop functioning for some days. As Imphal came under intermittent Japanese bombing attacks, people started fleeing to interior areas. There was complete chaos and lawlessness with the killings of several persons and destroying of houses during the attacks. On the other hand, refugees from Burma, mostly people of Indian origin, thronged Manipur on their way to different parts of India. Some of these people who included Tamils, Punjabis, Bengalis, Gujaratis, Malayalis, etc, have settled at the border town of Moreh in Manipur's Chandel district.

With a view to liberate India, the combined forces of Japanese and Indian National Army (INA) attacked Manipur and then Naga hills district of Assam in March 1944 against the British forces deployed in this region. Kohima, the headquarters of Naga hills, fell after a fierce fighting while hill areas of Manipur were captured by the invading forces.[123] Though the INA raised the Indian flag at Moirang, about 45 kms south of Imphal, on 14 April, 1944, the allied powers ultimately defeated the invading forces. Owing to difficult terrain, bad weather condition and lack of supplies, the Japanese forces lost their momentum while 14th army division under the command of General Slim who refused to surrender was given 'logistic'[124] support by air. The war soon came to an end. following surrender of Germany and consequent atomic bombings on Hiroshima and Nagasaki in August 1945. What remains now is a thrilling small hillock,

[123]Merger of Manipur, Lt. Col. (Retd.) H. Bhuban Singh.

[124]Ibid.

locally known as Maibam Lokpaching, about 17 kms south of Imphal on Imphal-Tiddim road, where the allied and Japanese forces were locked in the fiercest fight during the war in this front. Japanese war veterans have constructed a monument at the foot of this hillock, also known as *red hill* under the title of 'India Peace Memorial.'

Irabot heard the sufferings of the people at Cachar, and was dismayed to learn the conditions of Manipur. As he returned home, following the withdrawal of order preventing him from entry in 1946, he found a completely changed Manipur with Imphal wearing a totally devastated look. All his supporters and friends were scattered because of the second world war in this front. It did not take much time for him to locate his followers. The problems did not deter Irabot from regrouping and regathering his followers particularly the workers of 'Praja Sanmelani'. A social organisation which he had earlier founded. They included Longjam Bijoy who had met him at Cachar. To organise the people in an effective manner. Praja Sanmelani merged with 'Praja Mandal,' also formed by him, and the two became 'Praja Sangh.' Praja Sangh was a political party set up with a view to arouse awareness among the mass. The slogan was; 'farmers should be the owners of the paddy fields.' As it soon gained momentum, this hurt interests of the landowners. His opponents worked hard to remove him from the political scene of Manipur, and decided to set up a political party to counter Irabot's movement. According to his biographers, Irabot wanted 'an independent and democratic Manipur with its own Parliament, Constitution and Cabinet. Instead of monarchical system, he wanted the representatives of the people, elected on universal adult franchise, to administer the state which, he thought, should follow the socialistic pattern of society.'[125] He wanted to make a strong Manipur with the people having the 'right to self determination' of their state. His thoughts and plans used to be reflected in his weekly journal *Anouba Jug*. A point which can not be

[125]See Chhatradhari 'Manipuri Itihasta Irabot' and Ritichandra 'Miyamgi Luchingba irabot'.

overlooked here is also the resolution which a committee of the Nikhil Manipur Mahasabha (NMM) had adopted in a meeting on 15 April, 1946. The resolution emphasised the 'right to self determination' though important subjects like defence, currency, communications, postal services and external affairs would remain in the hands of the central government.[126]

His opponents' attempts to remove Irabot from the political scene were intensified. Notwithstanding the repugnance by few opportunists, a large scale agitation was launched under his leadership demanding compensation for war victims, establishment of 'full responsible form of government,' merger of administrative units of hills and valley, setting up of dispensaries, equal distribution of wealth, reduction of land revenue, etc. He not only organised the movement but also vigorously campaigned to ensure implementation of the demands. Undoubtedly, he was a leader accepted by many people both in the hills and valley. The demand for release of Gaidinliu during the fourth session of the Nikhil Manipur Mahasabha at Chingalampak also made Irabot popular among sections of the hill people.

Under compulsory education programme, he set up schools in different parts of Manipur after the war. Around this time, those who did not subscribe to Irabot's ideas formed a new party called Manipur State Congress. This party was not a unit of the Indian National Congress and had no link with the INC. As the freedom movement against the British intensified at different parts of India, it also reached its zenith in Manipur. It was a question oftime only. The British knew that they had to leave the country one day. As the situation demanded, British Prime Minister C. R. Attlee announced in the British Parliament on 20 February, 1947 that India would become independent at a date before June 1948. At this, Maharaja Bodhchandra Singh realised that the state administration was to fall in his hands. With these things in view, he initiated some steps to streamline the judicial system, take over the hill administration from the

[126]Nikhil Hindu Manipuri Mahasabha (in Manipuri), L. Yaima Singh and R.K. Maipaksana Singh, p. 184.

President of the MSD and involve people in the administration. Towards the beginning of 1947, the concept of having a parliamentary form of government in. Manipur was born.

By an order in 1944, the chief court of Manipur was instituted, and in early 1947 the Manipur State Court's Act 1947 was implemented under which the Chairman of the chief court was designated as Chief Judge. Subsequently hill judiciary bench of the MSD was brought under the Chief Court. The revision court of Maharaja was now to be assisted by a judicial council. After dissolving the MSD on 30 June, 1947, Maharaja Bodhchandra Singh instituted a form of government known as 'His Highness the Maharaja in Council'. Former President of the MSD F. F. Pearson who was also the Chairman of the Manipur State Constitution Making Committee (MSCMC) became the first Chief Minister of the Council. With the implementation of the Manipur Hill People's (Administration) Regulation 1947 after approval of the draft prepared by the MSCMC, the hill administration was also brought directly under the His Highness the Maharaja in Council. Again due to some internal problem. His Highness the Maharaja in Council was dissolved and an 'interim council' was formed with younger brother of Maharaja, Maharajkumar Priya Brata Singh replacing Pearson as Chief Minister. An important development preceded the installation of the new Chief Minister. Prior to this, the Maharaja while attending a meeting in Delhi 'signed the Instrument of Accession and the Standstill Agreement on 11 August, 1947. Original copies of the two documents signed by Maharaja Bodhchandra Singh of Manipur were still marked SECRET and are with the ministry of Home, government of India, in File Number F/375/45-Public'.[127] What is written in the original copies is obviously known to a very few people in Delhi. Under the instrument of Accession, the Dominion Government of India (at the time of independence) had a big role to play in the fields of defence, external affairs, communications, etc, of the state while the Standstill Agreement dealt with air communications, arms and

[127]See Bhuban Singh 'Merger of Manipur', p. 70.

equipment, control of commodities, currency and coinage, national highways, etc, under its Schedule.

Under the initiative of Pearson, the constitution of Manipur (later Manipur State Constitution Act 1947) was framed. The first election programme under the new constitution was announced with the last date of filing nomination papers on 25 April and the date of scrutiny on 19 May, 1948. As per the constitution, Manipur had an assembly of 53 members. However, the Chief Minister was to be nominated by the Maharaja from outside the assembly. Irked over non inclusion of some important points, Irabot stood against this constitution saying there was 'no article' guaranteeing 'independence of Manipur and democracy.' His Praja Sangh party also boycotted it on the same grounds. But, Manipur State Congress readily accepted and agreed to it. What could be noted was that all people were not allowed to cast votes to elect their representatives. Only the rich, Landowners and educated persons could exercise their franchise.[128]

Praja Sangh under the leadership of Irabot was the only political party before the formation of Manipur State Congress. With the coming up of the new party, competition for acceptance by the people was also stiff by the respective workers. Irabot had endeavoured to bring the people in hills and valley together. He had felt that the two parties could work together to achieve this. On 30 November, 1947, he convened a joint meeting at the Manipur Dramatic Union Hall in Imphal to parley over the issue. A.K. Shimray, president of Tangkhullong (a local Tangkhul Naga organisation), presided over the session. The meeting also decided to contact the leaders of the Nagaland-based Naga National Council (NNC), which was then fighting for an independent Nagaland, in order to bring peace in the region.

Under the Manipur State Constitution Act, 1947, the assembly elections were held in 1948. Although Irabot had objected to certain provisions of the constitution, the Manipuri leader took part in the polls. Why Irabot took part in the

[128]See Ritichandra 'Miyamgi Luchingba Irabot', p. 56.

hustings had not been clearly explained by anyone but it was believed that he must have wanted to bring about the change from 'inside'.[129] But this argument still lacks substance to prove the point. Krishak Sabha, Irabot's party which contested the election, won five seats while the Manipur State Congress secured 14. The party-wise break up was; Krishak Sabha 5, Manipur State Congress 14, Socialist Party 3, Hill areas 18, Independents (later formed Praja Shanti) 12 and nomination 1. It is noteworthy that this election was the first ever election held in Manipur or in any part of India on universal adult franchise. Contesting candidate was to be of 25 years of age while the age of the voter was to be of 21 years as on 1 March, 1948. As mentioned earlier, the voters were strictly restricted to certain category of people. Afterwards, a coalition government was thus formed without congress which could not form the government due to internal differences. The congress had then started working against the Manipur constitution. It also launched a movement for merger of Manipur with India, which was vehemently opposed by Irabot and the Maharaja.[130] Both Maharaja and Irabot strongly opposed the merger but they were not allies on the issue. Irabot also strongly opposed and turned down Sardar Patel's proposal for 'Purbanchal' to be formed by Manipur, Cachar, Lushai Pahar (part of present Mizoram) and Tripura.

Merger of Manipur with India

Events were unfolding fast, and it was becoming a certainty in 1946 that India would be independent soon. On 2 September, 1946 an interim government was formed with Jawahar Lal Nehru as the interim Prime Minister during which modalities for the future governance were chalked out. As time was ticking, Maharaja of Manipur and his ruling members were also keeping a track on all developments both in Delhi and London because this would also affect Manipur.

[129]See Tarapot 'Insurgency Movement in North Eastern India'.

[130]See Ritichandra 'Miyamgi Luchingba Irabot', p. 61 and Chhatradhari 'Manipuri Itihasta Irabot', p. 44.

Accordingly in London, the Indian Independence Bill was introduced, and it got the royal assent on 18 July, 1947. Under the Act, on 15 August 1947, two new independent dominions—India and Pakistan—came into existence.

It was a crucial period in the history. The then Governor of Assam, Akbar Hydari came to Manipur to study the political situation and explore the possibility for merger of Manipur with India. The government of India after hydari's visit 'knew' the minds of the Maharaja and that of the people. Merger of Manipur was not accepted by majority of the people. Dhabalo Singh, President of the 'Praja Shanti Sabha' which was the ruling party in Manipur, expressed in a memorandum to the Maharaja on 17 December, 1948 that 'Manipur is to remain as a state and autonomous unit enjoying responsible government with His Highness the Maharaja of Manipur as the constitutional head and with her sovereignty undisturbed.'[131] In another memorendum the General Secretary of the ruling party, N. Ibomcha Singh said, 'almost cent per cent of the people of the state were quite against integration or meger.'[132] Those favouring the merger were the members of the Manipur State Congress. The congress on 29 April, 1949 in Imphal, adopted the following resolution; 'the congress views with deep concern the present international situation specially the communist uprising in the neighbouring state of Burma and feels that the consolidation of the Government of India through integration and merging of native states, especially Manipur state which is an eastern gateway to India and which is now administered by a pro-communist and inefficient government, is urgently required.'[133] It was a sad moment for Irabot who was accused of fermenting unrest and could not stand against this. Most of the organisations he had formed were also banned though two of his organisations had jointly called a protest meeting at the Manipur Dramatic Hall in Imphal on 21 September, 1948 against the proposal of forming 'Purbanchal'. Responding to his call, a large number of people from Pungdongbam,

[131]Memorandum quoted in 'Merger of Manipur'.
[132]Ibid.
[133]Ibid.

about 25 kms north-east of Imphal, were coming to attend the meeting convened by the leader. It was when police attempted to prevent the people from 'attending the meeting, violence broke out. To contain it, the officer in charge gave a firing order and in the incident he himself was hit by a stray bullet fired by an 'untrained' policeman. The officer died instantaneously. By tbis time, Irabot realised that he could no longer remain or stay in the state and told his friends about this. No time was lost. The government of Manipur headed by Chief Minister Priya Brata Singh issued a warrant for arrest of Irabot who soon went underground.

Around this time, pressure on Maharaja Bodhchandra Singh by authorities of Government of India was increased to agree to the merger of Manipur with India. 'Except for the Manipur State Congress, the public, in general, was not in favour of Manipur continuing as a part of India, but preserving its own constitution and council of ministers and monarchy.' The Government of India was also informed of every development by its intelligence department. It was at this point that the government was keen to 'install a right man as the *Dewan* (agent of the Dominion Government) of Manipur and interfere in the internal administration of Manipur as much as possible as a test case.'[134]

It must be pointed out here that some insurgent organisations particularly those of Meiteis operating now in the state asserted that the people in general had not wanted the merger with India as was, according to them, evident from the fact that the merger issue was neither discussed nor approved by the state government formed after the election. Without delay, the Maharaja was called to Shillong, the capital of present Meghalaya. He arrived there on 17 September, 1949 to discuss with the Governor of Assam Sri Prakash about the relations between the government of Manipur and the Dewan. The Dewan, as mentioned above, was an agent of the Dominion Government of India and his 'loyalty was not with the Maharaja.' Major General Rawal Amar Singh was the Dewan in Manipur at that time. While

[134]See Bhuban Singh 'Merger of Manipur'.

at Shillong, the Governor of Assam and other authorities exerted maximum pressure on Bodhchandra Singh to sign the merger agreement. At this Bodhchandra Singh said he wanted to go back to Manipur and consult his people on the issue particularly with the council of ministers elected by the people, but his proposal was 'turned down politely.' The Governor of Assam who had been instructed by Sardar Patel that the 'merger agreement must be signed positively during this particular visit of Maharaja to Shillong' requested the Maharaja to finalise the merger business within the next 'one or two days.' The Government of India was so determined on the merger of Manipur with India that Sardar Patel 'even hinted' (to the Governor Sri Prakash) the presence of a senior-ranking army official at Shillong. Finally, the agreement on the merger of Manipur was signed at Government House, Shillong on 21 September 1949 and accordingly Manipur formally merged with the Indian Union on 15 October, 1949.

Consequent upon the merger the Praja Shanti Sabha coalition government was abolished and the Government of India sent the first Chief Commissioner to Manipur. It was a shattering news for Irabot who was 'utterly shocked' on hearing that Manipur had merged with India. He then decided to follow a 'new policy' from that day. It was a crucial stage in the political annals of Manipur. Rawal Amar Singh came to Manipur as the first Chief Commissioner. In the meantime, the idea of a revolution was born among the communist members. Without losing much time, Irabot left Manipur for Burma following the crackdown on the communist members. His biographers point out that the purpose of his going to Burma was manifold. Having contacted with some friends, he wanted help from Burmese Communist Party to fight for an 'independent socialist republic of Manipur.' At that time, the Burmese Communist Party was also fighting against the Burmese Government (now Myanmar Government). Besides Burmese Communist Party, Communist Party of Burma and People's Comrade Party were also fighting against the Burmese Government but they could not join hands. By his skill and power to organise the people, Hijam Irabot brought leaders of different Burmese organisations together and formed a 'United Front.' As a part of his strategy to step up movement, he signed an agreement with the 'united front liberation Government of Burma'. People's Comrade Party, Burmese Communist Party and Communist Party of Burma signed the agreement on behalf of the United Front. Under the agreement, the three parties agreed to give some 'occupied territory'[135] including Kabaw valley and Angoching to Irabot.

Working hard to pursue his goal, the Manipuri leader set up 'Manipur Red Guard' army to carry out his plans into action. However, old age and unsuitable climatic condition took their toll and Irabot fell sick with typhoid at his 'headquarters' at Tangbo village. All out effort was made by his Burmese friends to save his life and they despatched men to fetch medicines from Mandalay and Yangon but. the great Manipuri leader who wanted a strong Manipur, breathed his last on 26 September, 1951.

Major Underground Organisations and Small Militant Outfits

Nearly one and half decades after the death of Irabot, about 200 Meitei youths set out for the then East Pakistan (now Bangladesh) with a main object to approach and receive the training on guerrilla warfare from the Pakistani authorities. And to fight for 'an independent Manipur'. The youths, who were once termed 'revolutionary youths' by the government of Manipur, took the view that Manipur was forcibly merged with the Union. Most of these youths are now no more as they died due to ill health, or were either killed in clashes with security forces or gunned down later in factional fights. But some of the insurgent organisations which were formed are waging an armed struggle to what they called 'liberate Manipur.'

[135]See Chhatradhari 'Manipuri Itihasta Irabot'.

According to an intelligence report, about, 19,590 insurgents and extremists were operating in both valley and hill areas of Manipur by 2001. While the report estimated about 9070 insurgents in the valley, about 11,510 others were agile in different parts of the hill areas of the state, new Cachar hills and Nagaland. In addition to this overall figure, sympathisers or 'over ground workers' were four or five times the total number of insurgents and extremists, the report pointed out adding that the number of arms including highly sophisticated weapons such as AK 47, rocket launchers, etc, possessed by the insurgents was about 11,635. It estimated 4,975 weapons for insurgents who were operating in the valley of Manipur while about 6,660 arms were in the hands of militants in the hill region including parts of Nagaland and new Cachar hills of Assam. And going by the report, the over ground workers or sympathisers of the outfits ranged between 78,360 to 97,950 in the region. These estimates, according to the report, included the two factions of the NSCN which also operated in parts of new Cachar hills of Assam and Nagaland in addition to some areas of Manipur. In Manipur alone, about 10,000 underground members including those insurgents who kept going in and out of the state were operating in addition to the members of the two factions of NSCN. It meant that the number of overground sympathisers or workers ranged between 40,000 to 50,000 out of the state's total population of about 23 lakhs.

Surprisingly, about twenty underground organisations including six or seven major insurgent outfits are waging armed struggle separately for 'common goal' of either for 'an independent Manipur' or for forming different smaller states by breaking up the territories of Manipur. There are also ample official evidences of some outfits having their training or base camps in neighbouring countries particularly in upper Myanmar; Sylhet region of Bangladesh, etc. The busting of three major underground camps of insurgents from Manipur by Myanmar army personnel at Tamu and surrounding places in upper Myanmar in November 2001 shattered some important underground groups in the state.

The Myanmar army personnel recovered more than Rs 2 crores in cash, two boxes of gold biscuits worth crores of rupees, and more than 1400 highly sophisticated weapons of United National Liberation Front (UNLF) and People's Liberation Army (PLA). There is considerable Manipuri population in Sylhet region.

The government of India held meetings on different occasions with Myanmar regime to jointly drive out insurgents from the north eastern region from upper Myanmar area. The same issue had also been taken up with Bangladesh government. It may also be pointed out that hard-core guerrillas have set up camps in interior and inaccessible hill areas bordering with either Myanmar, Mizoram and Assam. It would be really stupefying anyone outside Manipur when they come to know some of these more than twenty outfits are locked in underground factional fights.

Formed by some educated Meitei youths under the leadership of the late Arambam Samarendra on 24 November, 1964, UNLF with its armed wing Manipur People's Army (MPA) has been fighting for what it termed 'liberation' of Manipur and some of its neighbouring states along with other underground organisations in the Indo-Burma region from India. In its annual statement on 24 November, 2001. The UNLF said it had no alternative but to continue fighting for 'political future of Manipur and to determine its own path to social, cultural and economic development.' The major insurgent organisation said in the statement that its 'struggle for the right of self-determination is a political struggle demanding a political solution. And this is a struggle sanctioned by international law and practice.' The annual statement also said there 'is a growing realisation among the peoples in the Indo-Burma region (north eastern region of India and north western region of Myanmar) that they have a common historical destiny. The idea of a joint liberation struggle initiated by United Liberation Front of Assam (ULFA), UNLF and NSCN-K with the formation of the Indo-Burma Revolutionary Front (IBRF) in 1990, is slowly but definitely becoming a reality,' the statement said. During the last 37 years of its existence, the UNLF have never indulged in any terrorist activity nor will it ever be, in the future. Condemning the terrorist attacks in Newyork and Washington on 11 September, 2001, the Manipur insurgent organisation also opposed the 'human rights violations under the Armed Forces Special Powers Act 1958' now in force in the state. The statement said UNLF believes that a lasting solution to terrorism can be achieved only when people live in a more equitable world where the powerful do not use brute force to 'suppress the weak, where the cries of peoples still under' what it termed 'colonial occupation and exploitation, are heard and respected.'

A Manipur government report in 2001 said the UNLF's aim and object are to 'restore the lost political sovereignty of Manipur and her neighbours, to establish an independent sovereign republic comprising of Manipur and her neighbours, and to regain the lost territories of Manipur from Myanmar.' With an estimated cadre strength of about 2500, the report said UNLF has developed links with Revolutionary People's Front (RPF), People's Revolutionary Party of Kangleipak (PREPAK), ULFA, NSCN-K, Kuki National Front, President, (KNF-P), Kanglei Yawol Kann Lup, Toijamba, (KYKL-T) and Tripura People's Democratic Front (TPDF). The RPF is the political wing of the People's Liberation Army (PLA). While Rajkumar Meghen, popularly known as Sanayaima, is the Chairman of the UNLF, Khundongbam Tomba alias Sunil or Pambei is the General Secretary of the underground organisation by the time this book was written.

With an aim to what it called 'secede Manipur from India and form a separate sovereign state of Manipur.' PLA which also later formed RPF as its political wing was first established on 25 September, 1978 under the leadership of the late Nameirakpam Bisheshwar Singh. Having an estimated cadre strength of about 3000, RPF/PLA is now headed by its Chairman Irengbam Bhorot alias Chaoren while Manoharmayum Pravinkumar alias Ngouba is the Vice-Chairman of the outfit. The PLA also aims 'to regain the lost territories of Manipur and to unify the people of

Mongolian origin of south middle Asia'. It has also developed links with some other underground .groups in the north eastern region of India including Kangleipak Communist Party (KCP), NSCN-K, ULFA, TPDF and the PREPAK. Like PLA, PREPAK was set up on 9 October, 1977 at Koubru hill in the north-western of Imphal by the late R.K. Tulchandra Singh. With a strength of about 1500 members now, the underground organisation is led by its chairman Achamba Singh alias Subhash while Palliba Singh is the General Secretary. What must be noted here is that the office bearers of some underground outfits changed very often following either split in the organisation or due to their killings in the encounters with security forces or in underground factional fights. PREPAK's main aim and object are, according to the official report, to 'free Manipur from India and establish an independent sovereign state of Manipur, to introduce job-oriented education, land ceiling and panchayat systems, and to abolish capitalism. 'The three major underground outfits—UNLF, RPF and PREPAK—which have been separately fighting for 'an independent Manipur' for over three decades have formed a common front called Manipur People's Liberation Front (MPLF) on 1 March, 1999 with an aim to 'remove the slow progress of liberation struggle because of lack of unity among the revolutionary parties.' Sanayaima of the UNLF is the convener of the MPLF while Sanasam Gunen alias Phalguni, the Secretary General of the RPF, is the publicity-in-charge of the front. Underground Kanglei Yawol Kann Lup (KYKL) was formed at the Prepak headquarters in Bangladesh on 25 May, 1994 by a combination of breakaway groups of UNLF, PREPAK and KCP with an aim to unite all the 'revolutionary organisations operating in Manipur and fight together in the struggle for independence.' However, it broke into two factions in May 1995-one faction led by Mutum Ibopishak Singh and another group by Achou Toijamba. While the Ibopishak faction is now known as KYKL, Oken, (KYKL-O) after the name of group's present leader, Namoijam Oken Singh alias Ingoba, Achou faction is called KYKL, Toijamba (KYKL-T). Both the factions were estimated to have a strength of about 400 members each. While KYKL-O has developed close links with NSCN-IM faction and Zomi Revolutionary Army (ZRA), the KYKL-T has ties with UNLF, RPF and PREPAK. The KCP was established on 15 May, 1990 by the late S. Maipak Sharma, a former leader of the PREPAK. It is now led by its Chairman Leibakmacha Singh while Ksh. Laba alias Noyon is the General Secretary. The other minor underground groups of the valley included the People's United Liberation Front (PULF). North East Minority Front (NEMF), Islamic National Front (lNF) and Islamic Liberation Front (Kanglei), While PULF's main aim under the leadership of one Azad alias Abdul Kalam is to protect the Muslim community from the attacks of any other community and has links with the NSCN-IM, NEMF said it would eliminate 'all communal elements whether individual or group who fostered or propagated ill-feeling or hatredness between the Meiteis and Pangals (as the Muslims are known in Manipur). The INF said it would fight against consumption of liquor, theft, dacoity, immoral trafficking, etc, in Muslim-settled area. Another group the Islamic Liberation Front-Kanglei (ILF-K) said it would join hands with different groups and take part in bringing peace and harmony among people besides helping other insurgent groups in their fight for the 'sovereignty of Manipur.' It was led by one F.M. Roj Alam. It may be noted that UNLF, PLARPF, PREPAK, KCP, both factions of KYKL, etc, are main outfits formed mostly by people from the valley, and have been operating both in the valley and interior hill districts. But some of these groups particularly UNLF and KYKL-O had been locked in deadly factional fights for six years mutually destroying and killing each other till the hostilities between the two were brought to an end on 12 June 2001 by the PREPAK which acted as an intermediary.

Some of the insurgent outfits operating in Manipur hills included NSCN and Kuki outfits. Established on 31 March 1980, the NSCN broke into two–one led jointly by Isac Chishi Swu, a Sema from Nagaland and Thuingaleng Muivah, a Tangkhnul from Manipur (NSCN-IM), and the other by S. S. Khaplang, a Pangmi Naga from Myanmar

(NSCN-K). Though cadres of the groups have been killing each other in factional fight since the parent organisation was split, the aim and object of the two factions are to 'liberate Naga areas of India and Myanmar in order to form a separate and independent Nagaland and to maintain a separate identity of the Nagas.' When they said 'Nagaland,' it included some hill areas of Manipur which are an inalienable part of the latter since the historic or pre-historic period.

In Manipur, as stated before, tribes were earlier known by their names and some of them, like Meiteis in the valley, are original inhabitants of the state. Intelligence reports estimated about 6000 members of the NSCN-IM as operating in some parts of Manipur hills, New Cachar hills of Assam and Nagaland while 3,500 members of the NSCN-K are active in some parts of Manipur hills, Nagaland and eastern Nagaland (Myanmar).

The NSCN-IM has developed close contacts with the KYKL-O, PULF, United Kuki Liberation Front (UKLF), Bodo Militant Group of Assam, Hynewtrep Achik Liberation Council (HANLC), etc, while NSCN-K has entered into alliance with UNLF, PREPAK, PLA, KYKL-T, ULFA of Assam and All Tripura Tiger Force (ATTF) of Tripura, etc, Underground Kuki National Army (KNA) with its political wing, Kuki National Organisation (KNO), aims at achieving an 'independent sovereign Kuki state's by carving out the Kuki-populated areas of Myanmar, and some portions of Thoubal, Ukhrul and Chandel districts of Manipur where Kukis have settled over the past decades. Based primarily at Myanmar border, the KNA was established in early part of May, 1998 at Molnoi in Myanmar under the chairmanship of Thongkholun Haokip and was, an official report pointed out, 'supported' by some important Kuki leaders from Manipur. It was estimated that the KNA had a strength of about 600 members who operated in some interior hill districts particularly Chandel, Ukhrul and Churachandpur. Another Kuki underground organisation, Kuki National Front (KNF) was formed on 18 May, 1988 but it split into two factions—one group known as KNF-President (KNF--P) is led by

Semtinthang Kipgen as the 'supreme commander of the organisation.' Both the KNF factions have a common aim of fighting for a 'separate state for the Kukis' to be known as 'Kukiland' by reorganising and dividing territories of Manipur. This 'Kukiland', according to them, will have a 'separate administration, court, economic rights, etc, according to the customary laws of the Kukis.' While the former had an estimated strength of about 200, the latter commanded a group of about 500 members. Both factions operate mainly in Kuki-settled areas of Churachandpur, Senapati and Thoubal districts of Manipur.

The KNF-P has so far no links with any other underground groups in the valley but the KNF-MC entered into alliance with PLA, ZRA, and ZRD (Zomi Reunification Organisation). With an aim and object of maintaining a separate identity of the Zomis comprising of Paite, Simte, Vaiphei and Tiddim Chintribes and to unite all Zomis scattered in different parts of India, Bangladesh and Myanmar, the ZRA was established on 7 May, 1993 at Phapjam in Myanmar. Thanglianpao Paite of Pangmol village of Myanmar is the President while Kamsuanthang Paite of Pearsonmun village under Churachandpur district is the General Secretary. The ZRA with a strength of about 500 members operated mainly in Churachandpur town, Thanlon sub-division of Churachandpur district, Barak valley and Cachar in Assam, Chimnuai and 'Laitui area in Chin state of Myanmar, and developed links with NSCN-IM and KNF-MC. Though both factions of the KNF did not agree on some points, the two along with ZRO, KNO and Hmar People's Convention-Democratic (HPC-D) have formed the Indigenous People's Revolutionary Alliance (lPRA) on 27 May, 2000 with what it called 'unity-victory' as their motto. At the time of the formation, the ZRO President Thanglianpao Paite was the President of the IPRA while Vipin Haokip was the Secretary. The IPRA operated in the Indo-Bangla-Burrna frontiers and its objective was to carry forward what it termed 'political aspirations of the Zo (Zomi) people.

Some hill-based 'minor' underground groups were HPC-D, Hmar Revolutionary Army (HRA). Kuki Liberation Army

(KLA) and UKLF. While HRA's interests were to protect Hmar community from the aggressive nature of the Kukis, Mizos and other larger communities, HPC-D was a group who opposed the signing of peace accord between some Hmar activists and the government of Mizoram on 27 July 1994 and has been fighting for a Hmar autonomous district council to be carved out of Hmar-inhabited areas of Mizoram, Manipur and Cachar district of Assam for some years. The KLA formed on 22 July, 1992 under the leadership of one Hernlal Gangte alias H. John of Molhoi Gangte village in Manipur's Bishnupur district with an estimated strength of 50 members has been fighting for a 'Kukiland' to be form'ed by Kuki-settled areas of Manipur, Nagaland, Assam, Tripura, Bangladesh and Myanmar. The KLA has developed links with the UNLF and Chin National Front of Myanmar and operated only in a small portions of Senapati, Ukhrul and Thoubal Districts of Manipur. The UKLF with an estimated strength of 60 members was set up in early part of 2000 under one Nelson Kuki alias M. Thangkholun Kuki as self-styled Chief of the army with an aim of fighting for a 'Kuki homeland' to be formed by Kuki-settled areas of India and Myanmar, and of abolishing the KNA and KNO in Manipur, The UKLF has entered into an alliance with the NSCN-IM and operated mainly in Chandel district of Manipur and Tamu area in Myanmar. Briefly, some of the underground organisations operating separately in parts of Manipur hill districts were the NSCN-IM, NSCN-K, KNA, KNF-P, KNF-P, KNF-MC, ZRO, ZRA and IPRA with an aim of either to merge some hill portions of Manipur with Nagaland or formation of 'an independent greater Nagaland' or for division of territories of Manipur to form 'Kukiland' or 'a Kukiland' comprising Kuki-settled areas of Manipur and Myanmar.

Some of the major underground organisations in the state are UNLF, PLA/RPF, PREPAK, KCP, KYKL-O. KYKL-T, KCP and MPLF, and have been fighting for an 'independent Manipur' for the past some decades while PULF, NEMF, INF and ILF-K are considered minor groups. The minor groups in the hills are HPC-D, HRA (A part of the Hmar Revolutionary Front), KLA and UKLF. How deep was the hatredness, animosity and vengeance among warring factions shall be dealt later. It also remains to be seen how far the UNLF and KYKL-O would refrain from fratricidal killings after the PREPAK-sponsored truce.

Well-Entrenched Groups

Before attempting any solution to the insurgency problem, it is very necessary to understand the background on which some of the major insurgent organisations had been formed in Manipur. According to some high-ranking security officials, there are what they termed several 'committed members of UNLF, PLA and PREPAK.' These organisations had not just been set up out of what they described problems arising out of sheer unemployment, corrupt practices in public life, frustration among youths, etc. The formation of these groups particularly the UNLF had some historical connection which can not be overlooked.

Not long after Manipur's merger with the Indian union, an underground group called 'Manipur Revolutionary Nationalist Party' (MRNP) had surfaced in 1953 and demanded 'restoration of independence status of Manipur.' But it soon died out following mass arrests of MRNP leaders and tightening of security measures across the state. It was after this movement that several educated youths with a firm conviction of 'continuing a long struggle' launched what they called 'historical mission of liberating Manipur and formed UNLF on 24 November, 1964' under the leadership of Arambam Samarendra. (Samarendra later gave up underground life, became a noted playwright, poet, social worker, theatre personality, etc, ... all rolled into one. He had tirelessly fought against social injustice including exploitation of women and other social evils, and his thoughts on 'decaying' Manipur society, culture, patriotism, etc, were reflected in his several plays, stories, poems, songs and other literary works. Such a rare figure, who had received several national literary awards, fell to bullets of two assassins while attending a social function at Salanthong near Imphal on 10 June, 2000). It may be pointed out that senior leaders of other insurgent outfits were once connected with the UNLF. Those in the powers that be should study 'all these things before trying to initiate solution to the problem.

UNLF first believed in what intelligence officials said educating the people about its cause, aim and object before taking up armed propaganda campaign. That was why that the PLA which took up arms in late seventies was more popular in early eighties. Cadres of different major underground outfits are termed as insurgents by the authorities. But, they (insurgents) called themselves as 'national freedom fighters', official sources said. It appears that a multi-pronged strategy is required to tackle the problem in the region.

Do the outfits get support from some sections of the public? The problem in the region is not just the law and order problem but an issue deeply connected with the historical past. It remains a fact, in spite of security personnel to throttle it, that huge number of people turn out either to take out a procession or participate in religious ceremony performed after the death or killing of an insurgent leader.

Intelligence sources said UNLF first concentrated on training its cadres, strengthening the organisation, collecting arms and seeking 'external help' to build up the outfit besides whipping up what it called 'patriotism' among young generation. Sources said the group could to some extent contact and develop the 'external sources' to continue their fight. The state government, according to sources, has also informed the centre about the UNLF's attempts to internationalise the issues by speaking at conferences of United Nations Working Group on Indigenous Populations at Geneva earlier. They spoke about 'self determination' at such international forum.

A senior central security official who is conversant with Manipur insurgency said UNLF and other major outfits were building up their arms by getting them from different 'foreign sources.' The arms of UNLF included anti-aircraft guns.

UNLF set up its arm wing called 'People's Liberation Army' (PLA) in 1967, imparted intensified training to its cadres in guerrilla warfare at different base and hill areas in 1975, framed a new constitution and decided to launch armed propaganda campaign in 1986. 'Military Affairs Committee' of the party was formed to step up armed propaganda campaign, said Manipur police officials, and UNLF renamed its arm wing as 'Manipur People's Army' (PLA) on 9 February, 1987 to avoid confusion in name with he PLA founded by Bisheshwar. Now, two factions of KYKL-KYKL (O) and KYKL (T)—have merged and is known as KYKL, police said. KCP is also active in some parts of the state. The UNLF, PLA and PREPAK have started fighting under a common banner named MPLF as narrated before. The MPLF has spread its network far and wide in this sensitive region. Will Manipur witness Kashmir-like situation? Only time will tell the answer.

(NOT TO SCALE)
INDIA'S
NORTH EASTERN STATES
CHINA
ARUNACHAL PRADESH
ITANAGAR
BHUTAN
ASSAM
GUWAHATI
NAGALAND
SHILLONG
DIMAPUR
MEGHALAYA
MANIPUR
IMPHAL
BANGLADESH
AGARTALA
TRIPURA
AIZAWL
MIZORAM
MYANMAR
MYANMAR

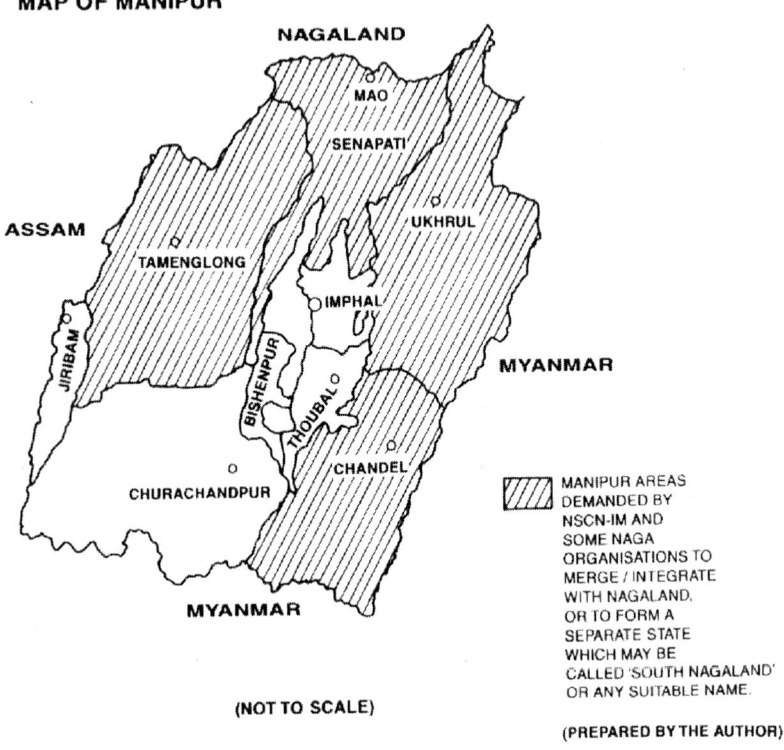
MAP OF MANIPUR
NAGALAND
MAO
SENAPATI
ASSAM
TAMENGLONG
UKHRUL
IMPHAL
JIRIBAM
BISHENPUR
THOUBAL
MYANMAR
CHANDEL
CHURACHANDPUR
MYANMAR
MANIPUR AREAS DEMANDED BY NSCN-IM AND SOME NAGA ORGANISATIONS TO MERGE / INTEGRATE WITH NAGALAND, OR TO FORM A SEPARATE STATE WHICH MAY BE CALLED 'SOUTH NAGALAND' OR ANY SUITABLE NAME.
(NOT TO SCALE)
(PREPARED BY THE AUTHOR)

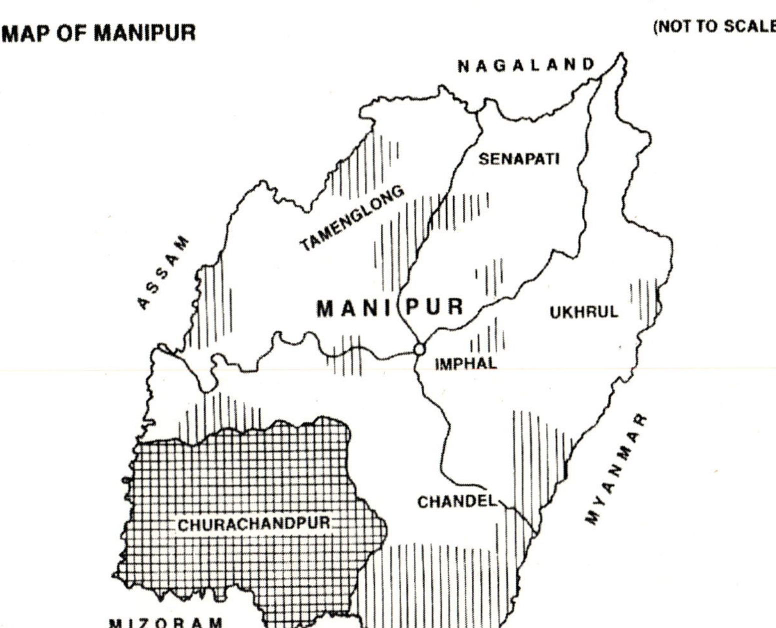

MANIPUR AREAS DEMANDED BY DIFFERENT KUKI UNDERGROUND ORGANISATIONS TO FORM A SEPARATE STATE WHICH MAY BE CALLED EITHER 'KUKI LAND' OR 'KUKI HOMELAND'.

MANIPUR'S CHURACHANDPUR DISTRICT WHERE ZOMIS (PAITE, SIMPTE, VAIPHEI, ETC.) WANT TO MAINTAIN A 'SEPARATE IDENTITY' SOME ZOMIS WANT TO FORM A UNION TERRITORY BY CARVING OUT THE DISTRICT OR MERGE PORTION OF IT WITH MIZORAM
SOME HMARS IN THE DISTRICT WANT A PORTION OF IT TO FORM AN AUTONOMOUS DISTRICT COUNCIL WITH HMAR AREAS OF NEIGHBOURING MIZORAM AND ASSAM.

CHAPTER IV

Killing Spree, Innocent Victims, Years-Long Ethnic Violence and Boundaries of Manipur

They were simply infants aged between four and one. Some of them were hurled up in the sky, and chopped to pieces while falling. The scenes were macabre and horrific. It was not a movie. More shockingly, most of the mothers witnessed the gruesome slayings of their own sucklings at Taloulong in Tamenglong district on 19 September, 1993. Four-year-old Phyalneichong Sithlhou was the oldest and the only girl among fourteen children who were slaughtered on that day.

There was nothing 35-year old Themneng Lhouvum could do to prevent the killings of her two sons, 3-year old Letboi Lhouvum and I-year old Paolenlal Lhouvum, in front of her eyes. As the news of 'Joupi massacre' had already spread to all Kuki villages in Manipur, inhabitants in interior villages including Taloulong in Tamenglong district felt unsafe and demanded security protection. In fact, several Kuki villages located in Naga-majority area had been served 'quit notice' by armed Naga activists to leave their villages within the stipulated time given in the 'notice'. Villagers of Taloulong, Selsi Burning, etc. in Tamenglong district had been disturbed and were restless following the 'quit notice'. The police and security forces, as stated before, had been far stretched and could not provide security to many who needed it.

A few days before 19 September, 1993, some Manipur Rifles personnel posted at nearby Tamei, according to village leaders, had told villagers particularly menfolks and boys from five onwards to flee the village because they were the main targets of the rival tribe. Accordingly, most of the menfolks and boys above five had already left the village either for Kuki-Majority Kangpokpi or for some safer places. That day, at around 9 a.m. the assailants equipped with sharp weapons swooped on the Taloulong Kuki village after most of the villagers had left, and set ablaze all the houses leaving only the village school-cum-community hall. While the attackers were ravaging the village, about 300 panic-stricken villagers mostly women and children were hiding in the school-cum-community hall. The villagers included women and children from nearby Buning and Jampi. Notably, the Manipur Rifles personnel who were supposed to repulse the attack withdrew to their post at Tamei on the ground that the strength was far less than the required number.

The attackers soon noticed the helpless villagers in the community hall. As the armed activists selected the male infants, the villagers started running towards the nearby jungles. Three mothers said in separate interviews with the author that their children whom they were holding were forcibly taken out of them before banging the infants on the ground and later cutting them to pieces in front of their eyes. Time may heal the mental agony of Themnem Lhouvum, 26-year old Kimnem Lhouvum and 38-year old Hoilam Kipgen but they will never forget that fateful day as long as they live on this earth because they were witnesses of the brutal killings of their own children. It was a touching moment but there was nothing the mothers could do to save their babies. 'Brothers, please do not kill the children,' pleaded women folks who knew some of the killers, and were trying to hide themselves at the corner wall of the community hall. Themnem Lhouvum said she knew one of the attackers and identified him as one Dara. His mother was a Kuki named Domneng and father was a Naga whose name was Anganbou. She requested him to spare the lives of at least some children. They were then beaten up and pushed backward. The armed assailants hunted for male infants saying these boys will 'revolt' against the Nagas one day while Kimnem was struggling hard to cover her son. While Hoilam Kipgen covered her 1-year old son, Tongkhohao on her back, Themnem wrapped her elder child with a cloth under her thigh while holding the younger one under her chest. The mothers did not let go the situation easily as they resisted to the maximum possible either by clashing with hands or sticks amid cries of mother, mother. Fourteen children lost their lives that day. Hours later, bodies of some of the fourteen babies which were scattered all over the places were seen being eaten by dogs, pigs and birds. Some weeping mothers in the melee could collect some bodies before running away from the place. They were later wrapped with clothes and put in the jungles by their mothers. Barring Phyalneichong and Letboi, the rest were aged between one and two.

It was a pogrom which had been termed by some as 'ethnic cleansing'. Reports of massacre after massacre, and burning of houses or villages trickled in from different parts of the state almost every day or week uninterruptedly from the early part of 1992. There were many untoward incidents which could have been avoided had the state government taken adequate precautionary measures after alerting the intelligence networks. In fact, the number of persons killed in the 'Joupi massacre' could have been lessened had the government forces acted swiftly after villagers were held up at the gate of Tamei village. The mass killings did not occur immediately. It took place in two phases 12 and 13, September 1993. Sarcastically, the government came to know of the killings three days after the villagers reported the incident. In the beginning, the media which had carried the story of 'Joupi massacre' were 'threatened' for publishing 'such alarming' news of killings of 87 villagers without cross-checking with the state government authorities who could not give a single line information on the worst incident up till the evening of 15 September, 1993. It was only after a Kuki body had submitted a list of missing persons to the police department and receiving a late evening intelligence report of killings of 'about 80 persons' at Tamei-Joupi area on 15 September 1993 that the state government came to know that some massacre had taken place. Interestingly, the 'Joupi massacre' were overshadowed by the killings of 13 persons including eight females on the same day at Gelnel in Sadar hills area of Senapati district because the report of the latter incident landed first at Imphal.

Inhabitants of Gelnel had been warned in the first week of September 1993 by the Nagas from nearby Nungai to leave the village at the earliest. They had been paying the 'house taxes' to Naga militants up till 1992 but they were upset since the ethnic clashes spread to interior parts of hill districts affecting mostly women and children. Their main occupation was cultivation at nearby fields and foothills. Some elders in the interior area viewed that Nagas wanted to drive Kukis away from their dwellings and encroach the arable lands around the village. The underground-supported Naga activists of Naga Lim Guard (NLG) took it that Kukis in the area were stumbling block in their march for forming a 'greater Nagaland' by integreting all Naga-settled areas in the north eastern region with Nagaland. It was a well-planned attack. Armed with highly sophisticated weapons, about fifty assailants barged into an isolated jungle near the village where some villagers mostly women folks and young girls were collecting woods, and forcibly herded them at gun point. Panic-stricken villagers could do nothing but to follow the 'orders.' Not much time was wasted. The pleas to spare them lost in the air. It was a grim scene as the assailants tied hands of the victims at their backs, made their faces lie on the ground and brutally shot at them from point blank range. All of them died instantaneously. Eight women and young girls who lost their lives in that incident were Lhingneng (68), Dimkhohat (28), Konneithem (22) and Nemhat (32) while male victims were Nehlal (60), Ngamlet (2), Lammang (4), Nengtinchong (6) and Lalchunglen (3).

It was like a mini war. Locally known as Hongmah, Khongbal Tangkhul is located at about 25 kms in the direction of north-east from Imphal. Situated on the slope of a hill about half a kilometre above the foothills, it is surrounded by Kuki villages of H. Khopipung one kilometre in the north, Chullouphai two kilometres in the north-west, D. Laikot two kilometres in the south-east, Aigizang two kilometres in the east and Jordanphai three kilometres also in the east. Meitei village Nongshum is about half a kilometre in the west, Guarding the village round-the-clock, panic-stricken inhabitants numbering about 300 had been having sleepless nights since they received reports of movement of armed Kukis in the nearby thick jungles in the first week of December 1993. Youths formed Village Volunteer Guard (VVG), made bunkers around the village, guarded it turn by turn with licensed guns and other sharp weapons. Some VVG members from time to time patrolled nearby jungles though they could not penetrate places close to Kuki villages. While elders were put on 12-hour 'security duty' from 6 a.m., the youths kept vigil during the night. Their plea for posting a unit of either para-military forces or Manipur Rifles fell on a deaf ear.

Armed Kukis knew that the village had been under the 'protection' of the VVG for the past some weeks and were waiting for an opportune moment to strike at this isolated Naga settlement. They had chosen Hongmahn because of its segregated location which is far away from other Naga villages. Thirst for vengeance particularly after the 'Joupi massacre' or killings at Gelnel, Taloulong, etc, the Kuki militants were determined to attack the village at all costs. Under the cover of darkness, about 100 well-equipped Kuki militants as spry as they were in thick hill jungles descended and surrounded the lone and secluded Naga village in the wee hours of 16 December 1993. The assailants took up positions in the early hours without the notice of the VVG, and lay in ambush. By dawn, they saw villagers going to nearby fields but they waited for 6 a.m.–the time the youths handed over arms to the elders. At 6.07 a.m. the Kuki assailants swooped down on Hongmahn and opened fire at the villagers from highly sophisticated weapons such as light machine guns, M 20 Rifles, AK 47 Rifles and started burning houses. Caught unprepared, the VVG activists suddenly took up positions and returned the fire. But they were on the defensive. The scene was like a war as the village within seconds turned to a battlefield. Children and women ran helter-skelter as every able-bodied person retaliated the Kuki attack. The exchange of fire lasted for one and half hour. Altogether eight persons were killed and five others sustained serious injuries. While 6-year old Tamang Samuel was burnt alive, 65-year old village leader Zimik Naongai, his wife Tuizarla (45) and daughter Thansingla (8) were among those killed. C.P. Paisho (50) who also sustained bullet injuries died on the spot while 16-year old Zimik Thanmi was caught and shot. Thanmi also died instantaneously. Later, secretary of the village Clarence Tharmi Ramson claimed that the empty cartridges of bullets recovered from the village filled a sack.

Perched on a small hillock, Keihao Tangkhul village is under Saikul police station in Senapati district in north Manipur, though the location of the village is next to Meitei village of Keithelmanbi which is about 20 kms south east of Imphal. A small stream, however, separates Keihao and Keithelmanbi. Like Hongmahn, Keihao with about 380 inhabitants stands isolated from other Naga villages and is surrounded by Kuki villagers of Nunambi, Somphel, Saichang, Molnom, Henjang, etc. As the two tribal groups were sharply divided and locked in deadly conflict, some Kuki militants had served 'quit letter' to Keihao villagers whose two members—a father and son-were earlier kidnapped and killed on 26 March, 1993. Seventy-year old Maleingam and his son, 35 year old Joseph Kasungnao were forcibly taken while colecting woods in the jungle and later chopped to pieces by Kuki assailants. This enraged the villagers who sought security protection but in vain. As they had nowhere to go in spite of the 'quit letter', they were prepared to face any eventuality. On 23 August, 1993, about fifty well-equipped Kuki militants crawled up the hillock during the night and burnt down at least 32 houses and grenaries. After some minutes they opened fire at the running villagers but only one person received severe bullet injuries in the dark. This incident shook the inhabitants in the remote village and many of them left for Imphal to live either with friends or relatives. However, some village elders and youths chose to stay back to 'safeguard' the village from further plundering or attack. For some months, nothing happened. Villagers thought at least the attention of the Kuki militants had been diverted to other Naga settlements. And they started reconstructing the houses and rebuilding the village.

The villagers had, however, miscalculated because the Kuki militants had been waiting for a gullible moment for the inhabitants. As in similar atacks earlier, about forty gun-toting assailants surrounded the village in the wee hours of 1 December, 1993 and sprayed bullets at the unsuspecting dwellers for more than one hour from 6 a.m. Miraculously most of the villagers escaped unhurt, and only three persons—Johny Kasung (25), Benjamin Chajao (25) and Alice Awungshi (27)-were killed by the bullets. In this case, the villagers could not retaliate as they did not have any weapons. The assailants also burnt down 65 houses, a government dispensary and a junior boys school before leaving.

'We don't know why we are fighting for,' asked 60-year old Mihileng Awungshi of Keihao. 'Earlier, we lived so closely and harmoniously but after the conflict, we looked at each other with suspicion,' Awungshi said. For 70-year old Thungalng Keishing, he did not know the reasons for fighting between the two tribal groups. However, he was slightly pressurised by the village youths present at the time of the interview with the author to say that the land had been the main cause of the current feud between Nagas and Kukis. 'We were friends earlier, and they cultivated at our fields.' Keishing said, adding that 'Kukis who came later said our lands belong to them.' 'The Naga armed activists supported by underground group wanted to form 'south Nagaland' by carving out and reorganising some Naga areas in some hill districts of Manipur and it is because of this reason that the armed Nagas or the so-called NLG (Guards of Nagas' land) had started killing Kukis who have settled in different places in the hills side by side with Naga villages for decades,' remarked L. Satkho, the Vice-Chairman Motbung Kuki village authority.

Ngariyan Kabui village is about 15 kms north-west of Loktak police station in Bishnupur district. It is situated at a segregated place and surrounded by some Kuki villages. On 29 September, 1993, about 120 Kuki militants penetrated the village at around 4.30 a.m and set afire at least sixty houses. As the villagers who were still asleep woke up suddenly and started running in all directions, the assailants opened fire kiling four inhabitants–L. Paodunlung (35). K. Lanchenlin Rongmei (48), L. Kakhujai (49) and K. Jangdinlu Kabuini (45) who was the lone female victim. Six Naga villagers of Thangland Akutpa village were killed by Kuki militants at Gairi Nepali village, about 10 kms from Senapati police station, on 30 July, 1994. Twenty four Kuki villagers were killed and 20 houses set afire hy Naga activists on 18 and 19 November, 1994 at T. phaichom village. Another 'shocking' incident was reported when six of seven Kuki women who went to collect woods at Khamunnuam village under Sadar hills sub-division were caught, tied their hands at the back and shot dead after forcing their faces on ground. The seventh one who was also shot in the same manner survived and narrated the gory tale. What is noteworthy is that the warring tribes have lived together for centuries, knew and slew each other at the instigation of the armed militants who belonged to both the communities. If a particular village were, as pointed out before, asked to carry out the felony against rival tribe, and if they did not do it, the inhabitants would be treated as 'traitors.' The militants sometimes punished even by eliminating those persons through whom the 'order' was communicated to the village for disobeying the diktat.

There are several examples of skirmishes, burning of villages, killings of villagers, exchange of fire between armed militants of both the communities, etc. They are not different from the beginning of the ethnic feud in the early part of 1992. The scale has enlarged, the bloody conflict has develped, the killlings have multiplied, the 'involvement' of vested interests has increased and general public in the state were deeply concerned. Nothing could stop or diminish the clashes.

'The ongoing clashes are posing a serious law and order problem as militants of both tribes take an active part in the fight, said an intelligence report in December 1995. 'While the NSCN (NSCN-IM) is recruiting training and providing arms to Nagas in the garb of villages volunteers, the same is true for Kuki militants who are all out to avenge the attrocities committed by the members of the NLG on their people, pointed out the report. As clashes intensified the sense of insecurity, fear and suspicion persisted in the minds of both the Kukis and Nagas, rendering regrouping of affected villages and people impossible. A number of villages were attacked with the help of the underground elements and casualties increased day by day. It may be pointed out that these attacks took place in the early hours of evening or in the morning though the time varied. The feud did not confine to a particular district or area but spread to all interior hill places. Despite strict security measures, killings proliferated to several villages in interior districts such as Buning, Dulen, Taloulong, Lasan, Joujangtek, Khoupum, etc, in Tamenglong: Tengnoupal, Sita, Laibi, Chandel, Sajik Tampak, etc, in Chandel; Lailong, Henglep and other villages in Churachandpur; Maphou Dam area in Thoubal; Khamjong, Chassad, Kamu Saichang, Bongol Kuki, Leishan, Sanakeithel, Litan, Maokot Chamu, etc, in Ukhrul; and several others in Senapati,

Villagers in four Kuki villages of Kachaopung, Matiyang, Kilchinang and Phaimol, and Tangkhul village of Kashung-all under Chassad police station-had deserted while Phungyar under Kasom Khulen Tangkhul areas was severely affected. The ethnic clashes escalated till it reached its peak in the later part of 1993, and then began a downward trend and continued upto 1999. Uptil 10 December, 1995, 534 persons (391 Kukis and 143 Naga) had been killed and 4900 houses (2649 of Kukis and 2251 of Nagas) burnt down. The highest toll occured in 1993 wherein 320 people were killed (260 Kukis and 60 Nagas), 138 others injured (69 Kukis and 69 Nagas) and 3520 houses burnt down (2144 of Kukis and

1376 of Nagas). Between 1992 and 1999, 900 people had been killed (534 Kukis and 266 Nagas) while 480 others (257 Kukis and 223 Nagas) sustained grievous injuries. Altogether 5724 houses had been set afire (3110 of Kukis and 2614 of Nagas).

The 'alarming' situation had put the state police department and other security agencies including some para-military forces in a tight position very often but there was 'not much' they could do to prevent the 'butchering' of innocent women and children. All security posts, outposts, police stations and mobile parties were put on frequent 'maximum alert' one incident after another to prevent 'any retaliatory action or attempt by anti-social elements' from attacking isolated or rival villages. Authorities' concern could be discerned from a 14 January, 1994 crash message' to all superintendents of police, commandants and other relevant security officials in which the senior security officials were instructed to 'maintain law and order at all costs in the wake of the ethnic trouble and communal flare-up in Manipur state.' Security agencies were also instructed to inflict 'punitive fines' on villages which violated public tranquility, disobeyed government orders or sheltered armed militants or activists. Police stations or outposts were strictly instructed to react and counteract against any untoward happening in their jurisdiction or in the vicinity of the outpost. The government had warned security and police personnel that any deficiency in this regard would be taken as a 'serious lapse of expected duty.' 'There is definite requirement of change in approach and attitudes by all field officers and it is expected that they should rise to the occasion by producing much improved results,' said a police department order. However, in spite of heavy security measures or strict instructions to responsible officers, the killings of civilians, burning of houses or of villages continued undiminished.

At one point of time, the state police department in a 15 January, 1994 report to the state governmnt appeared to be 'desperate and hopeless'. The report stressed the need for political leaders of various hues, affiliations and communities to put up a 'united front to dissuade and condemn' such activities (of killing innocent folks or burning of villages) and to work concertedly for the sole goal of bringing peace in the state. It said the police and security forces had been trying to contain and control the 'ethnic conflict prevailing in Manipur state between Kukis and Nagas of which Tangkhul Nagas are prominently involved' and pointed out that looking at the historical, political and economical backgrounds of the conflicts betwen the Kukis and Nagas, it was clear that security forces alone 'will not be able to solve the problem except for the fire-fighting task that they are carrying out,'

Despite stiff security measures, the number of victims kept multiplying day by day, or week after week. It was when both warring groups had grown tired after a long spell of bloody killings and counter slayings that there was a sign of decline in the year-long intra-tribal strife towards the end of 1999.

One thing is very clear in Manipur. It was mostly innocent children, happless women and incapacitated old folks who had been the victims of the ethnic violence between Nagas and Kukis, and Kukis and Paites in the nineties. it is obvious that they were the 'soft targets' of the attackers, and their killings revealed how deep the hatredness had imprinted on the minds of the two antagonistic tribes. As mentiond before, the killings recalled and resembled the 'tribal warfare and headhuntings' in the olden days as most of the victims were unarmed, helpless and attacked suddenly by the opponents. There were frequent wars among different groups of warring 'Naga' tribes in the olden days with the bigger tribes annihilating the smaller ones. And it was the Kings and their forces who, without any discrimination, protected the smaller tribes from the forays of bigger ones. Of course, there were revolts and wars but there was no such thing as 'ethnic cleansing or violence' in Manipur. The Kings were looked upon as saviours and protectors by the tribes who paid tibutes also. At the same time, the people in the valley also gave gifts and presents to tribal village chiefs making thus the kingdom powerful and united. The Kings also treated tribal subjects equally and their protection from being attacked by bigger tribes was main concern of the rulers in those days. It was the normal practice of the King or the ruler to send Manipuri forces instantly whenever the report of the attack on smaller villages by big ones was received. The erring tribes were punished by burning down their village, properties destroyed and tributes exacted. Many smaller tribes were thus saved from bigger ones who for fear of reprisal by the king's forces stayed away from the habbit of killing the weaker tribes.

It all started with the idea of breakin up Manipur by some tribes who belonged to both 'Nagas' and 'Kukis' on the ground that hill areas were 'not given proper attention.' They, however, overlooked the points that the longest-serving Chief Minister Manipur has ever had was from Ukhrul hill district and that the portions of the huge amount of money sanctioned for development of hill areas were either drained out to hill militants or pocketed by the 'privileged few' from the hills. It was not only in the hills but also in the valley that the major portion of the money meant for development went into the pockets of the few or were extorted by the militants. Moreover, the development work in most cases could not be executed effectively either in the hills or in the valley because of 'interference or huge extortion' by the militants. The religion had also to some extent parted the people earlier though this can not be an issue now because of increasing interactions among various communities in a secular society and education spreading even at interior places. Manipur society is known for non-communal nature and reflected when a leader from Muslim community which constituted about five per cent of the population was elected the first Chief Minister after Manipur became a state in early 1972. There are also several villages and places in the valley where different tribes have settled over the decades while people from the valley as per the present laws and system have been barred from settling at the hill areas. It is also noteworthy that Ukhrul district also produced another well-known Chief Minister.

It should also be understood that most of the senior officials holding key positions in the backbone of the Manipur administration, state secretariat, hailed from hill districts because people in the valley, though they are in majority, hardly got through open all India competetive examinations since they competed with those candidates in the 'general category.' In a backward state like Manipur, facilities provided for 'quality and sound' education remained inadequate besides lack of devoted and highly-skilled teachers. Apart from having many senior all-India level officers, hill districts have also produced two chief secretaries while none from the valley was qualified for that post.

Some persons belonging to different 'Naga' tribes, according to memorenda submitted to the central government, first wanted to merge portions of hill areas where these tribes have settled with neighbouring Nagaland. And if it was considered 'infeasible or unjustified', their idea was to form a 'state of their own by reorganising Manipur territory with a separate administrative unit'. In plain words, they wanted four hill districts—Ukhrul, Senapati, Tamenglong and Chandel—either to merge with Nagaland or form a 'state.' The 'separate state,' they said, may be called 'south Nagaland or any other better name,' The reasons they cited in memoranda were that the British had 'divided the Nagas.' As stated earlier, tribes in Manipur were known by their tribal names such as Kabui, Mao, Maram, Tangkhul, Anal, Moyon, Chiru, Maring, Kom, Khongsai, Hmar, etc, and the word 'Naga' which the British had applied, as mentioned before, to some tribes in the then Naga hills (Present Nagaland) of Assam was started using in Manipur to denote some original tribes only after the state was subjugated by the colonial powers in 1891. Before that the word was never heard of by the people in the state which, unlike other north eastern states, has a separate, distinct and unique history of its own. The same was the case for the word 'Kuki' also. What is to be noted is that Manipur with its present boundaries or even slightly more than this was still an independent kingdom when the British had brought the rest of the country including Assam under their rule.

In a memorendum submitted to the late former Prime Minister Indira Gandhi on 26 July, 1968, the 'Naga Integration Committee' (NIC) said 'integration of all Nagas within one administrative unit will definitely strengthen the hands of the administration of the state of Nagaland and the solution of the present trouble there (Nagaland) would become much easier, and urged the centre to look into the matter regarding integration of Manipur Naga areas with Nagaland'. Interestingly, a prominent member of the then NIC later became Chief Minister of Manipur and ruled the state for about a decade in the eighties and early nineties during which the leader had never made the 'integration' a public issue. A very important point has come up regarding the integration of 'contiguous Naga areas' with Nagaland. Some 'Nagas' argued that as per 'clause 13 of the sixteen-point agreement arrived at between the Naga People's Convention and the government of India in July 1960', the 'contiguous' Naga areas should be 'consolidated.' Here, it must be pointed out that the NPC delegation which had signed the agreement at the time of formation of Nagaland (which was carved out of Assam) placed on record' that the Naga leaders expressed the wish for the contiguous areas to join the new state (of Nagaland which was formed in 1963). Some counter-argued that when the NPC's wish for integration of continuous areas of Nagas had nothing to do with Manipur because Assam and Manipur had two sharply different and distinct historical backgrounds, and that Nagaland was created out of Assam. Moreover, in the same agreement, it 'was pointed out to them (the NPC delegation) on behalf of the government of India that Artices 3 and 4 of the constitution provided for increasing the area of any state, but that it was not possible for the government of India to make any commitment in this regard at this stage.' The clause of the agreement is very clear.

The All Tribal Students' Union Manipur (ATSUM) in a memorendum submitted to the Prime Minister on 18 July, 1980 demanded 'creation of a separate state' by reorganising the hill districts of Manipur because the hill people were what they termed 'systematically exploited and neglected'. How some hill tribes have looked at the plain people could be gauged from a memorendum submitted to the late former Prime Minister Indira Gandhi on 23 September, 1969 by Tanghkul Students Conference (TSC). The TSC had said 'the political motive of the state government' (Manipur government) was to what it termed 'Meiteinise (Meiteis of the valley) all the hill people of Manipur' when some of their demands including making of Tangkhul language compulsory upto class eight were not fulfilled. However, tribal languages are now taught in the schools in Manipur. It has been stated that there is a 'feeling of oneness' between the common hill and valley people and pointed out that it was only some 'vested interests who are trying to divide Manipur' that are driving wedge among different communities in the region. The perception of some tribal activists who alleged that the hill people were 'ignored' seemed dubious of their stand as some leaders from. the hills who had demanded integration of four hill districts of Manipur with Nagaland later became cabinet ministers. And how far they had worked for the development of hill region remained 'questionable' and below expectation. It should be pointed out that the tribal leaders from hill districts were deeply involved in the state administration or in any policy making decision body right from the beginning. Hill leaders were not only included in the constitution drafting sub-Committee which had drafted the Manipur State Constitution 1947 but also in the Hill People's (Administration) Regulation 1947 drafting sub-committe. Under the Manipur State Constitution Act 1947 which was approved by the Maharaja in early 1948, the rules for the elections to the state assembly (before Manipur's merger with the union) provided that the representatives returnable from General, Hills and Mohammadan constituencies shall be in the ratios of 30:18:3

respectively. After independence, and before merging with the Indian Union, elections in the valley under the said constitution were held on 11 and 30 June, 1948 for which the results were announced on 14 July, 1948. In the hills, the polls were held on 26 and 27 July, 1948 and the results announced on 6 August, 1948.

It was not only some 'Nagas' who wanted disintegration of Manipur. Some 'Kukis' also demanded formation of a 'Kukiland' by fragmenting the territories of this tiny land of 22,327 sq kms. The so-called 'Kukiland', according to 'underground' Kuki National Front (KNF), was to be formed by carving out the districts of Churachandpur and Chandel, Sadar hills area in Senapati and Jiribam in Imphal East districts respectively in Manipur and some parts of Nagaland, Mizoram and Assam. Though they 'incorporated' some parts of the three states of Assam, Nagaland and Mizoram, major chunk of the Manipur territory was to form the proposed 'Kukiland'.

The main reason, this 'underground' group cited for the proposed 'Kukiland' in a memorendum submitted to the President of India on 24 September, 1992, was that living with plain people (Meiteis) had caused 'great inconvenience' for the Kukis whose culture, religion, language, social life, customary practices, literature, etc, were 'distinctively' different from the Meiteis. However, it has not been properly explained what had actually caused them bothersome by living cheek by jowl with plain people in the state where majority population always played a great role in bringing harmony amongst various communities. Apart from the KNF, how some other Kuki underground outfits are demanding for formation of 'Kukiland' by reorganising Manipur territory has also been stated earlier. What caused the tribal ethnic conflict was that the area which some Nagas wanted to carve out to form 'southern Nagaland or a separate state' from Manipur included some Kuki settlements and the area which some Kukis hoped for formation of 'Kukiland' was also settled by Nagas. It was on this backdrop that what was termed 'ethnic cleansing' was started by armed militants. It is sad to say that hardly any tribe have thought of building a strong Manipur by maintaining good age-old relations and living harmoniously as before.

Kukis' participation in both civil and police administration has been considerable. 'There are more number of Kuki officers in the central government services in the state administration than that of all communities put together,' said a state government note to the central government when asked to comment on the allegations that Kukis have not been given due participation in the state administration.

In Manipur, there is no particular area or place where it is known by tribe inhabiting there. There are no Meitei-inha bited, Kuki-inhabited, Naga-inhabited areas, Muslim—inhabited areas. For instance, Muslims are in majority at Lilong area in Thoubal district, but it is never known as Muslim-inhabited Lilong area. There is hardly a district where a particular tribe or community have solely inhabited in Manipur. In the hills, Nagas and Kukis live side by side or are mixed up in Tamenglong, Senapati, Ukhrul and Chandel districts. Notwithstanding the fact that they have lived for centuries in propinquity, sharing at times weal and woes, the two could not be recouniled since Naga underground activists, alleged by the Kuki Council (KC), were 'harassing' the Kukis. 'This is for the reason that they (Nagas) want to have exclusive possession of areas they consider to be a part of Nagaland and can not tolerate the presence of Kukis,' said a memorendum dated 21 October, 1987, submitted to the Prime Minister by the Kuki Council. What can not be ignored was that militant organisations of both the communities were behind the bloody ethnic conflict which had claimed several lives till 1999.

Is Manipur a dreamland which anyone can hope to fragment and distribute it among various tribes or communities. What must not be overlooked, some state well-known historians pointed out during interviews with the author, is its 2000 year-old written history and how the forefathers had shed blood and sacrificed their lives to build this multi-racial, multi-ethnical and multi-cultural state which is known for its non-communal trait. Manipur belongs to the people of Manipur historically, geographically, and there is no particular or specific area which can be identified with or portioned for a particular tribe or community in the state, they told the author. No other people on earth will come and work for betterment of Manipur or for social harmony of various communities in the state except its people—Meiteis, Kabuis, Marings, Tangkhuls, Kom, Koireng, Khongiais, Thadous, Anals, Moyons, Lamkangs, Vaipheis, Paites, Hmars, Meitei Pangals, Mao, Maram, etc, who all live in it. Having heterogeneous characteristic and at the same time homogeneous with 29 tribes who speak 19 dialects, Meiteis, Muslim, and different tribes live in an egalitarian and pluralistic society. The evils of discrimination on grounds of religion, race, caste, sex or place of birth are not present in this tiny state in India's north eastern region. This ancient state was not built nor divided into districts or sub-divisions or villages on communal lines.

A Manipur government intelligence report said Naga underground members have been collecting 'annual tax' of Rs 10 per house in some hill districts of Manipur since the beginning of the underground movement a few decades ago. The collection was a 'symbolic gesture' to show that the other hill tribes were also supporting the movement launched by some armed Nagas to break up Manipur and merge either some portion of it with Nagaland or form a separate state. In 1992, the October 2000 report said, the NSCN-IM faction increased the 'annual house tax' to Rs 100 per house from Kukis and demanded another Rs 1000 per year from each chief of every Kuki village for the creation of what the report called 'southern Nagaland' (to be formed by four hill districts of Chandel, Ukhrul, Senapati and Tamenglong). At the same time, the villagers had also been 'ordered' to pay three years' arrears of Rs. 300 per house which the poor villagers could not afford, and complained to the state government authorities against extortion demand. This was seriously resented by the NSCN-IM, said the report.

The refusal to pay 'house tax' by some Kukis at Moreh, an important Manipur border town with Myanmar in Chandel district and trade centre, angered some NSCN-IM activists who viewed the 'defiance' as an act to challenge the 'authority' of the Naga underground organisation. The NSCN-IM also took that some Kuki militants were supporting their villagers in interior parts of Manipur. The situation became 'very tense' in early 1992 because some Kuki inhabitants had been threatened with dire consequences if they did not pay the 'house tax' which, the interior dwellers felt, was also much more than what the Naga villager were paying to the Naga militant faction. It was not one sided. At this time, some militants of KNA were extorting money from Maring inhabitants of Satang, Wakshu, Phaison and Chaktong villages at Indo-Myanmar border villages in Chandel district. In early 1992, some militants of the KNF had also served what was termed 'vacation notice' to villagers of the Chatrik village in Ukhrul district.

The recent ethnic feud started from the border town of Moreh, which is situated at about 120 kms south-east of Imphal and is considered to be the gateway of India to south-east Asia. Moreh is an important commercial centre and a major route for smuggling of arms and ammunition, and a border point often used by armed militants and insurgents while crossing into Indian territory from across the border or infiltrating into neighbouring Myanmar from Indian side. This town became a centre of conflict between the KNA and NSCN-IM as each wanted to control over the area. Tension ran high in the area as KNA apparently 'wrested' the town from the sway of NSCN-IM faction sometime in early 1992. The enmity between the two became visible and intense as the time went by.

The spark was provided when a 21-year old Kuki youth, Onkholet Haokip was kidnapped by armed Nagas from Moreh, and later found murdered on 3 June, 1992. The Naga militant group claimed that Haokip was killed in a shootout between the KNA and NSCN-IM at Bongiang village which is about seven kms from the border town, and that he was a volunteer of the KNA which, however, insisted that the victim was an 'innocent' villager. Soon followed attacks and counter-attacks, killings and burning down of houses across hill districts. Suspected Kuki militants kidnapped K. Kodun Maring and A.S. Khayao from separate places near Moreh on June 9 and July 9, 1992 and their bodies were never found. There was a high tension following clashes of villagers of Taphou Kuki and Meremai Zeliangrong village under Senapati district on 30 August, 1992. And upto September that year, 4 Naga women and 12 men had been kidnapped by suspected Kuki militants out of which three could not be traced while one Maring was found murdered. Though the killing of Onkholet Haokip ignited to some extent the bloody clashes, in May 1992 three Kuki villagers had also been brutally murdered by suspected Naga militants, 72-year old Holkhojang Haokip at T. Molphei on 12 May, 70-year old Lhungkhothng at Phoilenching on 17 May in Chandel district and 33-year old Tongkholun on 26 May at Chammu in Ukhrul district.

Suspicion arose and animosity deepened between the two communities. As the situation was turning from bad to worst slowly, a ministerial team led by the then Deputy Chief Minister of Manipur, Rishang Keishing visited Moreh on 14 June and 4 July 1992 but it failed to restore confidence in the minds of the people and subside the communal tension. There was no sign of both sides withdrawing. In May 1993, Nagas at the initiative of the Naga-Umbrella organisation, United Naga Council (UNC), formed 'Naga Lim Guard' (NLG), a voluntary village defence force to what was called 'ensure security, to give protection of the Naga villages and to guard the villages when paddy cultivation was going on'. Whatever was the formations, militants belonging to both the tribes were behind the gory decimation which continued for almost a decade from early nineties and neither the central nor the state forces were able to keep back the warring tribes. 'Quit notices' were served to several villages by both sides and the rest is the history. Hundreds of villages were torched, houses burnt down, children orphaned, thousands rendered homeless, hundreds of women widowed, hundreds of innocent villagers kidnapped, butchered or shot dead. Vehicles stopped to hunt for rivals for killing, properties worth lakhs of rupees destroyed, and hills in Manipur were in flames.

The lack of application of uniform land law in the valley and hill has added problem in the state. The Manipur Land Revenue and Land Reforms Act 1960 is in force only in four valley districts of Imphal East, Imphal West, Thoubal and Bishnupur and in some parts of hill area. It does not cover the entire hill areas, and as a result no proper survey can be carried out in the hills for implementation of various development projects. In the hills, where the Kukis have settled, the village chief owns the land, plays an important role in distributing the land to individual. At the area where Nagas have settled, the land is either in the name of individual, group or the community. Even among Nagas, there is different system of owning or controlling the land in Tamenglong, Ukkhrul, Senapati and Chandel districts. Since the hill areas have not been properly surveyed, and if a development project was to be launched there, a huge land compensation is demanded by the tribals inhabiting around the area. The Section 2 of the Manipur Land Revenue and Land Reforms Act, 1960 says; 'it (the Act) extends to the whole of the State of Manmipur except the hill areas thereof; provided that the State Government may, by notification in the official Gazette, extend the whole or any part of any section of this Act to any of the hill areas of Manipur also may be specified in such notification.' When attempts were made to amend the Act to extend it to the whole of the state of Manipur (including hills) through legislation towards the end of 1980s during the regime of the late Chief minister R.K. Jaichandra Singh so that the Act would enable the government to conduct a proper survey of the hills before launching any project in the hills for development of the state, it could pot be done owing to stiff opposition from vested interests. The point that its extension to the hill areas would benefit the tribal villagers since every individual can have land in his or her name has not been made clear to the hill inhabitants.

As the clashes between Kukis and Nagas intensified, the UNC held an executive meeting on 22 October, 1992 during which '1972' was set as the 'base year for determining land ownership of the Kukis in all hill districts in Manipur.' 'To be a bonafide resident,' the UNC resolution said, 'a Kuki must have settled where he or she has been living before 1 July, 1972 and paying house tax to the government from that particular village.' The UNC meeting was presided over by R.K. Thekho, a former Manipur minister. The UNC resolution added; 'further, the Kukis may reside in that particular village on the condition that they give an undertaking to the original Naga village authorities (Nagas who have settled before Kukis) with copies to the concerned sub-divisional officer or deputy commissioner of that district to the effect that they (Kukis) will peacefully and loyally live with the next immediate Naga village by recognising the sole ownership and sovereignty of the Nagas over the land, and that they will not invite or allow any new settlers in their village. The Kukis must furnish this undertaking to the concerned persons and authorities within the month of November, 1992, failing which they must vacate their unauthoritiesed occupation of land and settlement and establishment of village within the month of December 1992 positively.' 'Those Kukis who settled after 1972 in the Naga areas must vacate the land and their settlement in the village by December, 1992. Any Kuki or their family who fail to comply with the above condition within the stipulated time will face the dire consequences at their own risk.' The UNC resolutions reveal the relations between the two leading ,tribes in Manipur.

Kukis counter-attacked the Naga version. Kuki Inpi Manipur (KIM), an apex body of Kuki organisations, in a statement in late 1996 charged Nagas of Manipur for 'concocting figures to justify their attempt to drive out Kukis and eventually to disintegrate Manipur.' 'At the same time a section of them (Nagas) appear to advocate peace to cover up their inhuman acts in the eyes of the the world,' said the statement issued to condemn the killing of 30 Kuki bus passengers by Naga militants at Jaluki area in Nagaland in December 1996. Protesting against the increasing attack on Kukis, KIM also withdrew from the Committee for Restoration of Normalcy (CRN) formed earlier with UNC to work for peace in Manipur. KIM had aleady been angered by an earlier incident. In a meeting of the CRN on 23 August, 1993 at the State Guest house at Imphal, both KIM and UNC had raised the issue of 'quit notice' served by the latter on 22 October, 1992 to Kukis with '1972' fixing as base year. It was alleged that soon after the 'quit notice', killings and burning of houses increased manifold. Peace process suffered a major setback when prominant Kuki leaders—So Pagin Kipgen (a retired army Major) and Lalkhohen Thangeo, the Vice President of the KIM—were killed in separate incidents in Imphal by suspected Naga militants. While Pagin was gunned down on 9 May, 1993, Thangeo was killed on 6 October, 1994. No doubt, the KIM and UNC could place common issues before them in the beginning and discussed them threadbare though the two sides could not arrive at a peace accord. Both sides were not sincere and honest in settling the issues could be seen from the events that followed. Things soon turned out differently. What exasperated the KIM was that Thangeo, a prominent member of the CRN, was kidnapped while coming out after attending a CRN meeting at Manipur Baptist Church at Chingmeirong in Imphal and later murdered. His body bore multiple stab wounds. Several statements or press releases issued by them were self-explainatory as each of two tribes hardly cited the crimes committed by each of them on the rival group. 'Kukis have no intention, plan or preparation to wage war against the Nagas. It is only a section of the Naga tribes that has been waging war against the Kukis, a KIM release said on 21 September, 1996, adding that Kukis had to organise themselves for 'self-defence and to protect their kith and kin, homes and villages. Despite losing 750 innocent lives, and burning of over 300 villages which had caused untold suffering to more than 25,000 displaced persons till 1996, KIM claimed it worked for restoration of normalcy.

The demand by the Kukis for creation of separate revenue district by carving out Kuki-majority Sadar Hills area in Senapati district was also the main reason for the present Naga-Kuki communal tension, said an UNC resolution on 22 October, 1992 claiming Nagas of different tribes such as Zeliangrong, Mao, Maram, Paomei, Thangal, Tangkhuls, etc, formed bulk of the population there. Some Naga organisations also alleged that the state government had failed to protect the rights of the Naga tribes. Commenting on it, the All Naga Student's Association, Manipur in an open letter to the Chief Minister of Manipur on 7 November, 1992 blamed the government for not providing adequate protection to Nagas and had said 'Nagas shall neither compromise nor surrender even an inch of land. On 22 October, 1994, the Naga Women's Union, Manipur described as 'senseless terrorist act and inhuman killing of the (thirty seven) innocent bus passengers (mostly Zeliangrongs) by the armed Kuki militants on 19 October, 1994 on the national highway number 53 between Kotlen and Sin am in Senapati district. This is the first and worst incident ever witnessed in the history of our land, the Union said in a statement. While any crime is to be outrightly condemned, the Union statement disregarded the killings of other people in the same district of Manipur. It also mentioned nothing about the 'Joupi massacre' which had occured in the same district of Manipur.

Beloved Kuki and Naga brethren, both overground and underground, said tribal leaders in an open letter on 27 July, 1996. 'Kukis and Nagas are Christians and believers in and followers of Jesus Christ, the only begotten son of God'. 'Kukis and Nagas belong to mongoloid race and thus they are racially and religiously one only, said the joint letter of Chief Minister of Manipur and Naga leader Rishang Keishing, his Excise Minister and Kuki leader Ngamthang Haokip, KIM President Holkhomang Haokip and UNC President G.Gaingam.' For the sake of our race, our state, our humanity and above all for the sake of our lord Jesus Christ, we call upon those involved directly or indirectly in Kuki-Naga ethnic clashes to stop forthwith all such acts and never more to return to the cult of violence. Enough is enough and it must be stopped here and now. Let us start altogether a new life of peace, harmony and amity among Kukis and Nagas. Let there be no more killings,' said the letter.

However, passengers continued to be pulled down from buses and butchered, innocent people including women and children torturned and killed and so many villages burnt and destroyed in spite of several appeals, public meetings to arouse opinion against the endless slayings, peace and solidarity march, peace meetings of Committee for Restoration of Normalcy, and heavy security deployment across the state. What is noteworthy was the seven-day Imphal-Moreh-Imphal 'Peace march' from 1 May 1993 in which thousands of youths from valley participated in it to bring peace and harmony in 'our beautiful motherland which is now under a cruel spell of ethnic violence.' The People including various communities rose to the occasion to restore love and confidence among the ethnic groups of Manipur and to bridge the gap and misunderstanding between the two major tribes in the state. Journalists, Politicians, voluntary organisations, social activists and various ethnic communities took part in the march. On way to Moreh, the participants in the peace march organised meetings with village chiefs and persuaded them to communicate to the militants about the senseless acts of violence. The response at some places such as Tengnoupal and Chandel was encouraging but it was one-sided. Since both the rival factions are Christians, the All Manipur Christian Organisation CAMCO) involved itself in an attempt to bring the warring groups to negotiating table. The prominent church leaders visited the affected areas in the hills pointing out the futility of killing and torturing each other and asked the two warring tribes to end the 'senseless violence.' But these anti-ethnic conflict campaign did not help much and all efforts to end the tribal warfare were in vain. Instead, attempts were made to implicate some other tribes in the continuing clashes between Nagas and Kukis.

It may be mentioned that speakers of 'Thadou' language and some other tribes accepted the generic term 'Kuki'. During the Naga-Kuki feud, some tribes and sub-tribes such as Paite, Zou, Vaiphei, Simte, Ralte, etc. which are together known as 'Zomis' and have linguistic affinity with the 'Kuki' tried to distance themselves from the latter. One obvious reason was that they preferred identity as Zomis to Kukis and second point was that the demand of Kukiland (sometimes also termed 'Kuki homeland') by the KNF included Churachandpur district where these tribes have settled. This enraged some Kuki militants particularly the KNF which also viewed Churachandpur-based underground outfits notably the Zomi Revolutionary Front (ZRA) as being supporter and sympathiser of the Naga militant group involved in the intra-tribal killings in Manipur hills.

There was an underlying mistrust between the Kukis and Paite tribes in Churachandpur district owing to various factors like paites' indifferent attitude during the Kuki-Naga clashes, said an intelligence report on 25 September, 2000. The influx of displaced Kukis to Churachandpur during the feud with Nagas had also resulted in a demographic imbalance in the district bordering with Myanmar and Mizoram in the south and west. This had caused enmity between the Kukis and Zomis from whom the former had expected some 'fraternal gesture' which, some Kuki militants viewed, was not forthcoming during the Naga-Kuki conflict. Irked by the lack of response, the Kuki militants also suspected some Zomi tribes as aiding the armed Naga activists, their sworn enemy, during the Kuki-Naga clashes. Kuki militants were also furious at the paying of 'house tax' by some Paites and Zous (Zomis) which, intelligence sources attributed, was the 'immediate root cause' of the Kuki-Paite ethnic (later KNF-ZRA) clashes in once peaceful Churachandpur district in 1997.

Till now Churachandpur was the only hill district which had not been affected by the intra-tribal clashes. Only a spark was needed to burn the whole of hills. The smouldering dissension between the two became known after the outbreak of the violence in which KNF activists attacked the Saikul Paite village in Churachandpur district and gunned down ten paites on 24 June, 1997. Since then, there had been a series of violent clashes between the two communities for about two years. While underground groups such as Hmar People's Convention (HPC) and Chin National Front (CNF) have 'severed' ties with the NSCN-IM for the latter's alleged communal atrocities against the Kukis, the ZRA and KNF have perpetrated the killings leading to communal outrage within the clans of the same community, 'said a KIM statement on 7 August, 1997. Attack and counter-attack continued deleterious to both the tribes.

The loss of lives, properties and houses of the Thadous (Kukis), Paite and other communities in Churachandpur district resulting from the misunderstanding between the KNF and ZRA is not a loss to the two communities alone but a great loss to the whole state, 'said four leaders from the district. In a joint apeal on 23 July, 1997, Chalton Lien Amo, President of Hmar National Union, Jainson Haokip, President of Kuki National Assembly, Lengpao Vaiphei, President of Vaiphei National Organisation and Thangkhanlal, United Zomi Organisation said it was not fair in the eyes of god to clash amongst the same group of people who came from one source, one linguistic community, practised one religion and lived under the same roof. What is perplexing is why numerous tribes or sub-tribes of same 'origin' are indulging in silly violence which have claimed several innocent lives. While the figures of victims, destroyed or burnt houses, etc, will speak of how serious was the conflicts among tribes, the tribal feud in Chura chand pur district ended after a 'ceasefire agreement' between KNF and ZRA in August 1997 and another 'peace accord' on 1 October, 1998. Under the agreement between the two underground groups in August 1997, the two sides agreed to cease all offensive activities including killing, kidnapping burining of houses, wanton destruction of properties, extortion of money, threatening and intimidation of any kind, etc., and under the 'peace accord' signed by two major social organisations of the two communities, KIM and Zomi Council (an equally important body of the Zomi people) in October 1998, both the parties agreed upon the following points: (1) That, the nomenclatures Kuki and Zomi shall be mutually respected by all Zomis and Kukis. Every individual or group of persons shall be at liberty to call himself or themselves by any name, and the nomenclature Kuki and Zomi shall not in any way be imposed upon any person or group against his/their will at any point of time; (2) That, any person who has occupied or has physical possession of any, land/private building /houses and quarters wrongfully and illegally during the period of clashes shall return and restore to the rightful owners, such lands and buildings; (3) That, no Kuki or Zomi militants shall indulge themselves in any forcible collection of funds, taxes, etc, against their counterpart nomenclature be it from the government officials, individuals, contractors, and business establishments. It may also be noted that Kuki-Naga clashes ended after both sides 'realised' the futility of senseless violence and were tired of killing each other. Will it occur again in future?

Is Manipur a 'very unfortunate' state? In a rare communal riot of its kind, killings broke out between Meiteis and Meitei Muslims in 1993 due to a wild rumour and misunderstanding' in 1993. On 2 May, 1993, three Meitei youths belonging to an organisation called the 'People's Republican Army (PRA) were assaulted by some Muslim villagers of Lilong Sambrukhong in Thoubal district, where they had gone to purchase illicit arms from oneillegal arms supplier, Md. Adon. They were beaten up, after an altercation took place between the youths and the arms dealers. After the incident, some passers-by (Meiteis) and the neighbouring Meitei villagers spread the rumours of molestation of some college students (Meitei girls) by the Meitei Muslims and assaulting of Meiteis by the Muslims, etc. The rumours led to a communal riot on 3 May, 1993 in which Meities assaulted the Muslim bus passengers, rickshaw pullers, pedestrians, etc, and on the other hand Muslims attacked the Meiteis wherever they got the chance. In the riot, 96 Muslims and 4 Meiteis died in the valley districts and 149 were injured. One hundred and one cases were registered by the police and 423 persons arrested in connection with the incident. Fortunately, it ended abruptly though healing of wounds took a bit long, and both communities are living harmoniously now as before.

Boundaries of Manipur

Once a powerful ancient kingdom, Manipur which had experienced the sorrow and vicissitudes of her long history had as a sovereign independent country entered into various international agreements, treaties and instruments with other foreign countries. As mentioned in chapter three, the 1470 agreement between king Ningthouba (also known as Kyamba) and king Choupha Khekkomba of Pongs in present upper Myanmar demarcating the boundaries between the two after conquering Kyang, a Shan principality in Myanmar, was the first of its kind. Boundaries of this ancient kingdom once extended far and wide than the present one. A rough idea of the earlier boundaries of the state has also been mentioned before.

The western boundary of Manipur had not been demarcated properly until the signing of the Anglo-Manipuri treaty in 1833 though Maharaja Gambhir Singh had occupied a large portion of Cachar area. Though Manipur had entered into an agreement with the British on 14 September, 1762 under which the aid of a contingent of British troops was promised to help Manipur recover its territories wrested by Burma, the treaty of alliance never came into effect. By the treaty of 1833, the western boundary became somewhat clear as the territorial extent under the 'treaty'[136] was confined to the two ranges of hills, the one called Kala Naga range and the other known as Nungjai range both of which are situated between the eastern and western bends of the

[136]See appendix.

Barak (river). The treaty fixed the 'the line of Jiri (present Jiribam area) and the western bend of the Barak (the Barak river) as a boundary.'

In the eastern region, the boundary of Manipur once extended to the Chindwin or Ningthee river which flows in upper Myanmar. Kabaw valley is a narrow strip of level land between mountains which form the eastern boundary and Ningthee river. The valley was divided into three divisions of Samjok, Khambat and Kule. Considered as an area rich in forest produce, possession of the valley was taken as indispensable for border security by both Manipur and Burma (Myanmar). Obviously both the countries had endeavoured to extend their sovereignty over the valley. And this had resulted in frequent border disputes between the two after the first Anglo-Burmese War (1824-26). How and when the area had been conquered and brought under Manipur territory has been stated. 'In olden times, the Kubo (Kabaw) valley was sometimes under Manipur and sometimes under Burma. It was in the possession of Burma on the outbreak of the first Burmese war (with the British), and had been so for twelve years before. For about the same period preceding these twelve years it had been in the possession of Manipur.'[137] What is to be noted is Marjit Singh had 'agreed to renounce all claim on the Kabaw valley' when he sought the assistance of the Burmese ruler to capture power in Manipur. It was perhaps because of this reason that the valley was 'in possession' of Burma at the time of the outbreak of Anglo-Burmese war. What is noteworthy is that nothing was mentioned about the Kabaw valley in the 'Treaty of Yandaboo' (February 1826 between the British and Burma after the war) though the valley had been taken by Gambhir Singh during the war. The treaty as stated before mentioned: 'With regard to Munnipore (Manipur), it is stipulated that should Gumbheer Singh (Gambhir Singh) desire to return to that country, he shall be recognised by the King of Ava (Burma) as *Rajah* thereof.' As nothing was mentioned about the boundary between

[137]See Mackenzie 'The North East Frontier of British India', p. 176.

Manipur and Burma, the government of India considered that 'all the places and territory in the ancient country of Manipur, which were in possession of Gambhir Singh at the date of the signing of the Treaty of Yandaboo, should belong to that Chief (Singh). The Samjok and Khambat divisions of the valley, as far east as the Ningthee river, were accordingly given to Manipur, and the Ningthee river formed the boundary between the two countries.'[138] During the war, Gambhir Singh had also driven out the Burmese who had retreated beyond Ningthee river from Kabaw valley. The British Commissioner in Sylhet, in a letter dated 19 April, 1826, remarked that the Ningthee was no doubt the original and natural boundary between Manipur and Burma.[139] The Burmese authorities had disputed the boundary by showing a 'wrong map' earlier but they were repeatedly told that the Ningthee river formed the boundary between the Manipur and Burma.

'At one point of time, the towns of Khambat, Woktong, Tammu, Mungsa and Samjok comprising the whole extent of the Kabaw valley from Khambat in the north were held by Manipuri posts.' The main reason why nothing was mentioned about the Kabaw valley in the Treaty of Yanda boo was that the British, according to some historians, had regarded the valley as a part of ancient Manipur. But, the troubles arose between Manipur and Burma after the Treaty over the possession of the valley.

Burmese authorities did everything possible to wrest Kabaw valley arguing that the valley in historic period belonged to Burma though it was objected to by the British who had pointed out to them that the region was conquered and brought under the territories of Manipur during the region of Kyamba. As the Burmese authorities persisted their opposition, the supreme government of the British India had appointed Captain Grant and Lieutenant Pemberton, the two British officers in Manipur, as Commissioners to settle and demarcate the boundary between

[138]Ibid.

[139]Ibid.

Manipur and Burma. In early 1828, .the two proceeded from Manipur and met their Burmese counterparts on the banks of the Ningthee but fruitful discussion could not be continued owing to rainy season. The two sides postponed the next meeting sometime in early 1829. Around this time the Burmese authorities sent a 'wrong map' to the British authorities at Calcutta showing Ningthee and Chindwin as two separate rivers. As the two British Commissioners proved the deception of the Burmese to the government of British India, the two were asked to proceed to the banks of the Ningthee to meet the Burmese Commissioners. The report of the two British officers was also forwarded to the British Resident at Ava (capital of Burma), Major Burney.[140] Interestingly, the Burmese authorities attempted to evade the meeting of 1829 on the plea that their Commissioners were busy collecting the money to pay the remaining part of the war indemnity. The British Commissioners fixed the boundary including in Manipur 'the only territories reconquered by Gambhir Singh, and from which the Burmese had been expelled during the war.'[141] The British Commissioners prepared a sketch of the boundary as per direction from their higher authorities and transmit a copy of it to the Burmese authorities with a declaration that they had fixed the boundary of Gambhir Singh's territory to the southward, the Ningthee being the boundary to the eastward. The Burmese were, however, invited to meet the British Commissioners in January 1830 pointing out to them that if they failed to come on the appointed date the boundary would be fixed in their absence permanently.[142]

Interestingly, the Burmese for the first time, 'no longer denied the fact of the re-conquest of Kabaw, but said that the retention of those territories recovered by the British armies formed no part of the Treaty of Yandaboo.'[143] In January 1980, the British and Burmese Commissioners met on the frontier during which the latter acknowledged the

[140]See Singh 'A Short History of Manipur', p. 254.

[141]See Mackenzie 'The North East Frontier of British India', p. 179.

[142]Boundaries of Manipur, L. Chandramani Singh, p. 11.

[143]See Mackenzie, p. 179.

incorrectness of the map they had earlier produced. However, the Burmese side did not agree to the boundary fixed by the British Commissioners earlier. The Burmese claimed that the Manipuris had sneaked into the Kabaw valley and taken possession of the country while the boundary issue was under discussion with Sir A. Campbell, the Commander of the overseas expedition, in the first Burmese war. Their argument was turned down by the British Commissioners who recommended in favour of Gambhir Singh stating that the valley was in possession of Manipur in earlier periods and gave facts and figures to support their statement.

Stating that the valley had been under them about 1300 years ago, the Burmese side said the Khambat and Samjok divisions belonged to them and rejected the possesion of the Kabaw valley by Manipur in ancient times as well as for twelve years upto the reign of Chaurajit Singh in 1813. The Burmese also said Khambat, Samjok, etc. were also not parts of Manipur before the conclusion of the Treaty of Yandaboo. The strongest argument put forth by the Burmese was that the 'Kabaw valley was separated from the authority of the Chief of Manipur and annexed to the Burmese Empire under the Burmese Governor for a period of eleven or twelve years before the First Anglo-Burmese War.'[144]

To support their contention, the Burmese side produced an 'old inscription on a stone in the Pagoda of Koungmhoohan to show that Samjok was subject to Ava in 1650 and denied that any grant of the territory eastward of the Chindwin was ever made to Manipur by the great grand father of the then Raja of Pong, an important and powerful Shan Kingdom of upper Burma.'[145] The Burmese claims were outrightly rejected by the British Commissioners who maintained that Kabaw valley belonged to Manipur and produced records from the chronicles of the state and proved that Kyamba, king of Manipur with Khekkhomba, king of Pong, agreed (the 1470 agreement between the two) to fix a

[144]Secret Consultations of the Government, 19 November, 1830, Nos. 4-11, quoted in the 'Boundaries of Manipur.'

[145]Ibid.

boundary between their countries bringing Kabaw under the territories of Manipur. Documentary evidences were shown to the Burmese Commissioners that.. '(1) The Pong Raja (king) was not a tributary of Ava 400 years ago; (2) That the Khambat and Samjok were tributaries of Pong and (3) That the Pong Raja then ceded to Raja Kyamba all the country comprised between the Naojeeree (Loijiri) and Muyalong Hills (Mungkhong Muwai) on the eastern side of the Ningthee river.'[146] Later in his book on 'Report on the Eastern Frontier of British India.' Pemberton wrote 'a tract of country was then made over to the Rajah of Muneepoor by the king of Pong, extending east to the Naojeeree, a range of hills running between the Moo and Kyendwen (Chindwin or Ningthee) rivers, which was then established as the boundary between the two countries, south, the limit extended to the Muyatoung or Muya hills, and north, to a very celebrated mangoe tree near Moonqkhum, between the Naojeeree hills and Kyendwen river.'

Both sides had agreed that the Burmese had been occupying the Kabaw valley for about twelve years before the outbreak of the Anglo-Burmese War because former Manipuri ruler, Marjit Singh when he sought the assistance from Burma to capture power in Manipur had agreed to renounce all claim on the Kabaw valley. But, the point at issue was that Gambhir Singh had driven out the Burmese after re-conquering the valley which had been a part of Manipur territory for centuries. The British Commissioners also told their Burmese counterparts that the conquest of the Kabaw valley by king Gambhir Singh before the Treaty of Yandaboo was correct because they were present at the time of the capture of Tamu. To support their points,' the two British officers also showed the printed narratives of the Burmese war, one dated 23 January, 1826, written from Tamu and the other dated 3 February, 1826 from Monfu on the western bank of the Ningthee river as proofs of their statement.[147] The Burmese obstinacy was revealed as the facts, figures and valid reasons put forward during the

[146]Ibid.
[147]Ibid.

discussions with the British commissioners could not be challenged properly by the former. As things were worsening since no solution was in sight. Major Burney invited Pemberton to Ava to discuss the issue with Burmese ministers. At Ava, Major Burney with the aid of Captain Pemberton argued and explained with solid facts and figures to the Burmese authorities to acknowledge the right of Gambhir Singh to Kabaw valley but in vain. However, Burney with the help of Pemberton could convince the Burmese authorities that: (a) Gambhir Singh re-conquered the valley; (b) the valley had at various periods been in possession of Manipur; (c) they admitted the incorrectness of their map showing Kyendwen (Chindwin) and Ningthee as separate rivers and acknowledged them to be the same, and (d) at the time of concluding the Treaty of Yandaboo, Sir Archibald Campbell neither recognised nor acknowledged the alleged right of the Burmese to the disputed' area. The Burmese also produced 'some untrue statements in the immediate past'[148] to show that the valley belonged to them.

At one point of time, it was stated, the Burmese had said if Gambhir Singh could be removed and place Marjit Singh on the throne of Manipur for under such an arrangement they hoped to maintain friendly relations between Manipur and Burma. Major Burney told them that the decision made by the government in favour of Gambhir Singh had already been reported to the authorities in England and as such the discussion could not be reopened.[149] In December 1830, Major Burney even 'hinted' to Burmese ministers who were hard pressed for money to pay the remaining balance of the war indemniity that the British might sacrifice a portion of the remaining instalment of tribute if the Burmese agreed to inclusion of Kabaw valley in Manipur and fix Ningthee as the boundary between the two. Considered as 'advantageous', the Burmese ministers listened to the proposal but none of them dared even to communicate their feelings to the king who, they knew, would burst out into a violent rage and

[148]See Singh 'A Short History of Manipur', p. 256.

[149]See Chandramani Singh 'Boundaries of Manipur', p. 15.

regarded the loss of a single foot of land as diminution of his authority and power.

Had there been a one line sentence about Kabaw valley in favour of Manipur in the Treaty of Yandaboo, the history of Manipur would have been totally different. The valley had been in the possession of Manipur for centuries except for some years during the period of Marjit Singh, and the unfortunate part was that the British whom Manipur depended for driving out Burmese from its territory ultimately conceded to the Burmese pressure. Despite vehement opposition from Grant and Pemberton who had strongly favoured inclusion of the valley in the territories of Manipur, there was a change in the stand of Major Burney. It was understood that the Burmese king did not like the British who, the king thought, were not only supporting the Manipuris but also wanted to give portion of his own territory. The point Burney had raised that if the matter of fixing Ningthee as boundary between Manipur and Burma was further pressed, it would precipitate another war was not convincing because Burma had just been defeated by the British. His change of stand was noticed when he questioned the wisdom of keeping Gambhir Singh in 'possession of an unhealthy and depopulated strip of territory which is divided from Manipur by a range of hills ... is worth the risk of thereby thoroughly disgusting the Court of Ava and accelerating another war.' Burney further remarked that 'there are grounds of probability that the determination of the Governor General in Council in favour of Munnipore may ultimately produce a collision between the British and the Burmese states.[150]

There was no doubt that the British Commisioners pleaded strongly for inclusion of Kabaw valley in Manipur. The supreme government was convinced of the right of Manipur to Kabaw valley but it concurred in the views of Burney when the Governor General Lord William Bentinck remarked ... to the humiliation of their pride and to their reduced if not extinguished power, I think it will be both

[150]Ibid.

generous and expedient to grant them this gratification. It is true that we give up the best boundary line, and the admission of the Burmese into the valley may tend to much more collision with the Manipuris, but with our superior power a better or worse military boundary is of no consequence whatever, and these boundary disputes if arising can lead to no war.'[151] And the final orders of government dated 16 March, 1833 were issued directing Major Burney to announce to the king of Ava that 'the supreme government still adheres to the opinion that the Ningthee formed the proper boundary between Ava and Manipur, but that, in consideration for His Majesty's (king of Burma) feelings and wishes, and in the spirit of amity and good-will subsisting between the two countries, the supreme government consents to the restoration of the Kabaw Valley to Ava and to the establishment of the boundary line at the foot of the Yoma Doung Hills'[152] (once known as Maring hills by the Manipuris).

It was a shattering blow for the Manipuris though Gambhir Singh was persuaded to accept the new arrangements on the plea that Manipur would benefit from it. One can imagine how the people in Manipur would have felt when the Governor General announced the decision of the supreme government on issue of Kabaw valley which, every Manipuri knew, had been a part of the state since the 1470 agreement. Grant and Pemberton communicated to the kind of Manipur about government's decision to 'pay Rs 500 per month as compensation for the loss of Kabaw valley and if circumstances arose by which the territory in question ever again reverted to Manipur, the compensation granted would cease from the date of such restoration.' It was the worst moment for the Manipuris particularly the Maharaja Gambhir Singh as Grant and Pemberton handed over the valley to Burma without the consent of the great patriotic leader on 9 January, 1834 after an agreement was concluded on the same day between the British Commissioners and

[151]See Mackenzie 'The North East Frontier of british India', p. 182.
[152]Ibid.

their Burmese counterparts. Minutes after hearing the 'saddest news', Gambhir Singh expired on 9 January, 1834, the very day on which the valley was transferred to Burma.

By the '1834 agreement'[153], the British Commissioners, Major Grant and Captain Pemberton, under instructions from the Governor General in Council made over to Woondouk Mahamingyan Raja and Tsarudauqicks Myookyanthao, Commissioners appointed by king of Ava, the towns of Tummao (Tamu), Khumbat (Khambat), Sumjok (Samjok) and all other villages in the Kubo (Kabaw) Valley, the Ungoching Hills and the strip of valley running between the eastern foot and the western bank of the Ningthee or Kyendwen (Chindwin) river. And the boundaries as per the agreement were demarcated as follows: that the eastern foot of the chain of mountains which rise immediately from the western side of the plain of the Kubo Valley. Within this line is included Moreh and all the country to the westward of it. On the south a line extedning from the eastern foot of the same hills at the point where the river, called by the Burmahs Nansaweng, and by the Munnipoorees Numsaeelung, enters the plain upto its source and across the hills due west down to the Kathekhyoung (Muneepooree river). On the north the line of boundary will begin at the foot of the same hills at the northern extremity of the Kubo valley and pass due north up to the first range of hills, east of that upon which stand the villages of Choeetar, Noongbree, of the tribe called by the Munnepoorees Loohooppa, and by the Burmahs Lagwensoung, now tributary to Muneepoor. What is to be noted was that the valley had been handed over to Burma in what appeared to be an, attempt to 'appease' them without making even the slightest reference to the Maharaja of Manipur, and avoid any possible war between the British and Burma. It had turned out to be a wrong calculation as the second Anglo-Burmese War broke out within 18 years of the transfer of Kabaw valley during the reign of king Pagan of Burma (1845-1852/1853) giving the British lower Burma.

[153]See appendix.

Notwithstanding the handing over of the valley to Burma, the relations between the former and the British continued to be unfriendly apart from frequent skirmishes between Manipuris and Burmese at the borders. Former Political Agent in Manipur Sir James Johnstone later on the issue of Kabaw valley observed: 'We had an agent, Colonel Burney (formerly Major), at Ava, and the Burmese who were not disposed to be at all friendly, constantly tried to impress on him the fact that all difficulties and disputes would be at an end if we ceded the Kubo valley to them, that territory belonging to Ghumbeer Singh of Manipur. Of course the proposal ought to have been rejected with scorn, and a severe snub given to the Burmese officials. It was not realised that a display of self-confidence is the best diplomacy with people like the Burmese, and with a view to winning their good-will we basely consented to deprive our gallant and loyal ally of part of his territories.'[154] The matter did not end there.

After Burma was annexted by the British, the latter did never decide to restore the valley to Manipur. While forwarding an application from Maharaja of Manipur, the Secretary to the Chief Commissioner of Assam wrote a letter to the Secretary to the Government of India on 14 April, 1886 pointing out that the question of ceding Kabaw Valley to the Maharaja was fully discussed by Chief Commissioner with Colonel Johnstone and Major Trotter at Shillong on 31 March, 1886 during which it was stated that the Shan population of the valley were opposed to the cession and that they threatened to leave the country if the cession was made. But this did not end Manipur's attempt to regain the lost territories. In 1932, Maharaja Churachand Singh and Manipur State Durbar contemplated for the restoration of the ceded territory of Manipur pointing out the 'reason which actuated its cession to Burma having been removed by annexation of upper Burma by the British government ... The territory, the state's right to which had been so clearly and emphatically recognised would have been restored in 1886

[154]See Johnstone 'Manipur and Naga hills', p. 87.

(at the third time of third Anglo-Burmese war giving the British colonial possession of Burma). His Highness and the Durbar fervently and confidently hope that with the pending constitutional changes the time has at last come when the British government will be prepared to consider the restoration to Manipur its old rights and status.'[155] It was during the reign of Bodhchandra Singh that another representation was made before the Chamber of Pricnes. It said '... the State (Manipur) is very gratified to learn that the Chamber of Princes are examining the question of ceded territories' and appealed for restoration of the Kabaw valley to Manipur.

In his speech of 18 October, 1948 before the legislative assembly of Manipur, Bodhchandra Singh said, 'this treaty (Treaty of 1834) left us a good heritage namely the Kubo valley of 700 Sq. Miles for which we now get from Burma (the British government) Rs 6,270 as annual tribute which according to the spirit of the terms of the agreement will cease when the area is restored to our state.'[156] However, in spite of so many appeals and efforts to restore the valley to Manipur, there was no change in the attitude and policy of the British government which continued to pay the compensation upto 14 August, 1947. The compensation was paid even after Manipur's merger with the union government in 1949 but the boundary problem between Manipur and Myanmar still remains unsolved. The Myanmar army personnel made an incursion and are occupying some area near Molcham village in state's Chandel district after mysterious disappearance of the border pillar No. 33 (the new number is 66) there. The area is now, claimed by Myanmar, and Manipur government's committee constituted to look into the issue and some disputed areas near Moreh and Namphalong in the district had sent a report to the centre. But, the matter still remains unsolved. Imagine what would have been the situation if the disputes had taken

[155]The Representation of the Manipur State which was laid before the State Enquiry Committee, 1932.

[156]Proclamation of His Highness the Maharaja of Manipur State 18 October, 1948.

place at Kargil, Siachen or any other point at Indo-Pak border in the western front.

The northern boundary once extended beyond the present one. In 1832, Gambhir Singh with a large Manipuri troops and British officers, Captain Jenkins and Lieutenant Pemberton, undertook a military expedition to the then Naga Hills which was later brought under British regime. In the olden days, the Manipuri forces penetrated into the hills and exacted tributes and during the reign of Gambhir Singh, wrote Johnstone in 'Manipur and Naga Hills' pointing out that several villages were 'brought under submission, including Kohima, the largest of all.' There was frequent military or other expeditions to the Hills from Manipur. In 1835, the forests between the Doyeng and the Dhunsri formed the boundary between Manipur and Assam.[157] This was again followed by a not-so-clear boundary line 'demarcated'[158] between Manipur and the then N aga Hills during the conference of Lieutenant Biggs, Principal Assistant in charge of Nowgong (Assam) and Captain Gordon, Political Agent in Manipur though Angami Nagas had a little regard for the Biggs-Gordon line. Clashes were not uncommon at the borders in those days.

It may be noted that the Naga Hills was later brought under the British and administered by a political agent whose headquarters was at Samagudting and his rule was confined only to a few villages in the area. The border affairs arising out of intermittent skirmishes, raids and counter-raids among the villages in the Hills had, at one point of time, reached to such an extent that the British government in 1851 wanted to hand over its administration to the government of Manipur. The then Political Agent in Manipur James Johnstone observed' ... failing any intention on the part of the British to annex the Hills, it would have been good policy to have reorganised the Manipur territory, and to have aided the Maharaja (of Manipur) to annex and subdue

[157]Political procedings, 11he Febraury, 1835, No. 90 (Manipur Archives).
[158]See Mackenzie 'The North East Frontier of British India'. p. 107.

as much as he could under certain restricitions.' 'Had this been done,' he wrote, 'the British should have saved themselves much trouble.'

A strong Manipuri force in March 1854 invaded the Angami area and ravaged the Mozuma village as they had earlier plundered some villages within the territorial jurisdiction of the government of Manipur. Mezeffina, another village, had in March 1874 sought the British protection because of frequent attack from Mozuma which later revolted against the former. To suppress the Naga village. Johnstone and a strong Manipuri force under the command of Manipuri leader, Balaram Singh marched there but Johnstone returned following reports of the Burmese attack on Manipuri post at Kongal at the border, leaving behind the Manipuri forces to aid the Political Agent of the Naga Hills. And again in 1879, following news of attack on the Political Agent, Damant, Johnstone and a large Manipuri forces rushed there to counter the Angami Nagas. No major incident was reported after that incident. But things changed and went different directions after the Anglo-Manipuri war of 1891 which brought a significant change in the territorial possession of Manipur towards northern frontier. As a result, the northern boundary of Manipur was confined to the Mao post which continues to be the boundary between Manipur and Nagaland.

In the olden days, the southern boundary of Manipur was 'vague and unsatisfactory.' '... its present boundaries, as far as they have been fixed, are, on the west, the Jeree river, from its sources to its confluence with the Barak, and from this point, south, to the mouth of the Chikoo or Toyaee, flowing from lofty ranges bordering on the Tripura country, falls into the Barak at the southern extremity of a range of mountains, three sides of which are embraced by the tortuous course of this river, said a government report in 1835. The Chikoo or Toyee river was also known as Tipai. The boundary line in the south was not well demarcated earlier.

Like at other border areas, Manipur also witnessed number of clashes, ravaging, plundering and killings between villages at. the border in the southern frontier. Often, Manipuri forces undertook military expeditions in the area because of frequent raids unleashed by the Lushais who devastated the villages within the territories of the state. At one point of time. Lushais took Tipai river as the boundary between Manipur and neighbouring areas in the south but this was not properly demarcated because tribes in the west of the river considered that they were in some way connected with Cachar in Assam.

In 1734-35, Maharaja Garibaniwaj set up a stone at the junction of Koowai, Toowai and Tanganglok rivers to demarcate the boundary of Manipur in the south.[159] There on the stone was inscribed in Manipuri character that the land on the northern side of Toowai river belonged to Manipur. During 1786-87, Maharaja Jai Singh confirmed the boundary settled by Garibaniwaj at Tipai area and went from Tipai to Chiboo, where he dug a tank and well for salt manufacture for the use of Kuki subjects there. Following frequent raids from Lushais in Cachar, Sylhet, Manipur, Tripura and were at the same time at feud with Kamhows or Sokties, a tribe living to the south of Manipur, the Governor General in Council in 1871 sent an expedition against the Lushais after seeking cooperation from Manipur. Maharaja Chandrakirti Singh also sent a Manipuri troop and the British officer, General Nuthal who was posted in Manipur. After the expedition, the tribes of Vonpilal, Poiboi and Vonolel were reduced to submission and 'tributes exacted from them.'[160] Peace prevailed for sometime. At this time, 23 village leaders from Poiboi, Lengkhum, Damboon, and Saileth came and declared themselves before Manipuri officials General Thangal and Balaram Singh and Nuthal that they were 'subjects of Manipuri king.'[161] There was a natural boundary, though not clearly demarcated, since long ago. 'Hence, that the river Toowai forms the boundary of Manipur is known from time immemorial to the Lushais and

[159]Assam Secretariat Confidential (1889), Governor's Secretarial Confidential Assam 1878-1950 (Manipur Archives).

[160]Same as 158, p. 160.

[161]Same as 159.

Kukis living there.'[162] It was thought that the boundary in south was the line drawn due west from where the Numsailong river enters Kabaw valley to the Tooyai or Chikoo river (the latter will be found to the extreme west and flows into the Barak river near or Tipaimukh.

In 1873, Chief of Lushai, Damboom visited Manipur though his trip was kept as a secret by the Manipur authorities. Having heard of his arrival, the Political Agent sent for Damboom privately. First the Lushai Chief did not turn up but he was later brought to Dr. Brown, the Political Agent. Both discussed the peaceful settlement of the Lushai-Manipuri relations. In the subsequent years, several Lushai chiefs, after Damboom, visisted Imphal. In one of their visits to Manipur, Damboom on the part of Poiboi, Daloom Muntri on the part of Lenkoom, Lalkoop, Raja of Lairuk, Konga, Raja of Punchoohi and Balool. Muntri of Dalkoon swore before the Maharaja and the Political Agent at Manipur, and other officers of the country that mutual friendship would always be maintained by them towards the British government and government of Manipur and agreed, for that purpose, to conclude a treaty with Chandrakirti Singh.[163] It was agreed by concerned parties not to commit acts of aggression against the British and Manipur subjects. But, the terms of the treaty were not followed by the Lushais themselves, and raids on villages in the territory of Manipur continued. And by early eighteen nineties, all concerned parties felt the necessity of demarcating a well-defined boundary in the southern part of Manipur. A boundary commission was thus formed with a view to demarcate a boundary line consisting of B.S. Carey, the Political Officer of Chin Hills in north-western part of Burma and A. Porteous, officiating Political Agent at Manipur, and both met on 27 January, 1894 at Tin Zin in the Kabaw valley.[164] The two decided to demarcate a boundary from Lunglen hill westwards to Tipaimukh. The proposed boundary ran the course of the

[162]Ibid.

[163]Annual Administrative Report of Manipur Political Agency, 1873.

[164]Annual Administrative Report of Manipur Political Agency, 1893-94.

Tin Zin river to its source in the Yomadung range thence for 4 miles south west wards the crest of that range and then the course of the Yangdung river to its mouth on the Manipur river.[165] This boundary was 'accepted'[166] by the government of India and officially approved it in 1898. And since then the territorial integrity of Manipur in this frontier remains the same till today.

[165]Ibid.

[166]Political documents (letter No. 1827, E. dt. 22 Oct. 1894) quoted in 'Boundaries of Manipur'.

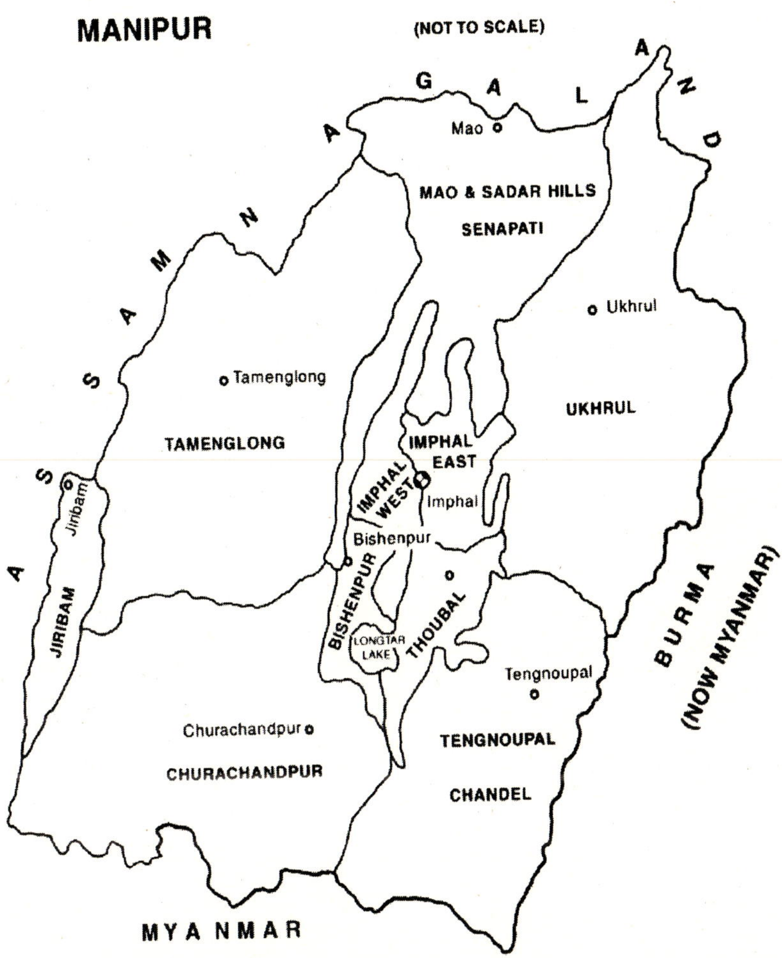

DISTRICTS: IMPHAL EAST, IMPHAL WEST, BISHENPUR, THOUBAL, UKHRUL CHANDEL, CHURACHANDPUR, TAM SENAPATI, JIRIBAM IS IN IMPHAL EAST.

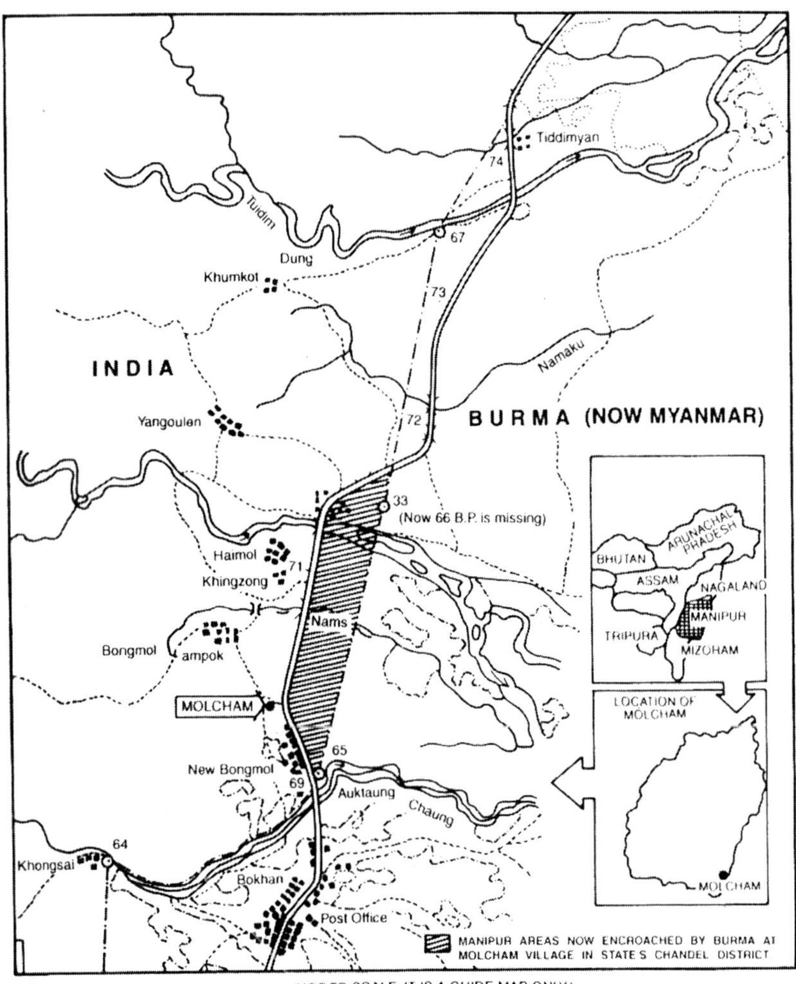

(NOT TO SCALE. IT IS A GUIDE MAP ONLY.)

CHAPTER V

Civilians at the Crossfire: Does Present Predict the Future

In Manipur where young persons can not remember in their lifetime when there had been peace and tranquility; innocent, law-abiding, unsuspecting civilians are sandwiched 'between army, para-military personnel, police commandos engaged in the counter-insurgency operations on one side, and militants, insurgents or guerrillas whom the government forces are pursuing on the other.

Since late seventies or early eighties when extremist-related violence had broken out on a large scale, there have not been a time when the underground insurgents were not fragile. Only when the former top leader of PLA. Nameirakpam Bisheshwor was arrested in July 1981, and later the 'commander in chief' of PREPAK, R.K. Tulachandra Singh was slain in an encounter with Manipur Rifles personnel in November 1985, people thought the underground movement was 'subsided and over.' After the killing of Tulachandra Singh, there was a lull on the insurgent activities of the once-dreaded PREPAK. PLA also suffered a series of setback as its successive top leaders were either arrested or killed one after the other. Public had assumed for the first time that it would take years to resurface the insurgency movement again. But it was not so. The underground activities remained dull only for some months.

In the beginning, the underground militants had concentrated their armed propaganda for what was termed 'an independent Manipur' in Imphal and surrounding areas but they later spread their activities to rural and interior Manipur where there was less deployment of troops.

Insurgents also fanned out to rural areas whenever there was heavy concentration of forces in the state capital, but they regrouped at any opportune moment to strike at any roving security patrol or an isolated outpost to make their presence felt. Frequent ambush on the forces, attacks on outlying security installations, snatching of arms from the police and other forces, encounters between insurgents and law-enforcing agencies, became a routine thing in a backward state like Manipur causing serious concern among the populace. It was true that the state administration, and more particularly its intelligence networks, were also caught flat-footed by the sudden eruption of secessionist violence and were at a loss in early eighties. In those days markets, shops and business establishments were closed minutes before or after sunset as people rushed in to their homes or dwellings to avoid any encounter or skirmish between insurgents and security forces which occurred mostly in the evening. Life was insecure. Everyone was concerned what would be the future of Manipur where people did not have much faith and confidence in 'the corrupt and inefficient' government as most of those in power were known for indulgence in corrupt practices, bribery or nepotism, and for self-centred work in spite of the alarming law and order situation prevailing in those days. It was said that every government job had its price tag with the rates varying according to the rank of the post. As the universities and higher educational centres churned out hundreds of graduates and post graduates every year, there was simmering discontement among educated, unemployed youths as they were facing an uncertain future. There was no big industry or factory which could provide large scale employment to the swelling number of educated youths and contribute to the economic development of the state. Educational institutions had remained closed for weeks if not months because of youths' unrest and student-sponsored series of agitations including anti-alien movement of the All Manipur Students Union (AMSU). AMSU was demanding detection and deportation of foreign nationals who over the past years had illegally infiltrated into Manipur from Bangladesh, Nepal and Myanmar. These nationals were seeking to earn their livelihood through their friends and relatives who have already settled in the state. And every parent was gravely concerned as frustration among the youths was growing.

Economy of the state as well as the economic condition of the common people were worst and remained far below expectation. There was or is no industry worth mentioning its name. The only major project which can be cited as an example is Loktak hydro-electric project which is run and owned by the National Hydro-Electric Power Corporation (NHPC). The project which is operated by water from Loktak lake is selling power to Manipur and its neighbouring states, and the state government's repeated requests to the central government to hand over the project to the state government has fallen into a deaf ear. If the project is made over to the state government. Manipur will benefit a lot and improve its economic condition to a large extent, feel some senior public leaders. For a backward state like Manipur where there are no resources but people live mostly on central assistance, the centre should give thought to the state's request for handing over the power project to the state government, they expressed. The financial condition of the state was so bad that sometimes the more-than-eighty-thousand employees went without salaries for months together. The central government which is blaming the state government for not properly implementing the development programmes has so far not initiated any major project worth mentioning its name and which can really improve the economic condition of the people. Above all, there is hardly any employment opportunity except the job provided by the state government, which was not only limited but was also given to those who could 'afford' it. Of course, there are persons who got to the lucrative government jobs by their sheer luck, talent and merit but the number was considered 'very few.' Corruption in public life made many a educated youth feel that their future is uncertain.

The situation in the hills was not different. The law and order was as bad as in the valley because of the activities of different underground organisations. In the name of launching agitations on various issues, the two national highways in the state, Imphal-Dimapur-Guwahati (number 39) and Imphal-Jiribam-Silchar (number 53), were blocked frequently by hill people causing extreme inconvenience to the general population, and creating 'division' between hill and valley people. As the two highways are the only land routes through which Manipur is linked with neighbouring states, people both in hill and valley were frequently cut off from the rest of the country. Even for a local issue, the highways were often blocked for an unspecified period, throwing the general population at the mercy of business persons who charged exorbitant rates for any essential commodity during the blockade of the highways. All essential items and other materials are transported to Manipur from outside the state through these highways.

Despite worsening the law and order situation and economic condition of the common people, major chunk of the funds allocated for development of the state, as mentioned earlier, continued to be pocketed by the few privileged. The progress of every development project was at snail's pace, or it took several years to complete any development work than its normal stipulated time. Moreover, how many major development projects have been completed according to the given schedule or are benefiting the people can be counted easily. The number of persons living below poverty line rose day by day as well as the educated unemployed youths. Students' unrest coupled with the government's failure to tackle various issues confronting the state not only crippled and severely affected the normal social and academic life but also resulted in the increase of number of drop-outs. On the other hand, those who did not have the purchasing power suffered maximum as prices of the man-made scarcity of essential items were soaring every day.

Simply, there was no hope for the poor people. With this social condition in the backdrop, hundreds of frustrated youths were joining the ranks of the underground organisations which had, in the early phase, received considerable support from some sections of the people. The centre's lackadaisical attitude towards development in the state, inadequate allocation of funds, using of forces to suppress any democratic agitation, long negligence to any major issue confronting the state further alienated the people in the region from the national mainstream.

While the 'independence of Manipur' for which the underground groups have been fighting for is totally a separate issue, many people hoped that the ultras would at least help 'clean' the rotten, impure, corrupted, divided, social and public life in the state. However, it turned out to be a miscalculation. Later, the huge extortion from the public by different underground groups alienated the latter from the former. One can well imagine what happened to those who disobeyed the underground diktat.

The atmosphere was thick, tense and heavy in Manipur in the early part of 1980 as life was not secure, and on the other hand more and more security forces were being rushed into the state to tackle the burgeoning underground activities. Troops were deployed at all strategic points, patrolling intensified at all vulnerable points and common people subjected to thorough combing operation by the newly-deployed forces who 'took almost every Manipuri' as either an extremist, insurgent, sympathiser of militants or anti-national people. The common people also looked upon central forces as 'inimical' to local inhabitants. A point which must be stressed is that in a democratic country like' India and present day world where what is happening in any remote part of the globe can be heard everywhere within no time, a proper policy to tackle insurgency problem should be adopted so that the ultras are automatically isolated by the masses without whose cooperation the former can not survive. If such strategy can not be chalked out and masses not won over, the insurgency will remain, and using forces' which may even attract flak both from national and international media in their course of duty will not bring any everlasting solution. Any misuse of the provisions of the Act under which the forces are deployed may be counter productive as more and more youths, unable to bear the torture or harassment, may join ranks of the undergrounds.

Manipur has undergone tremendous hardships in the past one or two decades. People can't openly criticise misfeasance, wrongdoings, misdeed of anyone having gun in his or her hand. There was a time when one couldn't express his or her opinion freely on some issues involving armed militants. Those who had voiced against them or expressed their views were either maimed or killed. So many precious lives have been lost. Some under ground actions including extortion from the public in the name of either 'road tax,' 'vehicle tax,' 'house tax' or 'donation/contribution to the party' annoyed many people but hardly anyone give opinion on the issue openly. Prominent leaders like veteran Communist Party of India leader Thokchom Bira Singh, and former Chief Minister and Manipur People's party leader Yangmasho Shaiza who was known for his opposition against any move to disintegrate the state were gunned down in 1980 and 1984 respectively. Attempts were also made on the lives of several political leaders including former Chief Ministers Rishang Keishing and R.K. Ranbir Singh, and former finance minister Laishom Lalit Singh.

As the ultras intensified the armed propaganda, army and para-military forces often staged flag march in early 1980. At the same time, people also stepped up their agitations against the proposal to impose the Armed Forces (Special Powers) Act, 1958 (as amended in 1972) to give 'extra powers' to the forces deployed in a 'disturbed area' while tackling militants, extremists or insurgents. Situation was simply grave. Both sides did not withdraw and ultimately, the Act which, under Clause 4, empowered 'any commissioned officer, warrant officer, non-commissioned officer or any other person of equivalent rank in the Armed Forces' was imposed after the entire state was declared 'disturbed area' under the Act in September 1980. If the said officer under the Clause 4 was of the opinion that 'it is necessary to do so for maintenance of public order, after giving such due warning as he may consider necessary, fire upon or otherwise use force, even to the causing of death, against any person who is acting in contravention of any law or order for the time being in the disturbed area prohibiting the assembly of five or more persons or the carrying on of weapons or things capable of being used as weapons or of fire-arms, ammunitions or explosive substances.' No amount of protests that the Act should not be imposed because provisions of the Act would be misused by those implementing it fell on the deaf ears of those in the powers that be.

Under the Act, the said officer may also 'arrest, without warrant, any person who has committed a cognizable offence or against whom a reasonable suspicion exists that he has committed or is about to commit a cognizable offence and may use such force as may be necessary to effect the arrest.' What is to be noted with emphasis is that 'no prosecution, suit or other legal proceedings shall be instituted, except with the previous sanction of the central government, against any person in respect of anything done or purported to be done in exercise of the powers conferred by this Act.' How many victims, their family or relatives who are mostly poor persons would go to Delhi and seek permission from the union Home ministry to file cases against the central forces? Even if they did manage to approach the central government, how many of them would be permitted to proceed against the forces under the said Act which was later termed by many social organisations, student bodies, political leaders, human rights activists as 'draconian and black law'. Every political party promised in their election manifesto to withdraw the Act from the state if they came to power but hardly anyone kept their word. As the troops deployed under the Act fanned out to rural and interior area, everyone in the state was gravely concerned about what would be the consequences of the implementation of this Act.

Twenty five kilometres to the north-east of Imphal, there lies a village called Pukhao Terapur. Inhabited mostly by Meiteis, the village is partly surrounded by hillocks and located at an isolated place which was also infested by the activists of the banned KCP (Kangleipak Communist Party), a communist-minded underground outfit. Like any other segregated Meitei village, Pukhao Terapur was as under-developed as anyone can imagine in a land-locked backward state like Manipur. Though not far-off from Imphal, there was no proper road, drinking water facility, electricity, health care centre nor any other essential service available at the village about two decades ago. Awareness for education among the youths was also very low as inhabitants lived mostly on agriculture and agricultural produce. Majority of the villagers were farmers.

One thing was clear. Whether it was at Pukhao Terapur, town area, other villages or anywhere, one could notice the gloomy face and concern of the people over the declaration of the entire state as 'disturbed area' after placing it under the Armed Forces (Special Powers) Act. Perturbed over the deployment of central forces even at the interior area, inhabitants were definitely unaccustomed to the sight of the heavily-armed army or other paramilitary personnel. There was also a communication gap between the security forces and the local inhabitants. As the situation was becoming grave, forces were also intensifying their mopping-up operations against the insurgents although the intelligence-gathering network on the movement or identity of the ultras was not as sound as of now. This was the scene in Manipur in those days.

Father of seven children, 43-year old Chandam Chaoba Singh was a simple, naive, uneducated, hard-working farmer of Pukhao Terapur. Though poor, he had a happy family with every member helping him much in the paddy field. And his sole aim was to raise children well and send them to a nearby village school so that, he thought, at least some of them would be able to earn their livelihood not by working round the year at the paddy field. He knew how hard the life of a farmer was in Manipur, and did not want his children to follow his footsteps. His wife equally had the same hope.

After a day's work, the Meitei farmer and family members were about to retire to bed when they heard some knocks at the door on 10 January, 1981. As his wife opened the door, within seconds, some para-military personnel forcibly entered the house, asked for Chaoba Singh. The farmer came out of the next room and he was asked whereabouts of some underground elements of the locality. Since he could not give them the answers, he was forcibly blindfolded and taken away with them. That was the last time his wife. Nungshitombi Devi saw her husband.

After waiting 13 days for her husband to return, Nungshitombi Devi submitted an application on 22 January, to the Deputy Inspector General of Police (Operations) to 'enlighten her about the whereabouts of her husband' but there was no reply to her request. With the help of some village leaders, she approached the police authorities to enquire about her husband but in vain. And finally, Nungshitombi Devi requested the local member of the Manipur Legislative Assembly, Y. Kulla Singh, who in turn raised the matter in the state assembly on 31 July, 1981 by putting a question: 'Is it a fact that the whereabouts of Chandam Chaoba Singh, S/o the late Gulamiat Singh of Pukhao Terapur who was arrested on 10 January, 1981, by the CRPF (Central Reserve Police Force) from his residence at about 7.30 p.m. is not yet known?' Chief Minister Rishang Keishing replied in positive by saying 'yes'. However, while answering supplementary questions, Keishing never mentioned that Chaoba Singh had been released. After this the issue became complicated with a serious problem arising when the Commandant of the 5 CRPF claimed that Chaoba Singh had been 'arrested on the night of 13-14 January and released at about 5.30 p.m. on 14 January, 1981.' However, the matter did not end here. Since Chaoba Singh did not return home, a question came up whether he had in fact been released as contended by the Commandant, who in support of his case, relied on documents produced by him—entries in the apprehension register, two situation reports of 14 and 15 January and a letter dated 15 January addressed by the adjutant of the battalion to the headquarters (Manipur) sector (army's office). These documents indicated that Chaoba Singh was captured on the night of 13 and 14 January along with two others, Tharongou Singh and L. Lala Singh, from the same area. Chaoba Singh and Tharongou Singh were reportedly released as directed by the army authorities after they were found 'white (word employed by security personnel when the arrested persons were found innocent). What is interesting is that Nungshitombi Devi contradicted the security version, insisted that her husband was picked up on 10 January night and that his whereabouts was not known.

Had Chaoba Singh been arrested on 10 January, 1981, as per claim of his wife, the Meitei farmer must have been kept in the custody of the CRPF for more than four days and was violative of the Article 22 (2) of the constitution of India which says: Every person who is arrested and detained in custody shall be produced before the nearest magistrate within a period of twenty-four hours of such arrest excluding the time necessary for the journey from the place of arrest to court of the magistrate and no such person shall be detained in custody beyond the said period without the authority of a magistrate. Was it because of this Article of the constitution that the CRPF had claimed that the farmer had been arrested on 13-14 January night and 'released' on 14 January evening to show that the security personnel involved did not act against the constitution? What is to be pointed out again is that Clause 5 of the Armed Forces (Special Powers) Act says: 'Any person arrested and taken into custody under this Act shall be made over to the officer in charge of the nearest police station with the least possible delay, together with a report of the circumstances occasioning the arrest.' If the CRPF version that Chaoba Singh had been arrested on 13-14 January night and released on 14 January was correct, why did not the security personnel hand over Chaoba Singh to the nearest police station as per provision of the Armed Forces (Special Powers) Act, and in this case to the Lamlai police station in present Imphal East district.

Nungshitombi Devi was relentless in her search for Chaoba Singh and filed a writ of habeas corpus at the Guwahati High Court which, for the first time, admitted such a writ after the promulgation of the Armed Forces (Special Powers) Act in the state. Senior advocate Laishram N andakumar Singh, pleading for Devi, said that documents produced by the concerned security personnel on Chaoba Singh's release had been 'manufactured' to suit the case of the Commandant of the 5 CRPF. The Court endorsed the view of the advocate and Justice B.L. Hansaria and Justice T.C. Das on 10 September, 1982 ordered the Manipur government and CRPF authorities to produce Chaoba Singh before the Court, and ultimately the matter reached the Supreme Court which again returned the case to the Guwahati High Court. The matter was finally settled following payment of Rs 2 lakhs as compensation to the family of the farmer by the relevant CRPF authorities 'with the knowledge of the Court.'

While the case ended without a happy note, the issue did not die down as various social organisations, student bodies and women's groups demanded restraint on the part of the security forces and immediate withdrawal of the Armed Forces (Special Powers) Act from the state. Government after government continued to be pressurised by the social organisations, women's groups, student bodies to withdraw the Act but no tangible effort was made in this regard by those in the powers. And slowly, Manipur was turning into a 'battle and killing field' with mostly unsuspecting, unarmed, innocent civilians becoming victims either in the 'crossfire,' 'encounter' or in the alleged extremist-related crimes. People who were unwonted to the sounds of gunshots, explosions of bomb felt no more panic as the security forces armed with the provisions of a 'draconian' law intensified counter-insurgency operations to flush out the ultras from the state particularly from the Valley.

Fifty-seven year old Ingudam Mangi Singh was a well-known artiste, and even acted in an international award-winning Manipuri film, Imagi Ningthem (My son, My

Precious). His role as a grandfather in the film is still regarded as superb performance by many. Mangi Singh and his friend, Jugindra Pebiya (a radio-artiste and playwright) were returning home after a drama practice when they met two other friends. Moirangthem Ingobi Singh (an school teacher) and Imobi Singh (an employee of electricity department) at around 7 p.m. on 1 May 1981 at Thouda Bhabok Leikai area on Imphal-Airport road. The four then decided to take an evening stroll in the area. Around this time, Manipur police commandos were chasing some armed militants in the same area in the darkness. At about 7.15 p.m., several gunshots were heard, and news spread like a wild fire in Imphal that four prominent underground members had been killed by state police commandos in an 'encounter.' A Deputy Inspector General of Police who later became the Director General of Police (Manipur) on his own told the author that four important underground leaders had been killed in the exchange of fire with Manipur police commandos that evening. When the story was about to be filed quoting the name of the official, another source said those killed were innocent citizens. When contacted the police official again, he said some arms were also recovered from the possession of the victims. It was a sad ending for the four civilians whose families were later given an ex-gratia payment of Rs 10,000 each since victims was innocent person. In another bizarre incident on 14 July, 1983, which could have been obviously avoided, one bullet, fired by a Manipur policeman, pierced three young men on a motorcycle, killing them on the spot. The incident occurred near the Lilong police station, about 10 kms south of Imphal, in Thoubal district on the Indo-Burma road. The three identified as Md. Ishlammudin Khan (26), Seram Thambal Singh (25) and Maibam Devananda (25) were shot dead on the alleged charge that they failed to respond to the policeman's challenge. Ishlammudin was a younger brother of a former Manipur Veterinary Minister Helaludin Khan.

There had appeared to be 'something' which was never made public behind this incident. The three on a motorcycle and five other friends were returning home after attending a party at Thoubal, about 20 kms south of Imphal, on that fateful day. The five others were P. Tikendrajit Singh, W. Ibocha Singh, Y. Iboyaima Singh, B. Joykumar Sharma and N. Khogendra Singh.

As they were nearing the Lilong police station, according to version of the survivors and some police officials, one policeman later identified as Tomba Singh abruptly came out of the police station with a loaded rifle. Another policeman, who followed Tomba Singh, commanded him, 'hey, don't go out .... wait ... wait.' Unconcerned about the command, the cop went straight to the main road, pointed the gun towards the eight young men. As they smelt danger, one of the youths shouted, 'Tachou (big brother) ... please do not shoot us. We are from Chajing (a place near Lilong), and we just went to Thoubal.' But, without heeding any attention to the pleas, the policeman (according to evewitness accounts) fired one round from point blank range, killing the three persons on the motorcycle. Only one bullet was fired but miraculously it penetrated the bodies of the three friends who died within minutes. When the firing was heard, the policeman who prevented Tomba Singh suddenly ran into the police station and locked the door. After the incident. Tomba Singh himself jumped into the compound of the station leaving the rifle on the main road. As the youths were known to the officer in charge of the Lilong police station, Gaya Singh and assistant sub-inspector, Ibopishak Singh, they repeatedly called out to these two persons. At last they turned out after about 40 minutes and were told the whole story. Had they come out in time and taken the victims to hospital, would any of them have survived? The state government, in spite of assurance that a judicial probe would be ordered to enquire into the incident, never kept its word. A senior police source later said this particular policeman had 'mistaken' the youths as 'extremists'. The killer policeman, according to sources in the department, was understood to have told his friends that, even if they (victims) were not extremists, he (the policeman) would not be punished citing some similar instances earlier. If the victims were extremists, he confided to some of his friends, he would be 'properly rewarded.' One can imagine how was the then prevailing situation in Manipur in those days. Even a more shocking similar incident had occurred earlier in 1982 involving a promising sportsperson. But nothing could stop what was once described as gun-crazy cops from killings of innocent persons in the name of tracking down the armed ultras in the region.

Hesitating for a moment, they were not sure whether the 22-year old youth was an insurgent, extremist, a militant or not when they heard him crying 'please do not shoot me. I am a football player' and begging for life. That was on 30 October, 1982. But, it was only for a few moments. Heavily-armed Manipur Rifles commandos who caught hold of Khaidem Imocha Singh pumped four or five bullets into the footballer. And in the next few agonising moments. Imocha Singh who was wearing sports uniform and returning home breathed his last with a shocking and piercing wail 'oh! mother.'

What was the fault of the sportsman? Lovingly called 'Maimu' by his close friends. Imocha Singh was coming back home after a short practice at nearby Chingamathak playground that hapless morning. On his way back, he was persuaded by some of his friends to attend the 'social science study course,' organised and conducted by the Singjamei branch of Communist Party of India (CPI) at a house at Ngakraba Leirak area. Most of the participants were youths and students of that locality. Maimu did not want to attend the course as he had some other work to do at home but since some of his close friends insisted, the footballer reluctantly agreed to join them. That day the topic on 'horrors of nuclear wars' was being discussed. For some illiterate, uneducated soldiers the word 'wars' may mean anything. And how recklessly the forces had been deployed in early eighties can be made out as there was not a single officer who would understand the topic of the course that day.

It was only some minutes after the session started that the participants to an utter surprise heard someone yelling 'kill them, kill them'. First the youths thought the commandos were chasing some militants who sneaked into the congested locality but soon they found themselves 'encircled and locked' by the security personnel. All the persons present were forced to lie down. 'Surprised and mistaken' by the topic (horrors of nuclear wars), the commandos who were not well-educated enough to understand the subject beat up the lecturer for what they termed teaching the participants to make bombs. As he was fully aware of the situation that the commandos would not understand the subjected, the lecturer though roughed up kept himself cool and advised the youngsters to maintain order. The place of occurrence was not in interior Manipur but only about two or three kilometres away form Manipur police headquarters. Disturbed over the strange nature of the forces, some youths out of sheer panic and fear started darting halter-skelter, Already angered over the youths 'learning to make bombs,' the commandos shouted 'do not move' as the young persons started running, and within seconds opened fire. Yumnam Nirmal Singh, a close friend of Imocha Singh, shuddered at the sound of the firing and tried to flee but he was soon caught at gun point. Nirmal Singh was given a thrashing by the commandos who continued firing. Nirmal Singh thought it was blank fire.

Security actions against the civilians followed very fast. Nirmal Singh and another friend, Khomei Singh were segregated by the commands who enquired about antecedents of Imocha Singh. When Nirmal Singh told them that 'Maimu' was not only a football player but also a dramatist, the young man was given another severe blow, and' was forced him to say that 'Maimu is a leader of the banned People's Liberation Army (PLA).' Refusing to say that, Nirmal Singh was tied up and removed to the nearby embankment of Imphal river. The men in uniform were also divided. Some commandos subjected him to 'severe torture' while some others strongly objected to it but he was 'kicked' like a football by many. Soon Nirmal Singh and Khomei Singh were taken to Imphal police station, about a kilometre away.

from the spot. Nirmal Singh who was produced before a senior official, told the official that the commandos had tortured him when he refused to say that Maimu was a PLA leader and narrated the whole story. Khomei Singh also told what had happened. Convinced about what they had said, the two friends-Nirmal Singh and Khomei Singh-were released, It was not the end of the story. The two now realised that what they thought was blank fire had actually killed their close friend, Maimu. There was nothing they could do but to shed tears for a friend whom they loved so much.

The killing of a young promising footballer sent a shock wave across Manipur particularly in the valley, and it was felt that the life was not secure since the large-scale deployment of the forces under the Armed Forces (Special Powers) Act. Imocha Singh was not only a sportsperson but also closely associated with Manipur Theatre Centre as a dramatist. Maimu was due to take part in a play of Manipur Theatre Centre to be shown at the All India Short Play Competition at Allabahad in February 1983. What irritated the people particularly those close to the victim was a press release issued by the Manipur police department after the incident. It said 'Khaidem Maimu Singh (not official name Imocha Singh) was killed in the exchange of fire between extremists and police personnel.' 'The extremists,' the release said, 'opened fire on the police.' This was a common phrase later used by security authorities whenever any extremist, militant, ultras etc killed in any encounter with the forces. The police release further mentioned that the 'deceased was member of PLA unit three as per documents seized by army from extremists at Kadampokpi operation on 13 April, 1982.' (At Kadampokpi, near Imphal airport, an encounter took place between army and PLA during which several senior PLA members including its top leader, Thoudam Kunjabihari Singh were killed and many incriminating documents, weapons arid ammunitions recovered from the spot). The police press release said the commandos went to Ngakraba Leirak area to raid PLA members following information that extremists were holding a meeting in the area.

Did Imocha Singh become an 'extremist' after his death as per the 'documents' recovered from Kadampokpi area? Before the 30 October, 1982 incident, Maimu had been freely moving about and there was no intelligence report against him at that time that he was involved in underground activities. It may also pointed out that the Kadampokpi operation during which the reported documents were seized had taken place many months ago. Many felt that the 'mistake' made by those concerned should have been admitted to avoid further complication and to restore public confidence in the law-enforcing agencies. It is a fact that no enquiry has ever been held on the death of any extremist or insurgent in Manipur. But, another official release dated 2 November 1982 said, 'the state government had decided to initiate an inquiry into the incident that occurred at Yumnam Leikai area on 30 October in which Khaidem Maimu Singh died.' The finding of the inquiry has never been made public. People no longer remained silent. A social organisation, Citizens Forum of Manipur strongly condemned the killing of Maimu, and in a memorendum submitted to the then Prime Minister, the late Indira Gandhi, pointed out that 'indiscriminate killing of innocent people and later describing them as insurgents has annoyed the general people in the state' and 'innocent people often fall prey to the excesses of the security personnel.' It was not only the central but also the state forces who were allegedly involved in the 'security excesses' on civilians. And for the first time, after Manipur's merger with the union in 1949, common people became aware of the facts that human rights in the state were being violated in early eighties in the name of searching armed extremists. It was not only the security forces but also the armed underground activists who used civilians as shields against the forces.

Though the central forces had been called out to 'aid the civil administration in a disturbed or dangerous situation,' many questions came up whether the forces were operating on their own, or 'with cooperation' from the state forces. As lack of coordination was noticed among the forces, it had been stressed on many occasions the need to conduct joint operations, share intelligence gatherings amongst various forces engaged in the counter insurgency operations and inform the civil police in the respective area about the search of militants. The massive combing operations launched to drive out insurgents in early eighties were mostly conducted by the central forces. Army or combined forces of army and para-military forces, after receiving any tip-off about the clandestine movement or infiltration of ultras in a particular place, would surround and cordon off the area mostly in the wee hours to avoid detection of troop deployment. Early in the next morning, all the menfolks of the locality would be called out to a nearby field, playground, roadside or any open area where each and everyone was subjected to identification parade before masked squealers who knew their former comrades-in-arms. The hooded persons may also be a local leader or an intelligence official who knew the identity of the armed militants. The process was not only time consuming but caused extreme inconvenience to the general public. What was most shocking was that the informers who identified the extremists or underground elements sometimes pointed their finger at people whom they had personal enmity. During the combing operation, no person was allowed to either come into the area or go out of that. It was not only the security forces who had intensified counter-insurgency operations. The underground militants also stepped up their armed propaganda even at the crowded place, sometimes using public as shields against the security forces.

People in Manipur are sportive and very fond of playing competitive games either at local, district, inter-district or state-level. Football. Hockey, volley ball, badminton, boxing, weightlifting and other athletic games are very popular in this north eastern state. Moreover, Manipur has also produced some well-known national as well as international sportspersons in spite of the various hardships and inadequate facilities available in the state. Now-a-days, instead of celebrating some festivals or on any other opportune occasion, they organise competitive games at various places. And in one such game, a volley ball match between the teams of Manipur Rifles and Border Security Force was organised at Heirangoithong area in the outskirts of Imphal on 14 March, 1984. About 3000 local enthusiastic men, women and children were watching the match which was also witnessed by seven or eight well-armed CRPF personnel. For half an hour, the match had been continuing very well with all the spectators deeply absorbed in it. But, all of a sudden at about 4 p.m., about 15 unidentified extremists fired upon the CRPF personnel who were on 'law and order duty' at or near the venue of the match, killing one CRPF constable and causing injuries to five CRPF personnel on the spot. The extremists snatched three self-loading rifles (SLR), one grenade firing rifle with 100 rounds of SLR and 5 rounds of 303 ammunitions from the CRPF personnel. Thirteen civilians were also killed in the incident. General people were outraged at the killing of 13 spectators including children. As several social organisations, public leaders and eye-witnesses demanded a judicial inquiry, the state government had no alternative but to finally submit to the public demand. A Manipur government notification dated 25 June, 1984 said 'the extremists allegedly continued fire while retreating and security personnel returned fire for about five minutes, and in the course of it some extremists or security personnel or both fire at the crowd of the spectators killing 13 civilians and causing injuries to 36 others with bullet injuries on the spot.' As the government of Manipur took a serious view of the incident and was satisfied that it was a definite matter of public importance involving law and order in Manipur, and the matter required a detailed inquiry into the causes and circumstances leading to the incident and also to find out the persons responsible, a commission of inquiry later known as Heirangoithong Firing Inquiry Commission headed by the then District and Sessions Judge of Manipur Y. Ibotombi Singh was constituted under the sub-section (1) of Section 3 of the Commissions of Inquiry Act, 1952 (Act 60 of 1932). The terms of the Commission were, briefly, to inquire into the cases and circumstances leading to firing incident, find out as to who fired upon the crowd of spectators and the persons responsible for the incident.

Interestingly the government version differed from the finding of the Commission of Inquiry. According to the Commission of Inquiry finding, the CRPF personnel led by platoon commander, Sushil Kumar were witnessing the volley-ball match between the Manipur Rifles and the BSF teams and they were 'not on duty.' The other CRPF constables were PP Kumaran, K.V. Kunnikrishnan, Tarsem Singh, Padeiya, Riyayat Ali, Bachan Singh and Jagdishchand. Barring Sushil Kumar and Jagdishchand, the rest were fully armed. As the spectators including the CRPF personnel were concentrating on the game, some armed extremists attacked the security forces with a 'sole object' to snatch their arms by firing some rounds from small arms like pistol and revolver, injuring Kunnikrishnan, Kumaran, Tarsem Singh, Riyayat Ali, Bachan Singh and Padeiya. Padeiya succumbed to injuries on the spot. As there was stiff resistance from the central forces, the militants could take away 'only three self loading rifles and one grenade firing rifle and some ammunitions.' The extremists then fled away after a brief encounter. The finding said Jagdishchand who took a weapon from Kunnikrishnan, and Kumaran became wild at the sight of the dead body of Padeiya and their wounded comrades and 'in order to avenge the death of Padeiya and wounds of their colleagues fired several rounds upon the crowd of spectators at the playground thereby killing and wounding the innocent spectators.' The Commission of Inquiry blamed Sushil Kumar for not restraining CRPF personnel from firing in the crowded area after the militants had run away and fixed three CRPF personnel responsible for 'most of the killing and wounding of innocent spectators' and also the extremist for 'illegal activities'. However, the Commission made no recommendation as to against whom what legal action should be taken up saying its duty was 'one of fact finding.' There was no mala fide intention in quoting portion of the Commission's finding which may affect the interests or tarnish the image of some quarters but what is at issue is many common, innocent people have lost their lives in the conflict between armed persons in the past two decades. How many more victims will there be? Only time will tell.

What later came to be known as 'Heirangoithong massacre' shocked the people across the state as they were now sure that the life was not safe in Manipur. Anytime anything may happen anywhere. On 9 July, 1987, militants belonging to National Socialist Council of Nagaland (the then undivided NSCN) attacked and killed nine jawans including a junior commissioned officer of 21 Assam Rifles at their post at Oinam village in Manipur's Senapati district. Ninety self-loading rifles, twenty sten guns, ten light machine guns, two 'two inches mortar' and a large quantity of ammunitions were looted by the Naga militants. However, security forces recovered seventy per cent of arms and ammunitions which were taken away by the NSCN militants, said a defence press release on 14 August, 1987. But, during the course of the counter-insurgency operations 14 persons lost their lives. 'After the incident of 9 July, 1987, as many as 14 civilians lost their lives, alleging their involvement in NSCN activities,' said a Manipur government memorandum submitted to the Union Home Minister in connection with the Oinam incident. It was pointed out that those who lost their lives were Seva, P Shanglong (54), Th. Wakhao (48), L. Yaho (55), Wacha (58), PL. Ring (32), Rangkhew (50), Mathomi (30), Esow (30), Shunai (29), Khua (40), Lokho, Sosang and Th. Thava. Security forces said eight of them were killed in encounters while the rest making an attempt to escape from army custody. 'Similarly, it is not clear as to how the arrested persons could make an attempt to escape from army custody,' the memorendum said. Post mortem reports of many deceased persons showed that bullets were fired at the back of their heads. And there was no end to the violence.

Examples of civilians being killed in either crossfire, encounter or extremist-related crime are many. An old woman vendor was killed by a stray bullet accidentally fired from the rifle of a reckless CRPF jawan who was on law and order duty on 24 April, 1980, even before the declaration of the state as 'disturbed area.' Two days after, following an ambush in which three CRPF personnel were killed by suspected activists of the PLA at Patsoi area, about 15 kms west of Imphal, the central para-military forces enraged over the slaying of their colleagues came out in large number from nearby Langing camp and launched a massive combing operation at Patsoi area during which, according to a report of a parliamentary fact-finding committee, four innocent persons were shot to death.

What was the motive behind the attack on the security forces or the police commandos by the unidentified militants at the crowded areas? Some analysts felt the main purpose of striking the forces by the extremists was to capture arms and continue the armed propaganda. Another factor could be that the public's wrath, as a result of retaliatory action of the security forces, would turn against the law-enforcers. In most cases, it produced a negative effect as various social groups, women's organisations, public leaders, etc., appealed to armed underground youths not to attack, ambush security forces at people-gathering places, and stressed the need for the political solution to the insurgency problem in the state. It was the view of some analysts that security personnel, enraged over the killing of their colleagues by militants, would definitely resort to some kind of retaliatory action which may not be to the liking of the public. In such cases, definitely, the common public are at the crossfire between the security forces on one side and insurgents on the other. A question which still remains unanswered is whether the civilians are used both by the security forces and militants as 'pressure tactics' against each other, or not. Several law-abiding citizens have been killed even after knowing that they were innocent public. This is to drive the message home that if the security forces are attacked and killed, there would be civilian casualties. What is to be noted is whether the insurgents are trying to whip up the anti-forces, anti-government sentiment among the civil population by intensifying their extra-judicial activities at public places.

And people continued to be the victims of armed conflict. Two detachments from 119 and 79 Battalions of CRPF, comprising six persons each, were detailed on guard duty at the then Regional Medical College Hospital (now Regional Institute of Medical Science Hospital) at Lamphel in Imphal on 7 January, 1995 for protection of some injured CRPF personnel who were being treated at the hospital. The first detachment that was on guard duty at the medical ward comprised head constable Ram Dayal, constables B.L. Satpute, Ashok Desai, Basanta Rao Wali, S.K. Pandey and V.H. Yousuf. The other detachment deployed at the surgical ward comprised of naik Kartar Singh, Naik Mohan Das, constables Ratan Singh, Uma Shanker Rao, Puttu Lal and Ashok Kumar. All these personnel were issued self-loading rifles with 60 rounds of ammunition with each one of them.

At about 7 a.m., some three or four suspected militants opened fire at Yousuf at Sulab toilet complex of the hospital where he along with Ram Dayal. Pandey and Uma Shanker had gone for their morning ablutions. Yousuf was grievously injured. Immediately after that, CRPF personnel started firing at the suspected militants, and they were soon joined by the other CRPF personnel who came from surgical and medical wards. The firing continued for some minutes. A medical student from Arunachal Pradesh, Momi Riba, an employee of Sulab toilet, L. Pradeep Sharma, a driver, Wangkhem Upendra Singh, five auto rickshaw drivers, Saikhom Premchand, Hijam Khogen, R.K. Khogen, Angom Debendra and Koijam Rajendra Singh, and a rickshaw puller Md. Jakir were killed on that fateful day. Following extreme pressure from the public, the government of Manipur set up a Commission of Inquiry to enquire into the firing incident on 7 January, 1995 at the then RMC hospital complex, and the Commission was headed by a retired judge of Guwahati High Court, Justice D.M. Sen.

The report of the commission was very clear. 'The Commission on an appraisal of the evidence on record, the affidavits and the exhibits filed, finds there can be no other explanation for the death of the nine civilians and injury to another, except that they were fired upon by the CRPF after the militants had already retreated and when there was no further need for resorting to any firing by the CRPF.' The Commission report even mentioned whose shots killed whom pointing out that 'all firings by security forces must be controlled and aimed at definite targets.' There should be no indiscriminate or 'prophylactic' firing, in the sense that even in the absence of specific targets, firings can be legitimately resorted to. Instructions, the report said, should be issued to fire only when there are militants within their arc of vision and also when such militants are in the actual process of firing or mounting an attack.

As the injured CRPF jawan shouted 'mara, mara' (I am being killed, I am being killed), according to the report which quoted eye-witnesses to the incident, the other CRPF personnel guarding their colleagues who went inside the toilet and saw two militants running away. They also started shouting 'Bhaga, Bhaga' (they have escaped, they have escaped). These CRPF personnel from Sulabh toilet then reached towards the old gate of the RMC complex (a very crowded area) and shouted *hamara admi mara hai, sab Manipuriko maro* (our man has been killed: kill all Manipuris). At this time, the medical student (who was not a Manipuri but from Arunachal Pradesh), one worker of Sulab complex and a non-Manipuri (who had the feature of an Aryan) were coming towards the hospital through the old gate. While the non-Manipuri entered the old gate, the other two persons shouted that they were civilians and raised their hands from outside the fencing near the gate. However, the forces did not heed their pleas. Thus, Momi Riba and Pradeep Sharma became the first two victims of that day. On getting the bullet injury the Muslim rickshaw puller, Jakir cried 'Allah hu Allah' and fell down on the ground near the vehicle parking complex of the hospital. At that time, one of the CRPF personnel, the report pointed out, approached him shouting *kya Allah* and 'shot him again.' Jakir died at that place. The report also revealed minute details of how the other victims fell to the bullets of -the security forces. To prevent recurrence of such incident, the report suggested that the CRPF personnel 'must be warned that any deterrent, retaliatory or retributive firing or use of force is not authorised by law and may well amount to an offence of murder or culpable homicide.' The Commission recommended that further investigation of 'this unfortunate firing incident in the RMC complex should be entrusted to the Central Bureau of Investigation' adding that 'excessive or indiscriminate firing can never be deemed to be acts done in course of official duty or under the authority of any law.

What later came to be known as 'Tonsen Lamkhai massacre' and 'Malom killings' were both separate insurgency-related major crimes in which a large number of civilians were killed after the attacks on para-military forces by armed militants. What is to be emphasised is that these incidents of killing innocent civilians continued to occur in spite of instructions to the forces not to be provoked and not to harm the law-abiding citizens even at the difficult situation. The civilians were killed mostly in what was term 'crossfire' or 'encounter' though eyewitness accounts gave different version. It would remain so until and unless a court or a commission of inquiry proved otherwise. On 3 October, 1999, unknown militants ambushed a combined team of 81 CRPF and 35 CRPF at Tonsen Lamkhai area in Manipur's Thoubal district at around 1.15 p.m. killing seven CRPF personnel on the spot. The central forces, who were proceeding in nine vehicles to interior part of the district in connection with parliamentary election duty, also returned the fire killing an underground activist. According to first official reports and eyewitness accounts, the exchange of fire lasted for about 30 minutes after that the militants sneaked into nearby thick jungles. Minutes after the encounter, a bus carrying some polling personnel was also coming from a different direction. The CRPF personnel stopped the bus and asked the occupants to get down. Later, it was learnt that the bus, carrying 37 polling personnel including unarmed, security officials, was hired by the state government for transporting the personnel to three polling stations of Sugnu assembly segment for elections to the lower house of the Parliament. Panic-stricken occupants including unarmed security men at first refused to come out. However, the driver Nawab Ali (33), owner of the bus Bashir Ahmed (35), his friend Lherrudin (35) and Moirangthem Nilakomol, a peon of the district cooperative office at Thoubal who was a polling personnel, were forced out of the vehicle by the security forces. 'As we first approached Tonsen Lamkhai Chingjing, we heard sounds of firing from 1.15 p.m. and it continued upto 1.45 p.m., said Akoijam Mangi Singh, a polling personnel who was one of the passengers. 'Minutes after the shooting stopped, some angry CRPF personnel came to the bus which was parked near the ambush site and called out the civilians. Since I was in front seat. I Followed them. But when I saw the CRPF personnel kicking, hitting, beating the four of them (the driver, owner, his friend and Nilakomol) with butts I sensed danger and somehow managed to slip back inside the bus.' All four were taken to ambush site near a bus stand where, according to the lone survivor Nilakomol, they had been lined up before being gunned down. Another victim. Mangte Sangte of Tonsen village had been waiting for a bus when the shooting started. Three friends. Nandakumar, Kirankumar and Ibochouba of Sugnu Napet also got killed at the bus stand. While Ngaseppam Thanil and Sagolsem Brajamani of Uchiwa area who were coming back home in a truck, were killed by stray bullets, tenth victim Thinguiam Manglembi, a village girl, was roaming there at the time of the incident.

CRPF authorities denied opening fire at the civilians and maintained that all the ten civilian victims were killed in the 'crossfire'. Nilakomol who was injured in the firing said the security forces refused to let the bus go and instead forced the passengers to get down.'

They roughly pushed us, ordered us to raise our hand and suddenly started firing indiscriminately.' The first few shots missed but, as the firing continued, a bullet stuck my left arm. I fell down facing the ground. The driver of the bus fell in front of me; another person on my right and yet another behind me,' he said pointing out that he had never lost consciousness. Nilakomol who pretended to be dead got up when the state police personnel arrived at the spot, and shouted 'please save my life.' Later it was learnt that the ambush was carried out by the guerrillas of the Manipur People's Army (MPA), armed wing of the UNLF.

People were outraged over the killings of ten civilians at Tonsen Lamkhai, and various social organisations demanded holding of a judicial enquiry into the incident. The organisations including the All Manipur Students Union (AMSU), the biggest students' body in Manipur, also demanded immediate withdrawal of the Armed Forces (Special Powers) Act, 1958 (amended in 1972) from the state. Sit-in protests by womenfolks, demonstrations at various places and public meetings to arouse public opinion were organised across the state to register strong objection to the frequent killings of civilians in the name of tracking down armed insurgents and to exert pressure on the government to withdraw the Armed Forces (Special Powers) Act. The public also resented the activities unleashed by various underground organisations at the populated area.

Frequent killings of civilians in insurgency-related incidents were alienating the public from the security forces whose counter-insurgency operations needed the cooperation of the civil population to produce the desired results. Also it has never been made public what is the policy of the government towards tackling the insurgents in the region. Every political party, in their election manifesto, asserted that only a 'political solution' to the insurgency problem would bring ever lasting peace in Manipur. The central government, if necessary, should amend the constitution to guarantee protection of the territorial integrity of each state in the north eastern region, and also some provisions to protect the identity of the original inhabitants of respective state besides working for all round economic development of the region. For instance, intelligence reports point out, some section of people felt 'identity' of original inhabitants may be lost in some states in the region like the case of Tripuris in Tripura in view of the unceasing inflow of people from other big states, and mooted the idea of introducting 'inner line permit system' again in Manipur. Manipur had an inner line permit system under which people from other states cannot purchase land and settle in the state but that system was abolished about some decades ago. It has also been stated that while the security forces were suppressing the violent activities of the underground members, there should be vigorous implementation of job-oriented development programmes to distract the minds of the educated youths from joining the underground ranks. In any case, there is no clear-cut policy to deal with insurgency problem in the north eastern region particularly in the state of Manipur.

Hardly the dust fluttered by the Tonsen Lamkhai massacre had settled (the government decided to order a magisterial enquiry into the incident) when another similar incident shocked the public. In the beginning of the counter-insurgency operations in early eighties, it may be noted, if the civilians were killed by 'mistake,' they were earlier termed as 'insurgents,' 'extremists.' etc. But the innocent people who lost lives in insurgency-related violence in nineties or early 2000 would be acknowledged as 'civilian victims' killed in either 'crossfire' or 'encounter' between the security forces and armed insurgents. At the time of the Manipur assembly elections in early 2000, various underground organisations intensified their activities by planting bombs at the roads where security forces would pass, ambushing the personnel at several places, hurling grenades at the residences of some Members of Legislative Assembly (MLAs).

Greatly concerned over the increasing underground activities, the state government kept all police and security posts on full alert to detect the movement of the armed militants. In fact, free campaigning was disrupted. Intelligence reports indicated that the insurgents who had served notices to prominent legislators and ministers to 'donate generously' to the underground organisations were targeting those persons who failed to fulfil the underground demands. However, most of the underground outfits had earlier stated publicly that they had nothing to do with what they called 'India-sponsored elections' in Manipur. As the situation was becoming grave, army and para-military forces stepped up roving patrol, launched surprise and random checking of passers-by everywhere, continued mopping-up operations at any suspected area, arrested numbers of underground elements.

It was during this period that a patrol party of the Assam Rifles was returning from Nambol in Bishnupur district to Imphal on 2 November, 2000. As the para-military forces reached Malom area near Imphal airport at around 3.30 p.m. a powerful bomb earlier planted and concealed on main Imphal-Tiddim road by unknown underground elements went off injuring some personnel. The remaining irate jawans jumped from the vehicles and opened fire in different directions. Assam Rifles said its personnel returned the fire following an attack from the insurgents. Altogether ten persons including a woman and her two nephews in a nearby bus stand were killed. While the forces maintained that the victims were killed in the 'crossfire', eyewitnesses and 'first official reports' contradicted the version of the para-military forces. A magisterial enquiry was ordered by the government but its findings have not been made public. What came to be known as 'Malom killings,' the incident shocked, angered and provoked the public with various social organisations, women's groups, student bodies, public leaders demanding a judicial enquiry and immediate withdrawal of the Armed Forces (Special Powers) Act from the state.' People mostly women folks in thousands demonstrated against the killings of innocent civilians by launching sit-in protests across the state for months. How deeply hurt the sentiments of the people could be adjudged from the wide scale protests from various social organisations which also demanded the resignation of the then united legislature front ministry headed by Chief Minister Nipamacha Singh for 'failing' to protect the lives of common citizens. Protesting against the

'Malom killings,' a 32-years old women. Irom Sharmila went on fast unto death from 4 November, 2000 demanding immediate withdrawal of the Armed Forces (Special Powers) Act from the State, Sharmila, who was arrested on many occasions and kept in judicial custody, continued fasting more than a year even in the jail. In August 2001, a medical board was also constituted to check Sharmila's condition and report the matter to the state government since her condition became worst. However, the woman continued fasting in spite of persuasion by many including public leaders to stop her agitation. Sharmila hails from Kongpal area in Imphal East district and was an active social worker. Well-known political and other personalities visited the 'fasting woman' and persuaded her to stop the agitation though the cause was 'right'. Even some central ministers on tour in Manipur visited the fasting social activist who even attracted the attention of the national media. Interestingly, some of the political leaders who 'sided' with Sharmila and supported her demand remained 'silent' on the issue of withdrawal of the Armed Forces (Special Powers) Act when they came to power after the fall of the Nipamacha Singh ministry.

On 2 November, 2000, the day ten civilians were killed at Malom area, near the Imphal airport, two of the victims—52 year old Oinam Sanatomba and 35-year old Kanguiam Ngouba, both employees of the state food and civil supply (FCS) department—could have survived had they left the office as usual after the office hours. That day, the two from Malom area had decided to leave the office ten or fifteen minutes before closing to go for some private work. As they entered the 'cordoned off' area, they were asked to stop. Some gunshots were heard after that. At a nearby bus stop, 52-year old Laishangbam Ongbi Sana Devi was waiting for a passenger bus along with her two nephews. 18-year old Sin am Bocha Singh alias Gotomba and his elder, 25 year old Sinam Robin, an assistant teacher of Malom Megha High School. Bocha Singh was a winner of national bravery award. In fact, Bocha Singh and Robin were giving their aunt company who visited their house that day. While waiting for bus, they heard the sound of the explosion which was not far from the bus stop. Soon they found themselves in the cordoned off area, and local residents heard several gunshots in different directions. The place where the three got killed was about 200 metres away from the spot where two employees of the FCS department were gunned down. The other victims were 34-year old Amakcham Raghumani, a farmer, three students—18-years old Tokpam Santikumar, 15-year old Soibam Prakash and 20-year old Ksh. Inaocha, and 55-year old Gurumayum Bapu Sharma, an employee of state revenue department.

Of all the 'disappearance' cases, the Sanamacha issue had not only rocked the entire state with widespread protests from several organisations and different sections of people over the 'unknown whereabouts' of a school student who had been 'picked up' by security forces in late nineties, but it also attracted international attention and condemnation. It may be pointed out that 'disappearance' in the human rights parlance refers to the phenomena of abducting a person by agents of the state, and whose whereabouts are concealed and whose custody is denied by the authority. Various cases of 'disappearance' have come up in Manipur since the active counter-insurgency operations began in 1980, and in spite of intervention by the judiciary and court orders, several persons like Chandam Chaoba Singh, Kangujam Loken, Thokchom Lokendro, Yumlembam Sanamacha, Laishram Bijoykumar, etc. who all had been taken away by the security forces from their respective houses have not returned homes so far. It may be stated that underground members, their sympathisers were often subjected to severe torture after arrest to extract information on their activities; and those who yielded to such harassment, torment were taken along with the security forces to serve as 'informers' to identify their former friends, associates or sheltering places. It may again be pointed out that the picking up of any underground suspect or a civilian may be deliberate, a case of mistaken identity, vested interests of 'informers,' or for the reasons best known to the captors. What is to be noted is that many innocent civilians have fallen victims to the 'involuntary disappearances' in the hands of uniform personnel.

It was like a midnight knock on the door of the house of an opponent by secret police in either a communist-ruled state or Germany under Nazi. But, it happened in a backward region of a democratic country like India. Around midnight, there was knock on the door of the house of Yumlembam Jugol Singh of Angtha village under Yairipok police station in Manipur's Thoubal district on 12 February, 1998. Everyone in the family was surprised thinking who could be the persons knocking the door at the dead of the night. Seconds later, some familiar voice called 'Sanamacha, Sanamacha, open the door.' Thus the 15-year old Yumlembam Sanamacha, a school student, was taken away from his home by the personnel of 17th Raj Rifles who had also picked up the student's two other friends, Inao and Bimol, from the same village. As the news of arrest of the three youths spread across the village in the night, local leaders and women's group protested and demanded the immediate release of the three youths at the gate of the security post at around 1 a.m. on 13 February, 1998. Only Inao and Bimol were handed over to the nearby Yairipok police station. Suspicious over the manner of the security forces, hundreds of students and staff members of the Ramananda High School, Angtha village marched 3-kms in a protest rally from Yairipok police station to the army post while about 1000 people from Angtha village launched a sit-in protest in front of the Chief Minister's office at Imphal till 10 p.m. demanding safe release of Sanamacha on 14 February, 1998. This time, unlike in similar circumstances earlier, there had been spontaneous reactions from different organisations and sections of the people against the involuntary 'disappearance' of the village youth. Of course, people had amply demonstrated against the 'disappearance' of persons on many previous occasions. For months together, there had been agitations by various groups and organisations on the Sanamacha issue. Classes in educational institutions were boycotted indefinitely and sit-in protests, relay hunger strike, demonstrations, processions, etc. launched across the state demanding safe release of the student. Frequent 'Manipur bandh' was called to draw the anger of the public on the issue by the All Manipur Students Union. The AMSU also boycotted all the central government offices located in the state for months. The AMSU also organised what it called 'communication blockade' disrupting the transport services between Manipur and neighbouring states. Several memoranda were submitted to the central leaders including the Prime Minister, the Defence Minister, the state government and other relevant authorities demanding immediate release of Sanamacha. A complaint was also filed with the National Human Rights Commission on 15 June, 1998.

Following two separate petitions of habeas corpus filed by the public relations officer of the Chief Minister's Office and Y. Radheshyam, elder brother of the victim, Guwahati High Court on 9 March, 1998 ordered the District and Session Judge (Imphal East) to conduct an inquiry into the Sanamacha disappearance case and submit a report to the Court. At the same time, the state government on 12 March 1998 also instituted a Commission of Inquiry led by a retired judge under the Commission of Inquiry Act, 1952. As pressure from the public to release the youth was increasing. Chief Minister Nipamacha Singh announced on the floor of the assembly on 16 March 1998 about the inquiries being conducted on the disappearance of Sanamacha. This, however, did not pacify the public whose widespread agitation forced the member of Parliament, W. Angou Singh move a call attention motion on the Sanamacha issue in Parliament on 2 April, 1998. To lodge a strong protest against the mysterious disappearance of the village youth, local dailies appeared 'blank editorial' on 15 April, 1998. Public became more suspicious about the involvement of the security forces when a single bench of Guwahati High Court rejected the army's plea against the Commission of Inquiry instituted by the state government in April 1998.

A high level army court of inquiry led by the General Officer Commanding (Eastern Region) visited the house of Sanamacha on 28 July, 1998, and on 4 August principal bench of Guwahati High Court ordered the Commission of Inquiry (instituted by the state government) to continue its proceedings. The report of inquiry conducted by the District and Session Judge (Imphal East). M. Binoykumar under the direction of the Guwahati High Court said 'Sanamacha Singh was apprehended by an army column between 12th and 13th February, 1998 from his house at Angtha Mayai Leikai and that he was taken to the army camp at (nearby) Yairipok along with two others. The said Sanamacha Singh has neither been released nor handed over to the police after the arrest. There is no sufficient evidence to show that the said Sanamacha Singh was a member of (underground) United National Liberation Front at the relevant time.' In the meantime, the Commission of Inquiry also submitted its report to the state government on 25 September, 1998 but it has not so far been made public. Some human rights groups particularly the 'Human Rights Alert' moved heaven and earth to trace whereabouts of the missing youth, ultimately attracting the attention of the London-based Amnesty International and United Nations Commission on Human Rights.

In its report to the 55th session of the UN Commission on Human Rights, the UN Working Group on Enforced and Involuntary Disappearances as per the 'UN document E/CN.4/1999/62 stated "167 as follows: ... in Manipur ... grave concern has been expressed about attempts by the armed forces to prevent judicial inquiries ordered by the State government into the disappearance of a 15 year old school boy. Yumlembam Sanamacha, who was reportedly arrested by members of the 17 Rajputana Rifles on 12 February, 1998. Allegedly in many a cases of disappearance, the army has taken shelter behind the Armed Forces (Assam and Manipur) Special Powers Act of 1958, which, it is said, confers on the armed forces broadly defined shoot-to-kill powers and provides them with virtual immunity from prosecution .... In the case of the disappearance of the 15 year old school boy from Manipur, the Government replied that he had been apprehended by the security forces during a search operation on suspicion of belonging to a terrorist organisation, the United National Liberation Front, and had managed to escape when the security forces, who were taking him to be handed over to the police, had been attacked by members of 'Meira Paibis,' a women's organisation, seeking to effect the release of the persons apprehended. The government also stated that a case had been filed with the Imphal Bench of Guwahati High Court regarding the alleged disappearance and a counter affidavit had been filed by the Army.' But the issue remained unsolved as the authorities could not produce Sanamacha before the Court where the case was still going on.

About the 'disappearances' of Thokchom Lokendro and Kangujam Loken who had both been picked up on 23 September, 1980 by 15th Jammu and Kashmir Rifles from Singjamei Makha Pebia Pandit Leikai and Khongman Makha in Imphal, the supreme court (Criminal Appeal No. 580-581 of 1989) directed the District Judge. Manipur to conduct an inquiry to ascertain the facts. The inquiry report, submitted to the apex court, established that Loken and Lokendro were arrested by the 15th Jammu and Kashmir Rifles and 'were not released yet.' Thereafter, the supreme court passed an interim order on 2 August, 1991 directing the union government to pay Rs 1.50 lakh each to the two families and held that the state government was expected to take further necessary action to ascertain and fix the responsibility for the 'death or continued wrongful detention of Lokendro and Loken.' It was also expected to take all appropriate actions against each of the individuals including their prosecution for the offence committed by them, but no concrete steps in this regard have been taken up. For the mysterious disappearance of Laishram Bijoykumar, a former student activist, there had been public outcry for over six months demanding the revelation of identity of captors. Bijoykumar was picked up from his house at Thangmeiband in Imphal on 4 June, 1996 by some Hindi speaking persons in military uniform whose identity was not disclosed. In spite of moving a habeas corpus petition at the court, it has not been known who had abducted him, and for what cause. There are other insurgency-related cases of 'disappearance' of innocent civilians and the whereabouts of Khundrakpam Yaima alias Boyai (student) of Kwakeithel area in Imphal West district and Tayab Ali (a salesman) of Kairang Muslim Mayai Leikai in Imphal East district have not been known in spite hectic efforts to trace them. They are some of many such cases.

It was not only in the hands of the security forces that the civilians had become victims or suffered due to alleged security excesses, harassment, torture, atrocities. In Manipur, many civilians, law-abiding citizens have fallen prey to some armed insurgents who also harassed, tortured or shot dead either in cases of mistaken identity, of not paying the 'demand money', of defying 'underground order' or of involving in the activities of rival organisations.

When encountered, anybody would have taken them as army, para-military forces or police commandos either patrolling the national highway number 53 (Imphal-Jiribam-Silchar road) or checking the passengers travelling along the highway to detect the movement of armed militants. In fact, the two national highways, the other one being the Imphal-Dimapur-Guwahati road number 39, have been virtually under the 'control and mercy' of various underground organisations who extorted, collected 'vehicle, goods and road taxes' from any passenger buses and trucks passing through it. In spite of several protests, memoranda and appeals, the central as well as the state governments had failed to 'clear' the highways of any problem. As stated in chapter one, more security and police posts were opened along the national highway number 53 because of reports of frequent lootings, robberies, skirmishes between forces and armed militants, etc. And on 25 June, 2000, when occupants of a passenger vehicle on way from Imphal to border town of Jiribam, about 222 kms west of the state capital, reached Leingangpokpi near the border, they noticed about 20 persons in uniform whom they took as security forces guarding the oft-trouble national highway, As none of the men signalled to stop the vehicle, the driver although concerned over the 'silent' attitude of the uniform personnel was quietly and slowly crossing over the area when the armed group all of a sudden opened fire indiscriminately at the occupants from automatic weapons from a distance of about fifty feet, Nine passengers including two women and two non-Manipuris were killed, The innocent victims were: L. Manisang (30), H. Nobin (30), H. Nilachandra (30), Ajay Bengali, Shanti Devi, S. Roy, H. Copper (24), Angom Sanjoy (24) and the driver, Noren. Taken by surprise and outraged over the 'deliberate' killings of civilians along the highway, several organisations including a Kuki underground outfit demanded the revelation of identity of killers as the incident, many viewed, was likely to incite communal disharmony among some communities in the state. Public were 'utterly shocked and dumbfounded' when after some days on oldest insurgency organisation. UNLF, which was considered as the 'highly-disciplined and mature organisation,' owned up to the killings of innocent civilians by members of its armed wind, Manipur People's Army in what they described as a 'case of mistaken identity.' The matter subsided with an unhappy note notwithstanding the admission of their 'wrongdoing.' The outfit said the incident would be 'investigated further,' but gave no more details.

What has been mentioned here are some of many such examples to reveal that in many insurgency-related incidents involving civilian victims, it has been the public who suffered most in the armed conflicts in this tiny, north eastern state. It is very difficult to say which part of Manipur both in hills and plains is 'safe.' It is not only in some interior places but also in the urban areas that the underground's writ runs. Those who disobeyed the 'order' were either 'eliminated or punished.' This is the situation in Manipur where people are also found of celebrating any kind of festival in spite of even 'worsening' law and order situation. Are celebrating festivals more important than first understanding, analysing, discussing, studying the present 'many serious problems' confronting Manipur which is also facing a threat to its territorial integrity? Are people aware, before it is too late, of the problems the future generations will face? Who will give proper answer to these questions?

'Holi' used to be celebrated with pomp and gaiety, but now-a-days it has been replaced by various sports functions organised at different localities during the normally-five-day festival. After the festival, young boys and girls also performed 'thabal chongba' (a kind of traditional form of dance at the time of festival). The festival sometimes coincided with the final examinations of the high school leaving certificate, and social organisations including student bodies in such case and also for other reasons urged the people to limit the celebrations of the festival. On one occasion, the banned PREPAK in 2001 'prevented' the observance of the 'holi' festivities including 'thabal chongba' for not more than five days. What is interesting in Manipur is, sometimes local clubs, groups, bodies, etc., would issue 'notice or appeal' through local dailies saying.... 'dear brothers, sisters (in an apparent reference to underground members)... please allow us to perform thabal chongba on such and such date ... or this and that person has committed some crime, please punish the culprit, etc. etc'. For a person who has come from other states and seen such 'notice' or 'appeal' would perhaps feel that hardly anyone can go against underground diktat. Even for a personal cause, sometimes 'underground help' was sought. Is it an irony that sometimes members of the public instead of seeking justice from the government for correcting the 'wrongs done to them' either by any individual or groups, they 'approached' underground members to bring 'justice.' Why can't the authorities check and deal with these things properly? For instance, a girl was raped by someone. Instead of lodging a complaint with the police, the victim or her family would approach the 'armed persons' who, after 'doing their own investigation,' would bring them what some termed 'instant justice.' This type of example must not be taken wrongly. It is not to say that every person goes to the underground members either for 'instant justice' or for any kind of help. The insurgents also 'helped' those who sought their assistance for 'justice'—may be they are trying to win over the public. What is to be pointed out is that there are some people who sought underground help. There have also been instances that armed persons sometimes entered a house whose members were dead against the insurgents, and forced them to prepare food and slept the night. The security forces also subjected such family members to extreme harassment for 'sheltering' the underground members. Is not the situation complex in Manipur?

Even for newspersons based at Imphal, they sometimes faced difficulty not in filing stories by using not-so-advanced-communication set up in the region but in explaining the 'contents' of some stories which their colleagues at the metro desks found it a new and hard to believe. Some militants based at the hills have been, as mentioned before, extorting money from passenger buses and trucks passing through the national highways. Recently, the militants have 'increased' the rates of 'annual, goods, vehicle, road taxes, etc.' and local transports organisations particularly the All Manipur Road Transport Drivers' and Motor Workers' Union submitted memorandum in March 1999 to the Union Home Minister and other relevant authorities seeking 'protection' at the highways. They also pointed out that the militants 'collected' the money from places very close to security and police posts. The people outside the state may not believe that neither the state nor the central government provided security forces to the vehicles plying along the highways to protect them from paying 'underground taxes.' Considered as 'lifeline,' people in the state were, as stated before, often thrown to extreme inconvenience when blockade was launched on the Imphal-Guwahati and Imphal-Silchar routes.

In Manipur, some of the officials are also still in the old-fashioned manner of functioning, not adjusting themselves to the changing situation. What is again funny is that some so-called 'bureaucrats' whose ignorance and irresponsibilities have resulted in turning things against the government, appear to be not guiding the government in proper way. Why didn't the government and its machineries try to wean away public from seeking 'help from underground groups' and instil confidence in the minds of the people that the government was all out to protect the citizens at all costs? It should also let know the people that the government was prepared to help poor and needy by speeding up development programmes, provide employment to youths by effectively implementing the self-employed schemes, etc. There are many ways to improve small scale and cottage industries with little loan from the government. This will also give large scale employment to several persons in Manipur which is also known for handloom and handicraft products. How government agencies exploit small loan-seekers are also well known in the state.

PREPAK's call to limit the celebration of holi festival for five days from 9 March, 2001 was resented by some local clubs though they could not express it openly. Appeals were also made through the columns of local dailies to the underground organisations to allow 'thabal chongba' for more days before or after the holi festival. It was not known who were the assailants. Some unidentified gunmen opened fire at crowds participating in 'thabal chongba' at three different places in Imphal one day before the holi festival killing a 17 year old youth identified as Maimom Johnson and injured four others. The incidents which were the first of its kind, and shocked the public greatly, occurred simultaneously at Heirangoithong Maibam Leikai, Kiyamgei Heibong Makhong Lampak and Khaidem Makha Leikai Patsoi area, all in the outskirts of the state capital. Nobody had expected that the shots would be fired at the crowds by the unidentified gunmen. Growing concern among the members of the public over the killings of innocent civilians by armed persons was noticed as various organisations demanded the revelation of identity of the attackers. It was also clear that neither the nine victims at Leingangpokpi area on Imphal-Jiribam-Silchar highway on 25 June, 2000 nor Maimom Johnson was killed in crossfire between the security forces and armed insurgents. They like many others were also not the victims of underground factional fights.

It is a fact that many civilians have fallen victims at the hands of the armed persons but what is again noteworthy were the killings of journalists. Intellectuals, public leaders and social organisations in the state were greatly concerned over the attacks on media persons by unidentified gunmen. Were some sections of the 'armed persons' trying to gag the press by eliminating those whose writings, they thought, were against their interests.

It may be pointed out that the cause of the gunning down of Editor of a local daily, '*Manipur News.*' Thounaojam Brajamani who had expressed some views against 'some armed persons' in August 2000 at Imphal is still unknown to the public. Whether his 'elimination' was connected with personal enmity or for a cause is still not known. Brajamani who had founded the once-popular daily was shot dead by two unidentified gunmen at a place between Meino Leirak and Keisampat Thiyam Leirak in the heart of high-security Imphal town on 20 August, 2000 at around 10.30 p.m. while he was going to print his paper. No organisation or individual has so far claimed responsibility for the killing of the veteran journalist. However, in case of the Editor of a local journal '*Shan*' in Hmar dialect, H.A. Lalrohlu, who was shot dead on 10 October, 1999 at New Saikot in Manipur's Churachandpur district, the motive behind the crime was very clear. Hmar Revolutionary Front (HRF) in a statement on 14 October disclosed that its men had killed Lalrohlu and three others for 'working against the interests of the HRF,' an underground group whose aim is what they termed to 'protect' the Hmar community from the 'aggressive' nature of the Kukis, Mizos and other larger communities. 'Since it is the handiwork of the HRF no one should further investigate into the killings and we appeal to all concerned not to dig deeper into the matter,' said the HRF statement. What if public wanted to know more about the activities of Lalrohlu that led to his killing. In most cases, it has been one way communication.

An educated unemployed youth who started a taxi service after getting a loan from the bank, Laishram Gunindro was forced to take an injured underground member to the Catholic Mission Hospital at Koirengei in the outskirts of Imphal on 2 September, 2000 from Kangla Park in the heart of the town. Since then his whereabouts was not known for more than a month, and a joint action committee formed by the local residents of Gunindro's locality had exerted maximum pressure on the state government to trace the Maruti van driver. To a great shock and surprise to the public an underground group styled itself as the Kanglei Yawol Kann Lup (KYKL Kangjamba) in a statement on 18 October, 2000 claimed that Gunindro was killed for what the group called 'betraying' two KYKL (Kangjamba) men who were later arrested by Assam Rifles personnel. The body of the taxi driver who had been buried at Langol Ching area in Imphal west district was unearthed while some employees of the state forest department were cleaning forests and trying to plant bamboo saplings. There was nothing the people could do nor was there proper explanation of about how the youth had 'betrayed' the underground men. Several senior officials including Chief Engineer (works). S. Binoykumar Singh, Chief Engineer (public health engineering), Thingom Ibochouba, Loktak hydro electric project Chief Engineer, Subhas Chandra Ser, Director (health services), Surchand Singh, a telecom department engineer, Ambe. Director (Tourism), Dasarath Prasad (a senior Indian Administrative Service officer), an executive engineer of Singda dam project, A.K. Mathur, an assistant accounts officer of the project, T.K. Das, a contractor of the project, Phoni Bhushan Verma, etc., fell to the bullets of underground members belonging to different organisations. Refusal to concede to underground pressure was one of some reasons for eliminating these officials. According to high-ranking sources in the government, Prasad (shot dead in 1999). Ibochouba (12.8.1998), Ser (12.1.2000), Ambe (20.1.2001), etc, were known for their 'efficiency' in the respective departments. However, some of the officials had been eliminated for their 'activities' against the public interest; said sources. One can now well imagine how is the situation in the state where even the priests are not spared.

Public were stunned when armed militants brutally gunned down three Catholic priests who were working at the Don Bosco Training Centre at Ngariyan hill, about 10 kms south-eat of Imphal, on 15 May, 2001. It was not the first time the militants had killed the priests. The shooting down of Reverend Father Pali Akara Raphael (43), the Director of the Don Bosco Training Centre, his assistant Father Andreas Kindo (35) and another assistant, Brother Shinu Joseph (25) at one time after calling them out in the night not only shocked the entire people in the state but attracted international condemnation of the incident. Prime Minister A.B. Vajpayee was informed of the incident by the Catholic Bishops Conference of India which also strongly condemned the killings. The incident unnerved the Catholic priests when they were yet to recover from the shock they received in the wake of kidnapping and gunning down of Father Jacob Chittinapilly on 2 December, 2000 by two unidentified gunmen at Sugnu area in the state's Thoubal district. Sources in St. Joseph's Parish Church at Sugnu told the author that some underground members had demanded money from the Church authorities. In the case of 15 May, 2001 incident, police named KYKL (Kangiamba) activists as killers of the priests but the group denied the police version. According to police, the militants who demanded a huge sum of money argued with Raphael who gave them Rs 35,000. Angered for not paying the full amount, the armed persons threatened to kill the priests if the full amount was not paid. After some arguments, the militants took out their small arms, and shot at Raphael and Kindo from a point blank range. The two died instantaneously. At the sight of this horrible scene, Joseph shouted for help but he was also gunned down within seconds.

Sometimes majority of the government officials are in a fix-which order they should follow, the government or the underground organisationts). If they defied the former, they would attract penalty, and if they disobeyed the later, it would be the question of their lives. 'It has been brought to the notice of the State Government that demand letters and extortion notes have been issued by/in the names of the unlawful organisations to various offices, individual, government servants, businessmen and selected members of the general public,' said a Manipur government circular dated 7 April, 1999, signed by the Chief Secretary, H. Jel Shyam (now he is no more). The circular 'directed' the departments and government servants that 'such demand letters received from any unlawful organisation shall be deposited in original with the Director General of Police, Manipur as soon as it is received by them.' It also asked businessmen and the members of the general public who have received such demand letters to deposit the same with the DGP (Manipur) for 'further necessary action.' Under no circumstances any government department or government servants shall pay any money to the unlawful organisations in response to such demand letter, the circular said adding that non-compliance with this circular shall attract necessary suitable action. It may also be pointed out that extortion from the public or officials had been going on for the past some years, and some of the officials who had fallen victims at the hands of the underground members were also connected with the 'demand letters' served to them earlier. In the middle of May 2001, several officials of different departments including works, taxation, health and food and civil supply were arrested by the police for allegedly giving money to various underground organisations. The officials who were picked up for questioning included cashier of taxation, accountant and cashier of health department, six executive engineers and two clerks of works department, superintendent: and five store keepers of food and civil supply department. Obviously, such cases are many.

Factional Fights Among Various Underground Organisations

They called 'brothers,' 'friends,' 'revolutionaries,' 'compatriots,' 'freedom fighters,' among themselves, and were once comrades-in-arms. Together, they suffered hardships over the years in thick, inaccessible jungles, risked lives on many occasions, journeyed miles of rugged hilly tracks, pledged to fight for the 'motherland' till death separated them, attacked on enemies, stood against the opponents several times, spent uncertain moments at various camps in the deep bushes under constant threats from the government forces. They underwent the same training in guerrilla warfare, vowed to remain united through thick and thin to carryon the message of armed propaganda till the 'achievement' of their goal.

What tore them apart after years of fighting together against the government forces and other opponents still remain a mystery but they started calling one another as 'reactionaries,' 'spies of the enemies,' 'black sheeps,' 'destroyers of the national liberation movement,' 'agents of the government,' etc., 'Differences' which had cropped up among senior members over the style of functioning of top leaders and change of policy to compromise the underground 'cause' also greatly contributed to the birth of some underground factions and armed conflicts among them. By 2001, different underground organisations and factions were, as stated before, locked in internecine, bloody feuds which resulted in the heavy loss of lives in this trouble-torn state. They were gunning for each other wherever they met.

Since early nineties, there have been reports of 'youth (s) shot dead by unidentified gunmen,' 'youth called out and killed,' 'militants kidnapped and gunned down youth (s),' 'former underground men killed by unidentified persons,' 'underground men killed in factional fight,' 'unidentified youths killed and buried,' etc. etc. which filled columns of several local dailies almost everyday. Most of these reports were connected with the clashes between two underground groups, or within the factions. The enmity and animosity between underground factions were so deep-rooted at some point of time that their unending bloody clashes caused serious concern among various social organisations and women's groups who appealed to them to stop 'fratricidal killings,' However the warring sides would wait for any opportune moment to eliminate each other.

Considered as 'well-organised' underground organisation, the UNLF and some its former members who formed KYKL-O, backed by the NSCN-IM, had been engaging in a factional fight for some years until the PREPAK-sponsored truce between the two was reached on 12 June, 2001. Earlier, appeals from various organisations and public to stop the 'senseless killings' among the underground members had gone unheeded and warring sides called each other names. At one point of time, the enmity was so deep rooted that the members of the rival group were not only shot but killed after brutal torture. There are many such examples. Sometimes, innocent civilians also fell victims in the underground factional fight.

They came in military uniform in a vehicle in the night on 22 October, 2000 at Langmeidong area in Thoubal district, opened fire in the air causing panic among local population and threatened to shoot anyone who dared to come out. They beat up some people who were around Langmeidong market. Tension was high in the area as well-armed activists of the suspected KYKL-O were freely hunting for some UNLF members at Elangkhangpokpi and nearby Langmeidong area. In two separate incidents, three UNLF members-Wareppam Khingba alias Manikumar and Ningthoujam Ningthoujao alias Momocha, and Okram Kathokpa along with a civilian identified as Wakhom Shyamananda were gunned down on 20 October, 2000 at Elangkhangpokpi and on 22 October, 2000 at Langmeidong by suspected KYKL-O. What is particular about this incident was that the four victims had been severely tortured before they were gunned down. Local sources identified Shyamanda as an 'innocent civilian.' The KYKL-O had also earlier blamed the UNLF for eliminating its members who, the UNLF alleged, were in collusion with 'other enemies' trying to destroy the oldest underground organisation in Manipur. The KYKL-O denied the UNLF charges and also added that. Shyamananda was 'connected' with the latter. While the UNLF and the NSCN-IM have also been gunning for each other for the past some years, the latter also can not see eye to eye with member of the NSCN-K. While most of the NSCN-IM members were driven out of upper Myanmar area, NSCN-K is still maintaining some of its camps there. Over 300 NSCN cadres were killed during the factional fight between NSCN-IM and NSCN-K in upper Myanmar camps in 1988. As the killings between the two factions were continuing unabated and causing public concern, the NSCN-K in September 2000 offered the NSCN-IM a 'unilateral ceasefire' which was rejected by the latter saying 'the truce offer of NSCN-K is valid only in the present state of Nagaland.' NSCN-IM said its rival faction was trying to 'differentiate Nagas of Nagaland and Nagas of other areas.' However, a statement of the NSCN-K said since the ceasefire between the government of India and NSCN-IM was enforced only in Nagaland, its offered was also limited only to Nagaland, adding there was no question of differentiating the Nagas of Nagaland and Nagas of other areas. It also stressed the need for cessation of hostilities between the warring Nagas for bringing 'peace and unity.'

Some hill-based Kuki underground organisations were also locked in intra-party clashes. Small organisations like HRF and HRA are no longer active because most of its leaders have surrendered to the authorities. What is again to be noted is that remaining HRF men and HPC-D were also locked in factional fight. Manipur has truly become a killing field. Hardly a day has passed without the report(s) of killing a person or persons either in insurgency-related violence, intra-party clashes or ethnic feud. It also remains to be seen how far some major underground organisations of different communities, which are so far refraining from attacking each other, would remain 'neutral or stay away' from committing violence among themselves in this tiny state because their aims and objects conflicted one another. What would be the future of Manipur? It must here be pointed out that the armed struggles launched by some major insurgent outfits for 'an independent Manipur' or 'for secession of the north eastern region' remain a political issue and there should be a political settlement on these issues. Wiser minds should comment on these issues but onething is clear, involved parties should have the minds to settle the issues before beginning the 'political dialogues' and should adjust themselves even by withdrawing slightly from their declared 'aims and objects' or by amending some provisions of the constitution, if necessary.

Would not it be a 'big blunder' if the central government concedes to either the demands or aspiration of various small underground groups which wanted fragmentation of Manipur or some north eastern states into pieces to form so-called 'homelands' or separate smaller states (or union territories)? The problems arising out of it will never be ending. On the other hand, would all the more than 18 underground organisations, factions, groups, etc., meet and discuss jointly on the 'issues' for which they are fighting for? For the moment, it is very doubtful. At present, it is also very unlikely that some smaller groups would realise whether they are really fighting for a cause or not. Or have some underground faction(s) been formed to counter the major insurgent outfits? It appears that the present situation in the region is very complex. Manipur appears to be drifting towards an uncertain, anarchic, chaotic future. Who will brake it? The question does not have an easy answer.

APPENDIX-I

Anglo-Manipuri Mutual Defence Treaty of 14 September 1762

Articles of Treaty between Hurray Das Gussein, acting on behalf of Jai Singh (Maharaja of Manipur) and Mr. Harry Verelst, Chief of Chittagong Factory, on behalf of the British dated the 14 September 1762.

(Home Department Public, 1762, 4 October, Nos. 2-3)

Article No. 1

That said Jai Singh, his master, shall be assisted with such of English troops as from time to time can be spared for the recovery of such lands and effects belonging to the said Jai Singh as he hath been dispossessed by the Burmahs (Burmese).

Article No. 2

That for the assistance of such English troops the said Jai Singh is willing and ready to pay at the immediate expiration of every month all and every expense and contingent expenses of such troops then due so long as they may remain in his service.

Article No. 3

That the said Jai Singh is willing and ready to join with all his force the said English forces to obtain full and ample satisfaction for all and every injury the said English have from time to time suffered by the Burmahs at the Negrairje (Negrais) or any other place during the said

Burmah's administration when in any time in possession of Pegu.

Article No. 4

That the said Jai Singh will from time of signing these Articles, consider such injuries as have been done by the Burmahs (Burmese) to the said English as injuries done to himself and that the said Jai Singh will ever hereafter be ready to resent any new insult or hindrance the English trade or people may meet with at Pegu, the Negrairje or any other part or parts at present under the government of the Burmah Rajah or the Rajah of Pegu—also every other power or Government that may interrupt the free trade of every English subject passing into and through their countries.

Article No. 5

That the said Jai Singh will at all times fully consider every enemy to the said English as his own enemy and that the said English shall consider every enemy to the said Jai Singh as their enemy.

Article No. 6

That the said Jai Singh shall grant such lands as the said English may think proper for the building of a factory and fort for the transaction of their business and protection of their persons and effects in every part under his Government and that whatever part the said English may fix on for their factory and fort the said Jai Singh shall also grant a distance of country round such factory and fort of eight thousand cubits to the said English free of rent forever.

Article No.7.

That the said Jai Singh shall grant permission to the English for an open trade into and through his country/free of all duties, hindrance or molestation and that the said Jai Singh will ever protect and defend the said English.

Article No. 8

That the said Jai Singh shall not enter into any accommodation with the Burmah Rajah without the advice and approbation of the English nor shall the English enter into a separate and distinct treaty with the Burmah Rajah without previously advising the said Jai Singh.

Article No. 9

Should the English troops with those of Mackley be obliged to march against the Burmah Rajah in order to obtain satisfaction for their mutual injuries received and in consequence make themselves masters of the Burmah country the said Jai Singh doth then agree that should the said English then give him full possession of the said Burmah country he, the said Jai Singh will then make good to the said English all such losses as they have every heretofore sustained.

APPENDIX-II

Treaty of Yndaboo February 24, 1826

Article No. 1

There shall be perpetual peace and friendship between the Honourable Company on the one part, and His Majesty the King of Ava on the other.

Article No. 2

His Majesty the King of Ava renounces all claims upon, and will abstain from all future interferences with the principality of Assam and its dependencies, and also with the contiguous petty States of Cachar and Jyntea.

With regard to Munnipore (Manipur), it is stipulated that, should Gumbheer Singh desire to return to that country, he shall be recognised by the King of Ava as Rajah thereof.

(Signed Archibald Campbell) (L.S.)
Largeen Meonja,
(Woonghee)

(Signed) T.C. Robertson
Captain Royal Navy (L.S.)

(Seal of the lotoo)

(Signed) Hy. D. Chads
Captain Royal Navy (L.S.)

Shwagum Woon
Atawoon

APPENDIX-III

Anglo-Manipuri Treaty of 1833 Agreement between Rajah Gumbheer Singh and Commissioner F.J. Grant, 1833

The Governor-General and Supreme Council of Hindustan declare as follows: With regard to the two ranges of hills, the one called the Kala Naga range, and the other called Nungjai range, which are situated between the eastern and western bends of the Barak, we will give up all claim on the part of the Honourable company thereunto, and we will make these hills over to the possession of the Raja, and give him the line of the Jiri and the western bend of the Barak as a boundary, provided that the Raja agrees to the whole of what is written in this paper, which is follows:

1st: The Raja will, agreeably to instructions received, without delay remove his Thana from Chandrapur and establish it on the eastern bank of the Jiri.

2nd: The Raja will in no way obstruct the trade carried on between the two countries by Bengali or Manipuri merchants. He will not exact heavy duties, and he will make a monopoly of no articles of merchandise whatever.

3rd: The Raja will in no way prevent the Nagas inhabiting the Kala Naga and Nungjai ranges of hills from selling or bartering ginger, cotton, pepper, and every other article, the produce of their country, in the plains of Cachar, at the Banskandi and Oodherban bazaars, as has been their custom.

4th: With regard to the road commencing from the eastern bank of the Jiri, and continued via Kala Naga and Kowpum, as far as the valley of Manipur, after this road has been finished, the Raja will keep it in repairs so as to enable laden bullocks to pass during the cold and dry seasons. Further, at the making of the road, if British officers be sent to examine or superintend the same, the Raja will agree to everything these officers may suggest.

5th: With reference to the intercourse already existing between the territories of the British Government and those of the Raja, if the intercourse be further extended, it will be well in every respect, and it will be highly advantageous to both the Raja and his country. In order, therefore, that this may speedily take place, the Raja, at the requisition of the British Government, will furnish a quota of Nagas to assist in the construction of the road.

6th: In the event of war with the Burmans (Burmese), if the troops be sent to Manipur either to protect the country or to advance beyond the Ningthee, the Raja, at the requisition of the British Government, will provide hill porters to assist in transporting ammunition and baggage of such troops.

7th: In the event of anything happening on the eastern frontier of the British territories, the Raja will, when required, assist the British Government with a portion of his troops.

8th: The Raja will be answerable for all the ammunition he receives from the British Government, and will, for the information of the British Government, give in every month a statement of expenditure to the British officer attached to the Levy.

I, Shree Joot Gumbheer Singh of Munnipore, agree to all that is written above in this paper sent by the Supreme Council.

Dated 18th April, 1833
(A true translation)

Sd/-
Geo. Gordon, Lieut.
Adjutant, Gumbheer Singh's Levy
Signed and sealed in my presence

Sd/-
Shree Joot Rajah
Gumbheer Singh
(Seal)

Sd/-
F.J. Grant
Commissioner

APPENDIX-IV

Agreement Regarding the Kubo (Kabaw) Valley, 1834

First: The British Commissioners, Major Grant and Captain Pemberton, under instruction from the Right Honourable, the Governor-General in Council, agree to make over to the Woandauk Maha Mingyan Rajah and Tsarudangicks Myookyantheo, Commissioner appointed by the King of Ava, the Towns of Tammao (Tamu), Khumba (Khambat), Surjail, and all other villages in the Kubo Valley, the Ungoching Hills and the strip of valley running between the eastern foot and western bank of the Ningtha Khyendan (Chindwin) river.

Second: The British Commissioners will withdraw the Munnipore Thanas now stationed within this tract of the country and make over immediate possession of it to the Burmese Commissioner on certain conditions.

Third: The conditions are, that they will agree to the boundaries which may be pointed out to them by the British Commissioners, and will respect and refrain from any interference, direct or indirect, with the people residing on the Munnipooree side of those boundaries.

Fourth: The boundaries are as follows:

1. The eastern foot of the chain of mountains which are immediately from the western side of the plain of the Kubo valley. Within this line is included Moreh and all the country to the westward of it.
2. On the south a line extending from the eastern foot of the same hills at the point where the river, called by the Burmahs Nansawing and by the Munnipoorees Namsaulung, enters the plain, upto its sources and

across the hills due west down to the Kethe-Khyaung (Munnipooree River).

3. On the north the line of boundary will begin at the foot of the same hills at the northern extremity of the Kubo valley, and pass due north up to the first range of hills, east of that upon which stand the villages of Choatao, Naonghe, Noanghur of the tribe called by the Munnipoorees Loohooppa, and by the Burmah Lagumsauny, now tributary to Munnipoore.

Fifth: The Burmese Commissioners hereby promise that they will give orders to the Burmese officers, who will remain in the charge of the territory now made over to them not in any way to interfere with the Khyens or other inhabitants living on the Munnipoor side of the lines of boundary above described and the British Commissioners also promise that the Munnipoorees shall be ordered not in any way to interfere with the Khyens or other inhabitants of any description living on the Burmah side of the boundaries now fixed.

(Seal) Sd/- F.J. Grant, Major
Commissioners

(Seal) Sd/- R.B. Pemberton, *Captain*

Sunnyachil Ghat, Ningthee, 9th January, 1834.

APPENDIX-V

Agreement Regarding Compensation for Kubo (Kabaw) Valley, 1834

Major Grant and Captain Pemberton, under instructions from the Right Honourable the Governor-General in Council, having made over the Kubo Valley to the Burmese Commissioners deputed from Ava, are authorised to state:

1. That it is the intention of the Supreme Government to grant a monthly stipend of five hundred Sicca Rupees to the Rajah of Munnipore, to commence from the ninth day of January, One Thousand Eight Hundred and Thirty-four, the date at which the transfer of Kubo took place, as shown in the Agreement mutually signed by the British and Burmese Commissioners.

2. It is to be distinctly understood that should any circumstances hereafter arise by which the portion of territory lately made over to Ava again reverts to Munnipore, the allowance now granted by the British Government will cease from the date of such reversion.

(Sd/-)
F.J. Grant, Major

Commissioners

(Sd/-)
R. Boileu Pemberton, Captain

Langthabal Munnipore,
January 25, 1834

APPENDIX-VI

Manipur State Constitution Act, 1947

Whereas it is expedient to enact a law for the governance of the Manipur State, His Highness the Maharaja of Manipur is pleased to enact as follows:

Chapter I

1. *Title:* This Act shall be called the Manipur State Constitution Act, 1947.
2. Extent and application: This Act shall extend to the whole of the Manipur State inclusive of the Hill Areas saying that it shall not apply in any matter where a specific reservation of powers is made to any authority in the Hills under the provisions of the Manipur State Hill People's (Administration) Regulation, 1947.
3. *Government of the State by His Highness the Maharajah:* The territories for the time being and hereafter vested in the Maharajah are governed by and in the name of the Maharajah. All rights, authority and jurisdiction which appertain or are incidental to the Government of such territories are exercisable by the Maharajah subject to the provision of this Act.
4. *Succession:* Succession to the throne shall be governed by the Law of Primogeniture provided that the heir must be the legitimate son of a marriage recognised by the Council of Ministers. In the event of failure of heirs in the direct male line, His Highness the Maharajah shall, after consultation with the Council of Ministers and the Assembly, designate his heir.

5. *Attainment of Majority:* The Maharajah or his heir shall be taken to attain majority at the age of 21 years.
6. *Council of Regency:* (a) Where by reason of the Maharajah being a minor or where by reason of any mental defect or grave bodily sickness as a result of which the Maharajah becomes permanently incapable of exercising his powers, the Council of Ministers shall take steps to set up a Council of Regency which shall exercise those powers in the State and shall continue in office for such time as the Council may determine; (b) Notwithstanding the provisions of sub-section (a) above, the Maharajah in consultation with the Council of Ministers may, at any time or for any reason which may appear suitably, set up a Council of Regency to exercise his functions; (c) A Council of Regency set up under sub-section (a) and (b) above, may comprise of one or more persons as may seem desirably, the Regent or Council of Regency shall before taking office be required to take an oath before the State Assembly to be loyal to the State and to observe faithfully its Constitution and laws; (d) Where in any event it shall be necessary to set up a Council of Regency either for the reasons laid down in sub-sections (a) and (b) above or for any other reason or where for any reason the Maharajah has become incapable of exercising his powers before such Regency can be set up, the council of Ministers shall take whatever steps may be necessary for the governance of the State till such time as the Regency is created.
7. *Failure of heirs and disputed succession:* (a) In the event of failure of heirs in the direct male line and failure of the Maharaja to designate his heir under section 4 above, a joint extraordinary session of the State Assembly and the Council of Ministers shall immediately be convened and shall remain in closed and continuous session till it shall have determined by

a 75 per cent majority of the members present and voting, the person to whom the throne shall pass; (b) Where for any reason the succession to the throne is disputed, the Council of Ministers shall, on the death of the Ruler, take such steps as may immediately be necessary for the good governance of the State and shall refer the matter under dispute to the Chief Court for decision. Where any party is aggrieved by the decision of the Chief Court, an appeal shall lie to such authority as may be determined hereafter.

8. *The Maharajahs prerogatives:* (a) All family matters which are the Maharajah's sole concern as head of the ruling family, all matters which are his sole concern as the defender of faith and all matters connected with titles. Honours and palace ceremonial shall be deemed to fall within the Maharajah's personal prerogative and in such matters the Maharajah shall exercise full discretion subject to the provisions of the Constitution and law of the State. The Maharajah's prerogative shall not, however, be taken to comprise any matter wherein the legitimate interests of the State administration or a civil right sustainable in a court of law is involved. It will be within the prerogative of the Maharajah to remit punishment and pardon offenders subject to the provisions of the Manipur State Court's Act provided that this prerogative shall not prejudice the right of any individual to compensation; (b) It shall be the prerogative of the Maharajah and the Maharani that neither may be made answerable at law or subject to any legal proceeding in the State Courts. Their persons and property shall be inviolable; (c) Notwithstanding Section 8(b) above, it shall be lawful for the State 'Council in consultation with the Chief Court to draw up a statement of charges against the Maharajah or the Maharani where it is proved beyond all possible doubt that the Maharajah or the Maharani has been guilty of murder or any other

heinous offence or of any extreme political crime against the provisions of the Constitution; (d) On a statement of charges being drawn up under clause (c) above, the Council shall present it before the Maharajah or the Maharani and require satisfaction. Should satisfaction be not forthcoming the Council may refer the matter to such authority as may be determined hereafter.

Chapter II

9. *Definitions*

In this Act and Rules issued thereunder unless there is something repugnant to the subject or the context:

(a) State shall mean the Manipur State comprising the whole territory of Manipur as delineated in the maps of the Survey of India current at the date of this enactment.

(b) The Maharajah means His Highness the Maharajah of Manipur, the Constitutional Head of the State.

(c) Chief Minister means the office entrusted with the chief executive function of the State.

(d) Minister means a member of the Council of Ministers appointed under this Act by name or by virtue of his office to administer certain branches of the State administration and to perform the duties and exercise the power imposed and conferred upon a minister by this Act and Rules framed thereunder.

(e) Council means the State Council of Ministers constituted under this Act.

(f) Gazette means the official journal of the State by means of which important orders, notices communiques, etc., are published.

(g) Speaker means the President of the Assembly and includes the Deputy Speaker in the absence of the Speaker or in the absence of both, a member voted to the chair.

(h) Civil List means the appropriation of funds for the expenses of the ruling family and the privy purse of the ruler.

(i) Privy purse means such portion of the Civil List as is appropriated exclusively for the personal expenses of the Maharajah.

(j) Revenue includes all receipts of the State from State assets, from all lands, forest, taxes, fines, penalties, forfeitures, lapse and other sources.

(k) Rules means any rule issued under this Act.

(l) Fundamental rights shall mean those rights which the State people shall enjoy as of right under this Act.

(m) The pronoun 'he' and its derivatives are used of any person whether male or female.

Chapter III

The Executive

10. *Council of Ministers:*

(a) Subject to the provisions of this Act and subject also to the provisions of the Rules for the Administration of the Manipur State, the executive authority of the State is delegated to and shall vest in the Council of Ministers.

(b) Where under this Act or the Rules for the Administration of the State, it is requisite that the approval of the Maharajah shall be taken to any measure, the Chief Minister shall seek the approval of the Maharajah in person or in writing and shall obtain the Maharajah's orders thereon. Should in any case the Maharajah's approval be withheld, the Maharajah shall be pleased to inform the Chief minister in person or in writing and to communicate his reasons for withholding such approval in writing to the Council.

(c) The Council of Ministers shall consist of the Chief Minister and six other Ministers.

(d) The six Ministers on the Council shall be elected by the State Assembly subject to the proviso that two of these Ministers shall be representatives of the hill people of the State elected in such manner as shall be laid down in the Rules of Business of the State Assembly.

(e) The Chief Minister shall be appointed by the Maharajah in consultation with the elected Ministers on the Council.

(f) The Chief Minister shall receive letters of appointment over the seal of Maharajah.

(g) The Chief Minister in consultation with the Ministers shall allot portfolios.

11. The Chief Minister shall be President of the Council and the Vice President shall be appointed by the Council.

12. The Council of Ministers shall have a common seal and shall be jointly responsible to the Maharajah for the administration of the State.

13. The Council of Ministers and the Ministers individually shall exercise such powers and functions as may be assigned to them by or under this Act or under the Rules for the Administration of the State.

14. The quorum necessary for the transaction of business at a meeting of the Council shall not be less than three excluding the President.

15. The Chief Minister and Ministers shall, on taking office, swear an oath of loyalty and allegiance to the Maharajah in the following form:

'I (name of the minister) having been appointed as a Member of the Manipur State Council, do solemnly swear that I will be loyal and faithful and bear true allegiance to the Maharajah, his heirs and successors and that I will faithfully discharge the duties laid on me under this Act.'

16. A minister of the Council shall not be removable from office except in accordance with the provisions of Chapter IV below.

Chapter IV

17. There shall be constituted a State Assembly. The Assembly shall be elected for a period of three years and shall comprise representatives freely elected by the people on an adult franchise and on the principle of joint electorate. Elections shall be in such manner and by such franchise as may be laid down under the rules for the elections to the State Assembly provided always that the representatives returnable from General, Hill and Mohammadan Constituencies shall be in the ratios of 30:18:3 respectively with an additional two seats for the representatives of educational and commercial interests.
18. The State Assembly may debate all matters concerning the Government and well-being of the State which, in the opinion of five members of the Assembly, it is in the public interest to debate. The Assembly shall tender such advice to the Council of Ministers in any matter in which a majority of the members present, are agreed on the advice which shall be tendered provided that no matter touching the Maharajah's prerogative shall be debated and provided that the Maharajah may on the advice of the Council, veto debate on any matter where such course shall in the public interest be necessary.
19. The State Assembly shall not tender advice to the Council on any matter which is of primary concern to the hill people unless such advice has the support of a majority of the hill representatives in the Assembly.
20. Subject to the provisions of this Act, the Assembly may make rules for regulating its proceedings and the conduct of business.

21. Where in any case it is required to pass a vote of no confidence against a minister of the Council for his individual acts, a motion of no confidence, signed by not less than ten members of the Assembly and laying out in detail, the facts giving rise to the motion, may with the permission of the Speaker of the Assembly be moved. If such motion shall receive the support of at least 75 per cent of the members present and voting, it shall be forwarded through the Chief Minister to the Maharajah, who, unless there appear strong and valid reasons to the contrary which shall be recorded in writing, shall after consultation with the Chief Minister require the minister against whom the motion has been passed to resign.
22. Where in any case the State Council or the Maharajah is in the special circumstances of any case unable to accept the advice of the Assembly, the Maharajah or the State Council as the case may be, shall communicate in writing the reasons which have led to such course and shall give facilities for personal discussion of the matter with a representative or representatives deputed by the Assembly.
23. Subject to the provisions of this Act and the rules framed under it for the disposal of the Assembly business, there shall be freedom of speech in the Assembly and no member shall be liable to any proceedings in any court in respect of any speech or vote given by him in the Assembly or a committee thereof and no person shall be liable in respect of any publication by or under the authority of the Assembly of any report, paper, vote or proceedings.
24. No member of the Assembly shall be liable to arrest or detention in prison under a civil process: (a) if he is a member of the Assembly, during the continuance of the Assembly; (b) if he is a member of any committee of the Assembly, during the continuance of the meeting of the committee.
25. The elected ministers, the Speaker, Deputy Speaker and members of the Assembly shall receive such

emoluments as may be determined from time to time by the Assembly.

Chapter V

The Law Making Authority

26. The Law making Authority in the State shall consist of the Maharajah in Council in collaboration with the State Assembly acting under section 18, above.
27. When the Council or the Assembly consider that a law should be enacted the Council shall cause a bill to be drafted, which shall be laid before the Assembly and a reasonable time shall be given for consideration thereof. The Council then cause to be made such alterations or amendments as may be deemed necessary in the light of the advice tendered by the Assembly and the Chief Minister shall submit the Bill in its final form for the assent of the Maharajah.
28. On the receipt of the Maharajah's assent the Bill shall be published in the State Gazette and shall become an Act having the force of law.
29. Should the Maharajah in any case withhold his assent to a Bill, the Bill shall lapse as it had not been passed. If the assent of the Maharajah is not forthcoming within one calender month of the Bill being submitted to him he shall be deemed to have withheld his assent.
30. Where the assent of Maharajah to any Bill is withheld, the Council may cause the self same Bill to be introduced in the next session of the Assembly and if passed without amendment by a 75 per cent majority of the Assembly, the Bill shall be certified over the Seal of the Council and shall become Law.
31. Nothing in this Chapter shall be deemed to derogate from the absolute right of the Maharajah in Council to promulgate, the emergency cases, orders having the force of law without previous reference to the Assembly where the public interest in their opinion

demands that such order shall be promulgated provided that the first opportunity shall be taken of laying the order before the Assembly for consideration. Any such order shall not have the force of law for a period of more than six months.

Chapter VI

Finance

32. The revenue of the State and such other receipts as may accure from whatever source, less such reasonable percentage of the total real revenue as may be reserved for the Civil List, are placed at the disposal of the Council for expenditure on the Government of the State in the manner prescribed by State Account Rules saving that in every year a sum represents not less than 17 per cent of the average real revenue of the State for the proceeding three years shall be allocated for expenditure on the welfare and administration of the hill people.
33. The minister in charge of finance shall prepare an annual budget showing the estimated receipts and expenditure for the ensuing year classified under the prescribed heads of account and shall submit it to the Assembly within fifteen days of its meeting for the budget session along with a statement of account for the previous year.
34. The Assembly shall after considering the budget, submit it with their recommendation to the Council, who, having made such modification as may be deemed necessary shall submit it to the Maharajah for approval. Where any delay occurs in the granting of assent to the budget by the Maharajah and where such assent has not been obtained by the first day of the financial year, provisional effect shall be given to the budget as passed by the Assembly and funds shall be drawn against its provisions as it had received assent.

35. The Maharajah's Civil List shall be fixed at a figure equal to 10 per cent of the real revenues of the State over the preceeding three years, provided that no extraordinary revenues shall be taken into account when determining this amount and provided that no State revenue in excess of Rupees twenty lakhs shall be taken into account in any one year. The appropriations to the Maharajah's Civil List shall be non votable and shall not be the subject of debate in the Assembly.

36. No tax whatsoever shall be shown in the budget and no tax shall be collected by any officer of the State or by any person unless such tax has been imposed by due process of law.

37. (a) There shall be a State Auditor who shall be appointed by the Maharajah in Council on a nomination to be made by the Comptroller of Audit, Assam, or such other officer as may be deemed suitable. Such nominee shall be employed on contract for a period of not less than five years and shall be removed only by the Maharajah in Council in consultation with the authority making the nomination.

    (b) The conditions of service of the State Auditor shall be such as may be prescribed by the Maharajah in Council provided always that he shall not be eligible for any office of profit in the state after his retirement.

    (c) The Auditor shall exercise such powers and perform such duties as may be laid down in the State Account Rules.

Chapter VII

Hill People

38. The Council shall be responsible for the welfare and good administration of the hill people of the State and shall provide such funds for this purpose as may,

subject to the provision of Section 32 above, be deemed necessary, provided that the local authorities in the hill shall exercise such powers of local self government as may be laid down in the Manipur State Hill (Administration) Regulation, 1947.

Chapter VIII

The Services

39. The Council shall issue rules regulating the conditions of service in the departments of the State.
40. A Manipur State Appointments Board shall be constituted and the Council shall issue rule regulating the constitution, functions and procedure of the Board. The Board shall consist of not less than three members, one of whom must be a hillman and a chairman and shall be the final authority in all matters connected with appointments and promotions to the State service except in so far as specific powers may be reserved under this Act or the Rules for Administration of the State.

Chapter IX

The Judicature

41. (a) There shall be a complete separation of Judiciary from the Executive.
    (b) The Judicature of the State shall be as laid down in the Manipur State Courts Act, 1947.
42. The Chief Justice of the State and two Puisne Judges shall be appointed by the Maharajah in Council under the Royal Seal and shall hold office until the age of 65 years provided that:
    (a) A judge may resign his office.
    (b) A judge may be removed from his office by the Maharajah in Council only on the grounds of misbehaviour or infirmity of body or mind.
43. A person shall not be appointed as a Judge of the Chief Court unless he: (a) be a graduate in law and has

held judicial office at least for five years; or (b) is a barrister qualified in England of five years' standing; or (c) has for at least five years held judicial office in British India in a post not inferior to that of a subordinate judge; or (d) has for at least a period of ten years been a pleader of any High Court or of the Manipur Chief Court; or (e) be a person recognised a shaving a special capacity for the exercise of judicial functions.

Chapter X

Fundamental Rights and Duties of Citizenship

44. All citizens shall be equal before the law. Titles and other privileges of birth shall not be recognised in the eyes of the law.
45. The liberty of the individual shall be guaranteed. No person may be subjected to any judicial interrogation or placed under arrest or be in any other way deprived of his liberty, save as provided by law.
46. No person shall be tried save by a competent court.
47. No person may be tried except by a competent court who shall give full opportunity to such person to defend himself by all legal means.
48. All penalties shall be as determined by law.
49. Capital punishment may not be inflicted for purely political crimes.
50. No citizen may be banished from the State, expelled from one part of the country to another, and obliged to reside in a specified place save in such cases as may be expressly determined by law.
51. Every dwelling shall be inviolable save under express provision of law.
52. There shall be guaranteed to all people, justice, social, economic and political; equality of status, of opportunity and before the law; freedom of thought, expression of belief, faith, worship, vocation, association, and action, subject to law and public morality.

53. The practice of Arts and Sciences shall be unrestricted and shall enjoy the protection and support of the State.
54. Without any prejudice to the communities concerned, public institutions shall be opened to all citizens of the State.
55. (a) All officials of the State or of a local government shall be answerable before the law for their individual and unlawful actions.
    (b) Where damage is caused to an individual by the act of an official of the State or an official of a local government, such individual may use the State before the Chief Court and may seek redress save where such damage has been caused by a bonafide act of a State servant in pursuance of a policy duly laid down by a competent authority.

Chapter XI

General Clauses

56. Any provision of this act may be subject to amendment by the Maharajah in Council provided that such amendment is laid before the Assembly and receives the support of at least 80 percent of the member so the State Assembly present and voting, when such amendment is debated.
57. Where in any case circumstances arise which prevent the proper operation in law or in spirit of this Constitution Act, the Council may at their discretion refer the matter for decision to such authority outside the State as may be decided hereafter and the decision of that authority shall be biding.
58. The Court Language of the State shall be Manipuri or English.

Bodha Chandra Singh
(Maharajah of Manipur)

APPENDIX-VII

The Manipur Merger Agreement

Agreement made on this twenty-first day of September 1949 between the Governor General of India and His Highness the Maharaja of Manipur.

Whereas in the best interests of the State of Manipur as well as of the Dominion of India it is desirable to provide for the administration of the said State by or under the authority of the Dominion Government:

It is hereby agreed as follows:

Article No. 1

His Highness the Maharaja of Manipur hereby cedes to the Dominion Government full and exclusive authority, jurisdiction and powers for and in relation to the governance of the State and agrees to transfer the administration of the State to the Dominion Government on the fifteenth day of October 1949 (hereinafter referred to as 'the said day').

As from the said day the Dominion Government will be competent to exercise the said powers, authority and jurisdiction in such manner and through such agency as it may think fit.

Article No. 2

His Highness the Maharaja shall continue to enjoy the same personal rights, privileges, dignities, titles, authority over religious observances, customs, usages, rites and ceremonies and institutions in charge of the same in the State, which he would have enjoyed had this agreement not been made.

Article No. 3

His Highness the Maharaja shall with effect from the said day be entitled to receive for his life-time from the revenues of the State annually for his privy purse the sum of Rupees three lakhs free of all taxes.

This amount is intended to cover all the expenses of the Ruler and his family, including expenses on account of his personal staff and armed guards, maintenance of his residences, marriages and other ceremonies etc., and the allowances to the Ruler's relations who on the date of execution of this agreement were in receipt of such allowances from the revenues of the State, and will neither be increased nor reduced for any reason whatsoever.

The Government of India undertake that the said sum of Rupees three lakhs shall be paid to His Highness the Maharaja in four equal installments in advance at the beginning of each quarter from the State treasury or at such other treasury as may be specified by the Government of India.

Article No. 4

His Highness the Maharaja shall be entitled to the full ownership, use and enjoyment of all private properties (as distinct from State properties) belonging to him on the date of this agreement. His Highness the Maharaja will furnish to the Dominion Government before the first January 1950 an inventory of all the immovable property, securities and cash balance held by him as such private property.

If any dispute arises as to whether any item of property is thc private property of His Highness the Maharaja or State property, it shall be referred to a judicial officer qualified to be appointed as a High Court Judge, and the decision of that officer shall be final and binding on both parties:

Provided that His Highness the Maharaja's right to the use of the residences known as 'Redlands' and 'Les

Chatalettes' in Shillong, and the property in the town of Gauhati known as 'Manipuri Basti' shall not be questioned.

Article No. 5

All the members of His Highness's family shall be entitled to all the personal rights, privileges, dignities and titles enjoyed by them whether within or outside the territories of the State, immediately before the 15th August, 1947.

Article No. 6

The Dominion Government guarantees the succession, according to law and custom, to the *gaddi* (throne) of the State and to His Highness, the Maharaja's personal rights, privileges, dignities, titles, authority over religious observances, customs, usages, rites and ceremonies and institutions incharge of the same in the State.

Article No. 7

No enquiry shall be made by or under the authority of the Government of India, and no proceedings shall lie in any Court in Manipur, against His Highness the Maharaja whether in a personal capacity or otherwise in respect of anything done or omitted to be done by him or under his authority during the period of his administration of that State.

Article No. 8

1. The Government of India hereby guarantees either the continuance in service of the permanent members of the Public Services of Manipur on conditions which will be not less advantageous than those on which they were serving before the date on which the administration of Manipur is made over to the Government of India or the payment of reasonable compensation.

2. The Government of India further guarantees the continuance of pensions and leave salaries sanctioned by His

Highness the Maharaja to servants of the State who have retired or proceeded on leave preparatory to retirement, before the date on which the Administration of Manipur is made over to the Government of India.

3. The Government of India undertake to make suitable provisions for the employment of Manipuris in the various branches of Public Services, and in every way encourage Manipuris to join them. They also undertake to preserve various laws, customs and conventions prevailing in the State pertaining to the social, economic and religious life of the people.

Article No. 9

Except with the previous sanction of the Government of India no proceedings, civil or criminal, shall be instituted against any person in respect of any act done or purporting to be done in the execution of his duties as a servant of the State before the day on which the administration is made over to the Government of India.

In confirmation whereof Mr. Vapal Pangunni Menon, Advisor to the Government of India in the Ministry of States, has appended his signature on behalf and with the authority of the Governor General of India and His Highness Maharaja Bodhchandra Singh, Maharaja of Manipur has appended his signature on behalf of himself, his heirs and successors.

Bodhchandra Singh,
Maharaja of Manipur

V.P.. Menon
Advisor to the Government of India,
Ministry of States

Sri Prakasa
Governor of Assam, Shillong,
September 21, 1949

APPENDIX-VIII

Financial Outlays of Manipur Government

Annual Plan 1996-97 (Actual) Rs. in lakhs

(It would be very unfair to say that the Manipur Government has neglected the development works in the tribal areas. The amount indicates that adequate funds were allocated for proper development of the tribal area out of the total outlay. Tribal population is less than 40 per cent. There are many common facilities, which are located at Imphal (being the capital city), the benefit of which is also shared by Scheduled Tribe population and others).

Departments	*Total Outlay*	*of which flow to Tribal Sub Plan*
1. Agriculture and Allied Activities	2485.31	1211.00
2. Rural Development	1094.83	501.00
3. Irrigation and Flood Control	669.95	1594.00
4. Energy (Power, integrated rural energy programme, etc.)	4282.67	2629.00
5. Industry/Minerals	1228.23	274.00
6. Transport	7721.22	6182.00
7. Science and Technology	102.81	31.00
8. General Economic Services Planning, Tourism, Civil Supplies, etc.,	599.16	402.00
9. Social Services: Education, Sport, Arts and Culture, Housing, etc.	11451.93	1736.00
10. General Services: Works, Jail, National Highway, Police Upgradation, etc.,	863.93	34.00
Grand Total	35000.04	14594.00
Percentage	100.00	41.70

Annual Plan 1997-98 (Actual) Rs. in lakhs

Departments	*Total Outlay*	*of which flow to Tribal Sub Plan*
1. Agriculture and Allied Activities	2658.00	1270.00
2. Rural Development	1150.00	831.00
3. Irrigation and Flood Control	6570.00	3556.00
4. Energy (Power, integrated rural energy programme, etc.)	4365.00	2761.00
5. Industry/Minerals	1977.00	147.00
6. Transport	7736.00	4685.00
7. Science and Technology	116.00	47.00
8. General Economic Services Planning, Tourism, Civil Supplies, etc.,	925.00	510.00
9. Social Services: Education, Sport, Arts and Culture, Housing, etc.	11913.00	2152.00
10. General Services: Works, Jail, National Highway, Police Upgradation, etc.,	1090.00	191.00
Grand Total	41000.00	16150.00
Percentage	100.00	39.39

Annual Plan 1998-99 (Actual) Rs. in lakhs

Departments	*Total Outlay*	*of which flow to Tribal Sub Plan*
1. Agriculture and Allied Activities	2860.72	1375.81
2. Rural Development	671.00	346.77
3. Irrigation and Flood Control	7289.00	2284.27
4. Energy (Power, integrated rural energy programme, etc.)	3540.00	1678.91
5. Industry/Minerals	1773.27	305.91
6. Transport	6561.00	4070.00
7. Science and Technology	124.00	6.49
8. General Economic Services Planning, Tourism, Civil Supplies, etc.,	1899.00	1093.60
9. Social Services: Education, Sport, Arts and Culture, Housing, etc.	10740.34	3244.81
10. General Services: Works, Jail, National Highway, Police Upgradation, etc.,	1041.67	72.00
Grand Total	42500.00	16378.57
Percentage	100	38.54

Annual Plan 1999-2000 (Actual) Rs. in lakhs

Departments	*Total Outlay*	*of which flow to Tribal Sub Plan*
1. Agriculture and Allied Activities	2988.31	1701.30
2. Rural Development	980.05	429.52
3. Irrigation and Flood Control	9490.00	4841.00
4. Energy (Power, integrated rural energy programme, etc.)	3055.00	2670.53
5. Industry/Minerals	4484.10	983.97
6. Transport	7406.00	3667.00
7. Science and Technology	150.00	8.25
8. General Economic Services Planning, Tourism, Civil Supplies, etc.,	2187.00	1347.40
9. Social Services: Education, Sport, Arts and Culture, Housing, etc.	14961.45	3666.51
10. General Services: Works, Jail, National Highway, Police Upgradation, etc.,	1329.50	80.48
Grand Total	47500.00	19864.55
Percentage	100.00	41.82

Annual Plan 2000-2001 (Actual) Rs. in lakhs

Departments	*Total Outlay*	*of which flow to Tribal Sub Plan*
1. Agriculture and Allied Activities	4683.16	1987.19
2. Rural Development	1144.98	366.27
3. Irrigation and Flood Control	12831.72	75.64.00
4. Energy (Power, integrated rural energy programme, etc.)	6567.00	3385.93
5. Industry/Minerals	7643.05	1796.76
6. Transport	8337.03	3903.63
7. Science and Technology	355.00	11.35
8. General Economic Services Planning, Tourism, Civil Supplies, etc.,	2553.17	1492.00
9. Social Services: Education, Sport, Arts and Culture, Housing, etc.	20667.61	5128.91
10. General Services: Works, Jail, National Highway, Police Upgradation, etc.,	3412.70	118.52
Grand Total	68195.42	25754.56
Percentage	100.00	37.77

APPENDIX-IX

Civilians Killed in Insurgency-Related Incidents in Manipur

Year	Civilian Casualties
1997	205
1998	127
1999	112
2000	127
2001	140

Source: Official

ANNEXURE

Note for Supplimentary Work taken up under Heirok Assembly Constituency

Sl. No.	Name of the Work	C/Area	Remarks
1.	Impt of P/weir at Amukhong	40 ha	
2.	Impt. and extension of Heirok Litan Makhong Dam	60 ha	
3.	Constn. of P/weir at Nongdambi river at Salungpham Ukuthong Mapa	40 ha	
4.	Constn. of P/weir at Uyumpok Dam a/cAmukhong	30 ha	
5.	Impt. of P/weir at Malom	60 ha	
6.	Impt. of P/weir at Sikhong Bazar	30 ha	
7.	Constn. of P/canal at Heirok Litan Makhong	60 ha	
8.	Impt. of P/weir at foothill of Kotwall river	60 ha	
9.	Constn. of P/weir a/cAngom Thingel at Kakmayai	40 ha	
10.	Impt. of P/weir at Nongpok Sekami Awang Laimapa	30 ha	
11.	Impt. of Itok P/weir and remodeling to canal with gate	30 ha	
12.	Impt. of Itok Dam i/e irrigation canal providing of regulator gate existing structures	30 ha	
13.	Protection work of right side river bund at Chongabon	20 ha	
14.	Constn. of irrigation canal from Warungpham Ikhai Ukhongsang to Warungpham i/c 4 Nos. of cross drainage	60 ha	
15.	Constn of guide bund from Itok Dam to Chandrankhong and ressectioning of Itok river and constn. of protection work on both side of Chandrakhong	30 ha	
		670 ha	

Index